MW01089161

God Bless This Strip of Dirt

A Catholic's Spiritual Journey on the Appalachian Trail

By Kathleen Owens Stephens

There is a narrow strip of dirt that runs along the Appalachian spine of the Eastern US. It winds through heavy forests, up and down mountains, past hidden waterfalls, through picturesque bubbling brooks, and into and out of several small towns. It's sprinkled with rough, three-sided log shelters that provide some protection from the elements and, usually, some camaraderie on those nights when the beauty of solitude turns lonesome.

Every year a couple of thousand people shoulder heavy packs and attempt to walk from one end of this 2,000 mile long trail to the other, in one season. On April 1, 2013, I joined them.

Table of Contents

Introduction

WHY?

What would cause otherwise ordinary twenty-first century Americans to willingly give up the comforts and pleasures of home to spend months on end living in the woods, walking on blistered feet, carrying a heavy pack? To sleep on a forest floor, or on a dirty wooden floor, or suspended between trees in a thin bed of nylon instead of in their climate-controlled homes with clean sheets on pillow top mattresses? To willingly exchange hot soapy daily showers for an occasional furtive wipe down with a cold wet bandana? To trade the porcelain throne of a toilet for a squat behind the bushes and a handful of leaves? To replace the dangers of the morning commute with bugs, poison ivy, hypothermia, rattlesnakes, and bears?

Maybe it's not so hard to understand if the hiker you have in mind is a 20 year old male, flush with testosterone poisoning, youthful bravado, and foolhardiness. But what about if the hiker is a 54 year old woman, mother of four, grandmother of six, who falls closer on the activity spectrum to "couch potato" than to "outdoor adventurer?" That would be me. I will just lay that question of "why in the world..." to rest right now by telling you that there is no good answer to it. While I was hiking the Appalachian Trail I had many good conversations with hikers of different demographic groups around campfires every night. The conversations were wide-ranging and free-wheeling, on topics personal and profane, profound and practical, but I never heard one hiker ask another why they were on the Trail. There is an unspoken, tacit understanding that there is no single answer that can articulate the forces that drove or compelled us to leave our homes, families, jobs-- heck, society itself--and come to the wilderness.

To be honest, before I started my hike, when I was still trying to come up with an answer that would satisfy friends and family who asked why, I did compile a list of my reasons. Even while I was writing it I realized that it wouldn't satisfy anyone, not them and not myself. But here it is, as I wrote it on March 20, 2013, twelve days before I started my hike:

*To de-program myself from this crazy, over-mechanized world.

*To find silence and solitude, to reconnect to myself and to God.

*To attempt something that is challenging. To

challenge myself to do something that is inherently difficult, and that I have to accomplish on my own.

*To break out of the mold, the rut. To find a way of life that is different, with its own culture, daily rituals, and expectations.

*To attempt something physically demanding, while I can. I am healthy at age 54, and I don't take that for granted.

*To find simplicity and poverty. To live without luxuries. To strip life down to the essentials and see what is left. To see who I am without a job or family to define me and without belongings.

*To see the beautiful natural world without a filter. St. Francis said the beauty of nature is the footprint of God. I want to wake up in the middle of God's footprint every morning, and go to sleep in it every night, and live surrounded by it every day.

These are a few of my poorly articulated reasons for wanting to hike the AT. Each one contains a part of the truth, but none of them tells the whole truth. The whole truth of "why" is all of these reasons, and something else that just is. The Trail is there, and I want to walk it.

I realized even while writing the list that it wasn't the

whole truth. The problem is that the wrong question is being asked. The question should not be "why does a person want to hike the trail" but "why does one person want to de-program himself, to find silence, to attempt a challenge, etc, and another person does not." And that question is a bigger one than I can attempt to answer. But if we can accept that I wanted to de-program myself, find simplicity, etc, then my decision to hike the trail becomes understandable. Of course a person who wants the kinds of things on my list would choose to hike the trail! The aforementioned inconveniences (bugs, cold, lack of plumbing) become inconsequential when seeking something bigger, deeper. Modern life is so full of its own version of minor annoyances that it doesn't seem like a hardship to trade them in for a different set. I intuitively understood that there was more to be gained on the trail than the creature comforts I was giving up.

In retrospect now, three years later, I can see that I actually did achieve everything on that list that I naively compiled what seems like such a long time ago. For better or for worse, because stripping away all the trappings of modern life with which we insulate ourselves and coming face to face with our own true selves is not always pleasant. But if the glimpse I had of my own heart was in many ways a disappointment to me, the equally elusive glimpse I got of God's heart and His love more than makes up for it. I briefly encountered the pearl of great price and am forever changed by it, in ways that I am only just beginning to understand.

HOW?

Whew. It's a relief to leave behind the prickly question of "why?" and address instead the more straightforward question of how I came to decide to hike the Appalachian Trail. It all started with a book, given to my husband Mike as a birthday present a couple of years earlier. I didn't read it at the time, but eventually, while thrashing about for something, anything, to read (you readaholics will understand) I picked it up, read a couple of chapters, and was hooked. Not with the book, which presented a rather unflattering view of long-distance hiking, but with the Appalachian Trail itself. After a visit to amazon.com and a modest investment (which eventually became not-so-modest) I amassed a small collection of "trail journals." It seems that many people who hike the AT keep journals while hiking, have some sort of life-changing experiences, and end up publishing their journals. They are all different, and they were all fascinating to me. The seed was planted in my mind. I wanted to do this. But how? I wasn't a hiker. I wasn't an outdoorsperson, I wasn't even in shape, being 20 pounds overweight and plagued by bad knees. It didn't seem possible.

But I guess I'm kind of like the character of John Locke in the television show Lost--"Don't tell me what I can't do!" I looked for trail journals written not just by women, but by older women. There were plenty of them. And not just, ahem, "mature" women have hiked the trail, but small children, people in their seventies and eighties, and even a blind man. I was healthy, if not athletic. I could do this, I started to realize. It was possible. I started researching gear choices, and walking up the steep hill behind my house every day for practice. My husband Mike was on board from the beginning, once he got over his understandable surprise. He became my biggest cheerleader and my support system. We started saving money to compensate for the loss of my nursing salary for the six months we estimated I would be gone, and he willingly agreed to assume my share of the duties of our home business, making herbal soap and bath products. He had done some backpacking 20 years previously, when our children were small. I had declined to go with him because trudging through woods carrying a heavy pack did not sound in the least appealing at the time. His experience was helpful as he taught me how to use a camp stove and hang a food bag high in the trees to keep it away from bears. I started accumulating gear, a piece at a time, here and there, as I could afford it.

Eventually we went on a couple of actual overnight hikes, to allow me to use my gear and find any flaws in my system. As a result of these shakedown hikes I lightened my load and stepped up my physical training, and became convinced that I could do this. My adult children were also supportive, if a little bemused by their mother's latest hare-brained plan. Eventually there was nothing left to do but wait, throughout the long winter before my chosen start date of April first. Start date is important: too early and a hiker can encounter very cold weather and even snow in the north Georgia mountains and in the Smokies. Too late and you won't have time to make it to the end--Mt. Katahdin, in Maine, closes for the season on October 15. I really despise being cold, but I also knew that I wasn't a fast hiker, and wasn't capable of many 20 mile days. To hike the entire trail takes approximately six months if you can average 15 mile days. This sounded like an achievable goal to me, so April first seemed to be a reasonable start date.

The winter passed, slowly. I felt like I was walking through a swimming pool full of molasses. I went to work, I went to church. I went to my weekly book club. I played the dulcimer with my group on Tuesday nights, just as I always had. But the whole time my mind was tuned to April first, not the current date. I lived my life as usual, but I was waiting, waiting, for my hike to start. I already knew that my entire life was going to be forever divided into BH and AH--before the hike and after the hike. I continually rethought my gear choices and made little changes as the need arose. I had been communicating online with other hopeful members of the Appalachian Trail Thru-Hiker class of 2013 during that interminable period of planning and preparation. Many of them had started in March and so I was able to start reading their Facebook posts and online trail journals posted in real time by those hardy hikers who had started early. They were plagued by cold and frost and snow, and I fervently hoped for spring to arrive by April first. I was envious that their adventures had started while mine was still on hold, but the envy was tempered with compassion as they struggled with what was turning out to be a cold winter in the South, and a late spring. I turned in my notice at the hospital, and two weeks later walked out with all the contents of my locker in my bag. This was real--for the first time in 20 years I was unemployed.

Finally it was March 30. With the thirty-first, Easter Sunday, as a travel day, it was my last day at home. There weren't many last minute preparations, everything had been made ready weeks before. The day before Easter seemed like an appropriate day for the ending of one phase of my life, and the beginning of the next. I was ready.

Prologue

Beauty Spot Gap
May 21, 2013

My heart beat wildly in my throat, in my head, and like a jackhammer trying to escape through my chest. My hammock, normally so cozy and comfortable, felt like a coffin. The fear crept from my pounding heart to my gasping lungs and into the long muscles of my arms and legs, my neck and back, turning them into stone. Eventually the rigidity would become painful enough to enter my consciousness and I would make a deliberate effort to relax. This would last a few seconds, perhaps, but the tension would then creep back into my limbs until I was lying stiff as a board once again. I have never known such an all-encompassing fear. Intermittently I would try to regain some thread of control as I found myself spinning off into panic. These efforts lasted about as long as my efforts to keep my muscles from clenching.

For the first hour I prayed, and managed to keep a razor thin level of control. "Our Father, who art......Oh God, oh God! I trust You, I trust You. Help me to trust You more!" After that hour my faith, which I considered rock-solid, started to falter, and I tried to think of other, more secular, solutions. Using my cell phone was obviously impossible, but maybe I could send a text. And so began a series of wild, panic-stricken text message pleas for help as the thin grip of control that I had began to dissolve along with my faith. Without the stabilizing grounding power of prayer, I lost it, and it would be another hour and a half before I found it again. "It" being coherence, and a heart that beat at a rhythm approaching normal.

Finally, finally, I realized I was safe. I turned off my cell phone, always so careful to conserve the battery. My phone had not brought me any help. Had my prayers? I thought about God and was ashamed that it had only taken one hour to get me to turn from prayer to a phone for help. I wondered where He had been during my nearly three hour ordeal. I thought about God and added a touch of anger to my embarrassment and shame. I was confused and disappointed in myself, and deeply, deeply tired. I relaxed my achy muscles, shut off my weary mind, tied my tarp back down, and fell asleep.

The Hike

Springer Mountain to Hightower Gap
April 1, 2013

But it wasn't always like that. I was calm and confident on the day that I began my hike, Monday, April 1. The fact that it was April Fool's Day wasn't lost on me—I had been calling myself an April Fool through the long months of planning. I was a novice backpacker after all: 54 years old, 20 pounds overweight and out of shape in spite of my best efforts on the treadmill. I used self-deprecation as a shield, deflecting the incredulous responses of friends and coworkers as they heard of my plan to spend six months hiking through the wilderness. "Yeah," I'd say, "I don't know if I can really make it the whole way. I've got bad knees, you know. I'm just going to go as far as I can." But in my heart I knew, I had convinced myself, that I could walk the entire 2,180 miles. I knew that I was tough, that I was determined, and that I was stubborn. And that I was prepared, as much as you can be for such a thing.

Easter was on March 31, and I was hopeful that an early Easter meant an early spring. Mike and I attended mass on the Easter Vigil, Saturday night, at our home parish. I love the Easter Vigil, the quiet dark church growing slowly lighter as the tiny flickers of light pass up and down the pews as we share the flame from our little candles with each other, symbolizing the light of Christ entering the world. My anxieties about the next day were forgotten as I felt the peace of God's love all around me in the small, familiar church. The eternal words were read from the pulpit and I knew Who was in charge—and I knew that it wasn't me. I felt love encompass me, peace enter my soul. I may be a fool, but I'm also a child of the King.

The next day, Easter Sunday, we loaded the car—we didn't have much, my backpack and trekking poles and Mike's overnight bag—and drove the three hours from our home in Tennessee to Dahlonega, Georgia. Our four adult children and six little grandchildren came for the kick-off of Granny's Great Adventure. We gathered at Amicalola Falls State Park for a picnic lunch and an Easter egg hunt. The kids surprised me with thoughtful going away gifts and a cookie cake, and I was reminded again that I am loved, that I am blessed. I kissed the sweet, sticky faces of the grandchildren goodbye, and wondered: When I see them again in six months, will they be more changed, or will I? And so it was that I felt very calm, very confident, on Springer Mountain the next morning. It was a beautiful, sunny day, the perfect day to begin a hike. Mike walked with me from the parking lot to the summit of the mountain, which is the beginning of the Appalachian Trail. There was a small group gathered there, maybe 15 or 20 hikers, all clean and shiny and bristling with new gear and excitement. A ridge runner from the Appalachian Trail Conservancy was there dispensing advice and encouragement. We took some photos and walked back down the trail to the parking lot. It was time to say goodbye to Mike. Oh my goodness, this was real! This was happening! Could I really leave him at the parking lot and walk off into—who knows what? He made it easier for me, with a big hug and a smile, no tears, and a comment that registered with me as "Go get 'em, tiger!" (Honestly, I don't remember his exact words, but that's what it sounded like, to me.)

I did it. I turned around and walked off down the trail, alone. I felt a pang as I realized that he wasn't going to be there with me that night to listen to my stories, and another pang as I realized that he also wasn't going to be there with me to fix my gear, retie my knots, and throw my food bag high into the trees to protect it from bears. I swallowed the pangs of doubt and reminded myself of my months of preparation—the books I had read, the videos I had watched, the practicing I had done with my hammock and stove. I was ready. I was strong. I could do this!

So I walked on, my nerves all settled back into place after the momentary surge of doubt I had felt walking away from my best friend and safety net. Now, on to the adventure! The trail followed a fairly gentle grade down Springer Mountain. The forest had not yet awakened from the winter; there was no green to be found among the brown leaves on the ground, even though the sun shone brightly and the air was pleasantly mild, neither hot nor cold. There was a lively little creek that followed along beside the trail, the water bouncing joyfully over rocks. The world seemed sweet and fresh and optimistic, matching my mood. I occasionally encountered other hikers, usually as they came from behind me and passed me, and they were, without fail, jovial and good-humored. We all seemed to share the same sense of joy and freedom at suddenly being out in the fresh air actually doing the thing we had been talking about for months. We would exchange pleasantries and then walk on, each at our own pace.

I was enchanted when I came to little footbridges across the creek and stopped to take pictures of them, labeling them "my first footbridge," "my second footbridge," until I realized how silly that was. The truth was, I didn't know what to take pictures of because everything seemed photo-worthy. I was torn between two perspectives: the desire for a complete photographic record of my hike, and reluctance to spend time with my face behind the camera, being more concerned with documenting events than with experiencing them. I'm not a natural photographer, Mike has that role in our relationship. My camera was my smart phone, which was doing quadruple duty as phone, camera, Kindle, and computer to record my journal entries. I could then upload them to trailjournals.com for family and friends to follow along with me. I put the phone/camera back into the hip pocket of my backpack and walked on.

I stopped for lunch at another bridge over the creek, this one wider and more substantial than the log footbridges I had been admiring, with sides and handrails. I took off my shoes and socks and put my feet into the water just because I could, and then hastily reconsidered when I realized how cold the water was. It's important to take care of your feet when hiking long distances, keeping them clean and dry to prevent blisters and other foot funk, so I consoled myself that I was airing them out in place of soaking them. While leaning over the railing of the bridge after eating my gorp and cheese, my Reese's cup fell out of my hand and over the side. It didn't land in the water, though, but on the bank—and right side up! I took this as a sign that nothing could go wrong, and that I was the luckiest person in the world. An elderly gentleman hiker that came along right then asked me how I was, and I said that I was perfect. That every single thing was perfect. He smiled at me with an expression that said that he understood. After all, what kind of a world is it where Reese's cups can go sailing off bridges and end up clean and dry and ready to eat? A perfect world, that's what kind.

Feet dried, wool socks and hiking shoes back in place, I walked on. Once at the bottom of Springer Mountain, I had only to go up and over Hawk Mountain to finish out my first day. My plan for the day was to hike a modest 8.6 miles and stop at Hightower Gap on the other side of Hawk Mountain, there to meet my ride to the hostel. I had chosen to take advantage of a service offered by the Hiker Hostel in Dahlonega, and would be spending the first five nights of my hike at the hostel, with a real bed and a kitchen and modern bathroom facilities, and a hearty hot breakfast every morning. It seemed a good way to ease into the rigors of backpacking, hiking without camping, with a safety net, with training wheels. After breakfast each morning Josh, the hostel owner, would take me and the other hikers in my "slackpack" to the trailhead where we had stopped the day before. We would then hike the pre-determined miles and stop at the end of the day at the road crossing where Josh would pick us up and take us back to the hostel for the night. There were three other hikers in my slackpack arrangement—Janice and Pam, two women I had been communicating with online in the months leading up to the hike, and Pam's husband Seth.

As I came down Hawk Mountain and looked at my watch I realized that I was going to be late for our agreed-upon pickup time and kicked my speed up a notch. I really hate being late, and even more so if it inconveniences other people. I hurried on, mentally kicking myself for all the lollygagging I had done throughout the day, marveling at Reese's cups that land right side up and taking picture after picture of footbridges. Sure enough, as I burst huffing and puffing into the clearing at Hightower Gap, the van was already there, backpacks stowed in the back and every hiker in their seat, waiting. I apologized profusely, and they were all extremely gracious and generous, assuring me that they hadn't minded the wait, and oh, wasn't it a great day for a hike, and wasn't the weather perfect, and did you actually get a sunburn on your nose? We chattered happily all the way back to the hostel, giddy with the freedom and excitement of our first day on the Appalachian Trail.

Hightower Gap to Woody Gap
April 2, 2013

I climbed out of my bunk at the hostel early in the morning, excited to see what day two was going to bring. I picked through my meager belongings, deciding what to put into my green backpack for the day's hike. One advantage of slackpacking was that I didn't need to carry my full 24 pound pack. Most of the gear could be left at the hostel as I only needed to carry what I might need throughout the day. So I packed some food, my rain gear, water filter and water bottles (filled with water from the sink at the hostel), and a jacket. I could leave behind the rest of my clothes and food, the hammock, top and underquilts, and stove. I reluctantly added my headlamp and first aid kit, hoping that I would need neither of them but unwilling to take the chance. The phone went into my hip belt pocket as usual, along with the relevant page from the AT Guide.

There was great excitement among all the hikers

downstairs during breakfast. Another slackpack group consisting of seven or eight hikers from Virginia was a day ahead of us. They would be going home at the end of the week. Breakfast was a lively affair, as spirits were high. The food was excellent and plentiful—pancakes, scrambled eggs, oatmeal, with brown sugar, honey, raisins, and maple syrup. We ate from real plates and joked about how hard it was to be roughing it in such a fashion. The Hiker Hostel was beautiful, a modern log cabin with a fireplace and vaulted ceilings, and a wide, comfortable front porch. My room was upstairs and had four bunks in it, adjacent to a sweet little writing nook with a window, bookshelves, comfy chair, and a computer. The nook overlooked the living room and dining room. Downstairs from the main level was a kitchen for hikers with a dining area, a sitting area with a large television, more bunkrooms, and French doors to the backyard. Large framed photos of the trail covered the walls, and the entire house was immaculately clean. Josh and his wife Leigh had hiked the entire trail and were a wealth of information for us new hikers.

After breakfast, we loaded up into the van and Josh took us back to Hightower Gap, where we had stopped the day before. The mission for the day was to hike 12.4 miles to the road crossing at Woody Gap. The terrain included climbs of both Sassafras Mountain and Justus Mountain, about which I had heard some nasty rumors regarding their level of difficulty. In fact, the year before, Mike and I had hiked a short section of the Trail as a "shakedown" or preparation hike for me, and I had strained a groin muscle trying to climb Sassafras Mountain, ending that hike. Now I stood looking up at the same mountain and remembering the pain of that pulled muscle. I knew that I was in better shape than the last time I had walked the steep rocky slope, and that my pack was lighter, and that I was not going to try to rush as I had the year before. Sure enough, I got to the top of the mountain and started hiking down the other side, breathing heavily but otherwise intact. The other three members of my slackpack were far ahead of me, but that was all right. We had never met before the hike, and actually hiking together had never been part of the arrangement. I just didn't want them to have to wait for me at the end of the day again, so I made a determined effort to keep up my pace.

The weather was cooler than the day before, in fact it was a bit nippy, but the exertion of walking kept me quite warm and I didn't need to put my jacket on. The trail as a whole was not as kind and gentle as it had been the day before. Gone was the sweet little murmuring stream that had followed the trail and the gentle grades. This day's hike was steep, rocky, and dry. The only water to be found was at Justus Creek in the middle of the day. I stopped and used my water filter to replace the water in my bottles and ate my lunch. There were a few other hikers there, and we introduced ourselves and compared notes, but I was afraid to linger too long, always cognizant of the van that would be waiting for me at Woody Gap. So I kept my shoes on, ate quickly, and hurriedly packed up my stuff and got back on the trail.

I found that I couldn't walk quickly going uphill. It was just too hard. I got out of breath alarmingly easily, and the memory of the pain of that groin injury was just too fresh. I soon realized that I couldn't walk fast going downhill either; with a trail full of loose rocks I was afraid of turning an ankle, besides the strain that walking downhill put on my knees. So I tried to make up for my slowness on the slopes by speeding along on the few relatively flat sections. Between mountains I went at a near run, cursing alternately my own slowness or the speed of the other hikers in my slackpack. In this fashion and without rest stops or snack breaks I arrived at the bottom of Justus Mountain fairly pleased with myself and thinking that I must be in better shape than I gave myself credit for, as both Sassafras and

Justus hadn't seemed all that hard to me. They certainly hadn't lived up to their reputations. Then, proud, overconfident hiker, meet Ramrock Mountain. I had never heard of Ramrock, and I was peeved to find another mountain here in my way at the end of my day. Nothing to do but climb it, though. So up I went, stopping to catch my breath obscenely frequently, pulling myself up the side of the mountain by my trekking poles, and cursing under my breath (Dang! Shoot! Crap! Every dirty word I knew.) I pulled out the page of my AT Guide and looked for Ramrock Mountain. It barely registered as a blip on the elevation profile, unlike Sassafras and Justus Mountains. What was up? Maybe I was just tired because it was the end of the day, and I had been pushing myself relentlessly for so many hours. My feet hurt, my knees hurt, and I was tired of running and being out of breath. I hadn't taken the time to look around and appreciate my surroundings all day, always feeling the pressure of needing to hurry to get to the van. Besides, I was out of water, and thirsty. I really struggled on this section of trail.

Finally, as I was closing in on Woody Gap there was a section of trail described in the guidebook simply as "Springs. Many." I hadn't been overly concerned about being out of water because the van was only half a mile away. But there, springing out of the rocks, was water. It came out in trickles, in streams, gushing into little waterfalls, all coming out of the rock face on my left side, and falling down the mountainside on the steep drop off on the right side of the narrow trail. It was beautiful, and the sheer abundance of it made me laugh, my bad mood and discouragement forgotten in the joy of being reminded of the love of God who has created such a world where life-giving water flows out of rocks. I was reminded to look to Him for my needs, and for my cares and concerns. The psalmist wrote "To the hills I lift my eyes, from whence shall come my help." It doesn't say anything about vans. With a lighter heart and a lighter step I walked down the mountain to the waiting van.

Woody Gap to Neel Gap
April 3, 2013

The highlight of this day's hike was the dreaded Blood Mountain, the highest mountain on the Trail in Georgia. Word on the trail was that the ascent wasn't actually half bad, but that the descent was brutal—long and steep. Our distance for the day was a very reasonable 10.7 miles. Best of all was that our daily trek would end at Neel Gap, at the famous (in hiker circles) Mountain Crossings store. It's a charming, rustic stone building, built by the CCC in the 1930s. The Appalachian Trail itself runs right alongside the building, actually *through* the building, under an arch that connects the two parts of the building, the only place on the entire length of the trail that goes through a building. A landmark on the trail, at 30 miles from the starting point it makes a great place to stop and spend the night in the hostel and reassess your progress. Along with the hostel and the store, Mountain Crossings has showers and laundry facilities. For most hikers, who aren't slackpacking, it is the first contact with civilization since their departure from Springer Mountain. Perhaps not surprisingly, a great many hikes end there, the hikers having discovered after three or four days on the trail that backpacking is really not all that glamorous, after all. It's just hard, and dirty, and uncomfortable.

The store is an outfitter, which carries all the gear that hikers need, but it's also a gift shop and a book shop and sells food. These are all of my favorite things. I had visited the store the year before and was looking forward to spending a bit of time there at the end of the day's hike, and buying a couple of cute things to send home to Mike. I knew he'd like to have an AT decal on his truck, and maybe a book. And I was glad that I wouldn't be confronted with Janice, Pam, and Seth sitting and waiting for me in the van at the end of the day. They would instead be happily shopping at Mountain Crossings and enjoying the camaraderie of the other hikers. But first, I had to get over Blood Mountain.

So off I went, pushing myself as much as I dared. I couldn't understand why I walked so much slower than everyone else, and with a light pack on my back. How much slower was I going to go once I was carrying my full pack? I didn't feel like I was walking slowly. I felt like I was moving along pretty well, until another hiker would approach me from behind and walk around me effortlessly, chatting easily the entire time. I developed a routine. When I heard someone approaching from behind I would stop and step aside, as the trail is only wide enough most of the time for single file. When the hiker reached me I would smile and make some casually self-deprecating comment such as "Go on around me, I'm a slowpoke." The other person would chuckle and say something like, "Oh that's ok, I'm pretty slow, too." while they zoomed past as if they had been shot out of a cannon. I was chagrined, but determined that I was going to get stronger legs and better lungs, and that someday soon it would be me zipping along over the mountains. Meanwhile, I developed a strategy for the really steep uphill sections, when I was gasping for breath and looking at the trail ahead of me that just went on, and on, and on, up a mountain so high I couldn't see the top. I picked out landmarks. I would choose a big tree, or rock, or bend in the trail a short distance ahead and say to myself "You only have to go to that landmark. Then you can stop and catch your breath. But you have to keep walking to that point." Once I got there I would stop briefly, say to myself, "See, that wasn't so bad, was it?" and pick out my next landmark. This worked surprisingly well, and I was able to trick myself into climbing many mountains this way.

The trail was beautiful. I revised my earlier opinion that there was no green to be seen in the early spring forest. There was chartreuse moss on the fallen logs, and grass green pine needles on the evergreen trees, and dark emerald leaves on the rhododendrons. Poking up here and there through the dun-colored forest floor were the early spring plants—trillium, and bloodroot with its striking white flowers. Because the trees weren't yet in leaf the views from every overlook were amazing, miles and miles of forest covering the valley that swept out before me, reaching up into mountains that stretched off into the distance, as far as I could see. I loved that there was nothing man-made to be seen in the entire vista.

Even the trail itself was a thing of beauty, sparkling with mica. It looked exactly like someone had walked the trail ahead of me shaking glitter from a bottle all over the ground. The larger rocks either glimmered with their own sprinkling of mica or looked quite proudly out of place in their stark whiteness, as if they were competing with the little bloodroot flowers. Then I began to see that the marble wasn't always white but frequently had streaks of coral, peach, pink, and grey. What kind of world was this where even the rocks were spectacular in their showy beauty? It was a wonderland, and I was quite distracted from the pain in my feet and knees by the beauty of it all.

I stepped off the trail and into a rhododendron thicket, just because I was enchanted with the look of it. It was indeed hollow in the center, like a little room, surrounded by the sinuous branches of the rhododendron. I was enjoying feeling like a child in a secret fort, when I was joined by another hiker. "Hi, I'm Sunshine," she greeted me. "And this is Flycatcher," she indicated the little terrier, bouncing around her feet. I introduced myself. Sunshine, in contrast to other female hikers, was wearing makeup. Her hair was stylishly cut, and even styled, with evidence of a blow dryer, if not a flatiron. This little mystery was solved, however, when she went on to explain that she, like me, was slackpacking for the week, staying with a friend in the area, and enjoying the comforts of home (which presumably included mirrors and grooming appliances), while she could. She was friendly and reminded me of her dog. Like Flycatcher, she was small, cute, and bouncy. We chatted for a few minutes and then I said my goodbyes and exited from our little haven.

I moved along as fast as I reasonably could without courting injury. I no longer stopped for lunch, or rest stops. There is a physiological phenomenon frequent among new hikers, in which the appetite just entirely disappears for a while at the beginning of a long hike, even though a hiker burns typically five hundred calories an hour while hiking. I had read about it in trail journals and blogs before beginning my hike, but as a nurse I had discounted it, because it seems to defy logic and what I understand of the human body. But now I was experiencing it. Leigh from the Hiker Hostel had said she thought it was perhaps the body going into some kind of shock at all the new demands being placed on it. Some type of hunger strike, I suppose?

I could picture my body shaking its fist at me and saying, "You go lie down on the couch right now! Or else we're not eating!" I had no desire to eat anything at all. I wasn't nauseous, just not hungry. I was careful to eat a little something every couple of hours though, because I had heard of hikers getting sick from not eating. Hiking is physically very stressful, so I was mindful to nibble frequently, stay hydrated, and get plenty of sleep, to give my body time and the fuel to replenish itself. I carried my own homemade gorp in my pocket, along with beef jerky and cheese, and some squash and apricot leather that I had dried that tasted much better than it sounds.

I continued to struggle up Blood Mountain, landmark by landmark. At one point I saw a man hiking way up ahead of me, and to my surprise, I seemed to be gaining on him! This was a first for me and I dug down deep to keep hiking, thinking about what a novelty it would be to actually pass someone. I started planning what I would say when I got right behind him, to tactfully ask him to step aside so that I could continue my brisk march up the mountain. Should I discreetly cough to let him know I was approaching or just loudly shuffle in the dry leaves? Or maybe I could briskly call out "On your left!" like bikers do. And if he politely stepped off the trail to give me room to go around I would of course be very gracious, and if he attempted to apologize for his slow pace I would chuckle lightly and say, "Oh, that's all right, I'm a pretty slow hiker too." As I kept chugging along, slowly closing the distance between us, I was able to get a better look at him, and I realized that he was at least 20 years older than me, and that he was carrying a huge backpack that had to weigh at least 40 pounds. As I came up behind him he turned to look at me and I could see that he had a pale sheen of sweat on his face despite the coolness of the day. Although there was less joy to be found in the act with these revelations, I still wanted to pass him. But I was deprived of this pleasure when, just before I reached him, he sat down on a log to take a break. Drat! He took his pack off, smiled at me, and invited me to sit with him and rest. I politely declined, knowing that I would be seeing him again. He would probably pass me going down the mountain!

The descent of Blood Mountain was as advertised, long and steep. I felt pretty good coming out on the road at Neel Gap, except for the bottoms of my feet, which felt like shredded meat. I hurried over to Mountain Crossings, planning on doing some shopping, but my fellow slackpackers were waiting for me and ready to go, having spent as much time shopping as they wanted. I was disappointed, but embarrassed by my slow pace. It wasn't their fault that I was so much slower than they were, and I couldn't expect them to continue to wait for me while I poked around among the shelves. They were tired and eager to get back to the hostel to take their boots off and put their feet up. So I climbed up into the van, thinking that maybe, since we were starting back here in the morning, I could pop in and buy Mike a decal before I started hiking for the day.

Hogpen Gap to Neel Gap
April 4, 2013

A change in the plan for the day was announced at breakfast, caused directly by the weather--bitterly cold and rainy--and indirectly by my slow pace, although no one was crass enough to say it that way. The day's distance was the shortest of the entire slackpack, only 6.9 miles. But even at that distance it could be presumed that I would arrive at the destination some time after Pam, Janice and Seth. So in order to keep them from having to wait for me in the nasty weather, in or out of the van, we reversed our direction for the day, hiking from north to south. That way we would end up for the day back at the Mountain Crossings store at Neel Gap, surely a much more comfortable place for them to wait for me. We could resume our northbound hike on the next day from Hogpen Gap, which would be our starting point for the day.

Almost everyone who hikes the Appalachian Trail, or most long trails for that matter, hikes from south to north, "hiking with spring," as Earl Schaeffer, the first thru-hiker, called it. It makes sense, weather-wise. In hiker parlance, these northbounders are called nobos for short. There are sobos, hiking from Katahdin in Maine south to Springer Mountain in Georgia, but this route is much less popular. I looked forward to meeting some sobos further up the trail to hear their adventures, and ask their advice about the parts of the trail they had already covered. Our little slackpack group were to be sobos for the day.

I put my raingear on and got into the van, and Josh drove us to Hogpen Gap. We stepped out into the cold rain and started up the trail. Within minutes, as usual, the others were all ahead of me and I was walking alone. I felt a curious sense of exhilaration. The weather had been so excruciatingly lovely thus far, it hadn't seemed fair. *This* was real hiking, battling the elements. There is a saying,

"No rain, no pain....no Maine." This was definitely rain. I started up Wildcat Mountain, moving as quickly as I realistically could, both to try not to fall so far behind the others, and because the weather wasn't conducive to strolling and reflection. I got distracted by what looked like a pile of broken glass just off the trail, but when I stopped to investigate, I realized it was hail! Then I realized I could hear it, bouncing off rocks and trees, and my head. Walking on, I met a young hiker with whom I had crossed paths several times in the last few days. He had already met the rest of my slackpack so he knew why we were being sobos for a day, and walking the opposite direction from him. Our chat was brief since the weather didn't lend itself to conversation, but I obtained my trail name during this exchange. He had called me a tortoise the day before, when I bemoaned my lack of speed on the trail, and reminded me that, in the race between the tortoise and the hare, the tortoise always wins. I appreciated his kindness. Today, as he looked me up and down in my head to toe bright blue rain gear, he said, "Looking good, Blue Tortoise!" Voila, I had a trail name. Trail names are one of the traditions of long-distance hikers. They're fun, they separate you from your life in the Real World, and they help to differentiate between hikers such as Kathy from

Tennessee and Kathy from Pennsylvania.

I climbed up Wildcat Mountain as the wind continued to pick up. At one point I had to literally hug a tree to keep from getting blown off the trail as I got closer to the top of the mountain where the wind was gusting. I came out of the sparse cover of the leafless trees onto the rocky face of the top of the mountain. The ground was a smooth gray rock face, curving down and away off to my left. I didn't walk over to the edge to see what the drop off looked like. I don't like heights in general, and on this day that fear was justified, as the gusts were clearly strong enough to sweep me over the side. To add to the fun, the gray rock I was carefully making my way across was coated with a sheet of ice. To the right was more rock, waist high and covered by scrubby bushes. In spite of my eagerness to get across this windswept clearing and into the relative shelter of the trees on the other side, I stopped to take pictures of the little bushes. The leaves that still clung tenaciously to the bushes were encased in ice, and the sight was so starkly beautiful I pulled off my gloves and fumbled for my camera with stiff fingers. While I was at it I took a picture of the white blaze painted on the icy rock at my feet, reassurance that this barren rock was indeed part of the AT. The white rectangles, the size of dollar bills, were usually painted on trees. I returned the camera to its pocket, put the sodden gloves back on my hands, and scuttled forward to the tree cover.

The rest of the hike down Wildcat Mountain and up and over Levelland Mountain was relatively uneventful. I tried my new trail name on for size in my head, pretending that the hail and sleet pounding around me were the mountains' way of welcoming me, that they were calling out to me, "All hail, Blue Tortoise!" in mountainese. There was no question of stopping for water or a snack. But I wasn't really cold, except for my hands and my face. My clothing was entirely appropriate for the occasion, except for my gloves which were completely wet, and the exertion of hiking kept me warm enough. I decided that I would buy a pair of waterproof mittens at the Mountain Crossings outfitter at the end of the day's hike. I stopped to talk very briefly to hikers at times, all people I had been seeing off and on over the last few days, all wondering why I was now going "the wrong way". (I guessed that this meant they hadn't run into Janice, Pam, and Seth ahead of me. Oh dear, this meant that they were probably already at Mountain Crossings. Shoot. Speed it up.) My feeling of exhilaration stayed with me, and I found that for some reason I really enjoyed this day of hiking. Maybe it was just the novelty of being out and about in weather that people would normally strive to avoid. I seemed to be feeling a great sense of freedom. But I wasn't really free, they were waiting for me at Neel Gap, and I stumbled into the warmth of the store with a huge sigh of relief. But, deja vu, they were all waiting for me at the door and hustled into the van as soon as they saw me, eager to return to the comfort of the hostel and the chance to take off their wet hiking clothes. I begged for a few minutes to shop and ran into the store to buy some waterproof mittens, and in my rush didn't notice until later that I had bought extra large. For the rest of my hike I struggled with those giant size mittens! Fortunately I didn't have to wear them all that often. It did feel awfully good to get back to the hostel, peel off the wet layers and hang them up, throw the wet muddy clothes into the washer, put my boots on the boot dryer, and get into a hot shower. I considered the hikers on the trail who weren't slackpacking and would be spending the night out on the icy trail. I would be joining them in two days, with only one more day of the slackpack left. And as much as I appreciated the comforts the hostel provided, especially on this cold wet night, I was chafing at the restrictions of hiking at preordained times and for predetermined distances. I was looking forward to being pushed out of this comfortable little nest and spreading my wings to fly alone.

Hogpen Gap to Unicoi Gap
April 5, 2013

According to the pre-set mileage for the week-long slackpack, this day was to be our longest hiking day—14.3 miles. I had been nervous about this day's distance since I had started planning this slackpack the previous winter. The terrain was right for such a long day, however, with no steep mountains to climb until Blue Mountain at the end of the day. The majority of the hike was gentle, if long. We woke up early for the long day and got our start while the woods were still waking up. The air was misty with a barely perceptible rain, or maybe it was just the fog that softened all the sharp edges out of focus that caused the dampness. It was a face of the forest I hadn't seen yet, and it was a beautiful one. The trail was mysterious with wisps of low-lying clouds drifting among the trees and a beautiful, complete, utter silence and stillness. I looked around at this new version of the wonderland of the AT with the wide-eyed wonder of a child instead of the jaded perception of a 54 year old, and I knew that I was right where I wanted to be. Maybe the dampness on my cheeks was tears.

But I had places to go and trees to see, so off I went on the last day of the slackpack, knowing that even though I had to walk 14 miles on that day, for the rest of my hike I could walk as far or as little as I wanted to each day, that I could start as early or as late as I wanted, that I could linger wherever I felt called to. But first things first, so I charged down the trail. Eventually the sun came out, warming up the chilly morning air and chasing the wisps of fog away. The sky turned into the most vivid shade of blue I had ever seen, with clouds so white and fluffy they looked like the little pictures my grandchildren drew. It was as if the trail was grinning and apologizing for yesterday, trying to make it up to us. "But it's ok," I said. "I liked yesterday, too!"

I powered on down the trail, determined that The Waiting Van at the end of the day's hike wouldn't have to wait too long for me. I didn't stop, but moved quickly, eating gorp as I walked, sipping water, trying to think about anything that would take my mind off my aching feet and knees. It seemed that the rigors of hiking were beginning to catch up with my body, which was still 54 years old, after all, even if my mind was reluctant to admit it. I went over my plans for the next two days. From Unicoi Gap where I would be stopping at the end of the day and thus starting the next day, it was 16 miles to Dick's Creek Gap, where there was another hostel, the Blueberry Patch hostel. I thought I could hike the 16 miles in two days, at least I hoped I could average eight mile hiking days with the full weight of my backpack for the first time. Then I would stop at the Blueberry Patch and take a day off, what hikers call a "zero," meaning a day with zero miles hiked. That would mean staying at the hostel for two nights, but I felt like my body could use the rest. That would be day eight of my hike, and even God rested on the seventh day. I was satisfied with this plan, with the exception of the tug at my conscience caused by the possibility of missing church that weekend. I knew that there would be Sundays on the trail when I would be too far away from any established town to make it to Sunday mass, but I meant to try to minimize these. Missing the very first Sunday set a bad precedent for all the weeks to follow. I prayed as I walked, and asked God to help me figure it out, and plowed on, moving as fast as I possibly could. This kind of walking ironically seemed to be harder on my feet and knees than did the steep mountains, I suppose because being able to walk faster on the (reasonably) flat ground actually translated into more pounding than gingerly picking my way up and down steep slopes.

Going up Blue Mountain at the end of the day was actually not bad, but the descent felt like torture. It was a mile and a half long, down a trail that was muddy from all the rain, steep and rocky. My feet were screaming every step of the way. Finally I could hear the road down below, signifying that I was close to being done, but it seemed like an illusion, like an auditory mirage. I could hear it, but I couldn't see it, and I kept walking, down, down, down, expecting to see the road around each bend in the trail, but it was never there. So now the trail, so kind and gentle this morning, was playing cruel tricks! But I persevered and walked on, mostly because I had no other choice, and minced my way down the mountain until I finally came to the road, the van, and my fellow slackpackers, patiently waiting for me.

When we pulled up to the Hiker Hostel for our final night's stay, I could barely get out of the van because of pain. I hobbled in, tossed back some ibuprofen, had a hot shower, and then took up residence in a comfortable arm chair to massage my feet and legs. The tips of my toes were bruised from banging into the inside of my boots over the last five days and 52 miles, but they otherwise looked good. No blisters yet. I was in bed by eight thirty, even earlier than usual, my body just begging for rest. I was awakened several times during the night by pain in my knees and calves, sometimes sharp and cramping, sometimes dull and achy. I would try to stretch out the cramps and rub the aches, and got up twice to take Vitamin I--the ibuprofen I was counting on to help me hike on in the morning.

Hiker Hostel
April 6, 2013

When morning rolled around I realized I was not going to be able to walk the eight miles I had planned for the day. I needed to walk eight miles in order to be at Dick's Creek Gap in two days for my planned zero, but the cramps in my legs made such a feat unfathomable. But at breakfast, Leigh announced that there had been a cancellation for the night, a rare event in this, their busy season. That meant there was a bed available, and the pieces of my dilemma all dropped into place. "*Today* can be my zero!" I thought. I could take the whole day off, rest my poor feet and knees, attend mass in the evening (it was Saturday), and resume my hike the next day. "Thank you, God," I whispered under my breath, and "I'll take that bed," I said out loud to Leigh.

The van left, carrying away all the hikers including the members of my (previous) slackpack, and I was alone in the house. I went downstairs and took up residence on the couch, armed with two bags of ice for my knees, an icy cold Mello Yello, a blanket, and the remote to the television. I watched a movie in the morning, ate peanut butter and bananas for lunch, and dozed all afternoon. Mostly, I just didn't walk. I rubbed my feet and stretched my toes. I did a few simple yoga stretches, then retreated back to the couch for nap, part two. It felt luxurious and decadent, and like I was skipping school. When evening rolled around Leigh drove me to town so I could attend mass at St. Luke's, the charming Catholic church in the cute little town of Dahlonega. Afterwards, feeling peaceful and rested, and limping only slightly, I walked to a Mexican restaurant and bought a carryout plate of chimichangas to take back to the hostel. I had to get a taxi to take me back to the hostel which was a few miles outside of town. I wasn't going to walk it, and I wasn't emotionally ready to try hitchhiking yet, which is the usual method of transportation for backpackers in towns.

I got back to the hostel and ate my dinner while meeting a whole new group of hikers who had come in during the day, all fresh and green and excited to start their Appalachian Trail adventures in the morning. They were impressed with my 52 miles, which seemed funny to me as I felt as green as any of them. I went to bed early again, knowing that the *real* adventure began in the morning. But I felt rested and ready for it, and I was grateful to have been reminded that God still had His eyes on this little sparrow, who was now ready to fly out of her nest.

Unicoi Gap to Tray Mountain Shelter
April 7, 2013

As I put my fully-loaded pack for the first time into the back of the van to go to Unicoi Gap, I was reminded (as if I needed reminding!) that I was finally going to be truly on my own. For the first time I didn't leave the bulk of my belongings behind on my bunk at the Hiker Hostel, as I had for the past week, while setting out with a light "school style" backpack on my back, knowing that I would be returning at the end of the afternoon to a clean, warm and cozy hostel. Instead I had my "real" backpack, which I had named The Green Monster when in its full, loaded state. It weighed in at 24 pounds on the pack scale at the hostel, fully loaded with four days of food and two liters of water. That's about as heavy as I cared to go. I would have loved to have been able to shave a couple more pounds off the weight, but I had by this time been through the pack with a fine toothed comb and didn't feel like I could sacrifice anything else. I had even cut my comb in half to spare whatever fraction of an ounce that accomplished! But it felt manageable on my back. It was a good pack, a ULA Circuit, fitted to my body, and most of the weight was settled on my hip belt, not on my shoulders. Over the next couple of months I did manage to shave a few more pounds off, mostly due to replacing the winter weight gear with lighter alternatives when the weather warmed up.

Besides the increase in pack weight, this was the first morning that Pam, Janice, Seth, and I didn't start together. While they did always take off from our starting point much faster than I did, and I wouldn't see them again until the end of the day, still we did always talk on the ride to the drop off point, and compare notes at the end of each day.

But this morning I was in the van with all the new arrivals, and I was the only hiker to be dropped off at Unicoi Gap. I thanked Josh profusely, as he and Leigh had been wonderful hosts. But it was really time to spread my wings. He wished me well before he drove away, and I felt like my hike had finally started for real. I turned toward the trail, squared my shoulders under the unaccustomed weight of the Green Monster, and walked on.

I really loved the feeling that I could stop anytime I wanted and set up camp and spend the night. Or I could walk on late into the night if I so chose. I slowed down even more than usual, and I stopped for a long leisurely lunch for the first time since beginning my hike. The terrain was very challenging, with two mountains to climb: Rocky Mountain and then Tray Mountain, which at 4,430 feet high with a two and a half mile ascent, left me gasping and trembling. It was fairly early when I reached the summit of Tray Mountain, but I knew that I was done for the day, and would be stopping for the night at Tray Mountain Shelter, another half mile down the mountain. I was greatly relieved to finally reach the blue blazes that marked the side trail to the shelter, and curious and excited to spend my first night at a shelter. Shelters on the Appalachian Trail are rustic, three sided cabins, with the fourth side open to the elements. There are sleeping platforms, just wooden floors where hikers line their pads and sleeping bags up next to each other. Most shelters have picnic tables, cables to hang your food bags to keep them away from the bears, privies (outhouses), a creek, spring, or other water source, and a fire ring. At most shelters, hikers will have drawn a couple of logs around the fire pit for seating. And although in my "real" life I have often gone to great lengths to avoid having to use Port-a-potties, the privies seemed much more civilized when the only other alternative was to walk far enough off the trail so as not to be seen by any other hiker who might happen past. I wasn't planning to actually sleep in the shelters because I was uncomfortable with the thought of bedding down next to complete strangers, and because I had heard stories about the superabundance of very bold mice in the shelters, which would run across your face and nest in your hair as you slept. But I planned on staying at the shelter areas, setting my hammock up in the general vicinity, so I could enjoy the companionship of the other hikers. And a simple picnic table seems a marvel of engineering at the end of a long day in the wilderness.

I turned off the trail to follow the blue blazes down the gentle slope to Tray Mountain Shelter. Although it was only mid-afternoon when I arrived, there were already a fair number of hikers setting up for the night. I chose two trees near the shelter and hung my hammock. My discovery of camping hammocks the year before while researching my hike actually made my hike possible. I don't think I could have slept for too many nights in the one-person tents that are small enough to be carried in a backpack. It's not that I'm claustrophobic, the inside of a hammock, with the bug screen overhead, is actually probably smaller than the inside of a tent. It's just that sleeping on the hard ground, even with a good pad, felt miserably uncomfortable to me, and even worse was the stooping and crouching to get into the tent, and the crawling to get out of it. A tent needs flat, level, ground, with no rocks or sticks underneath, and then you have to hope it doesn't rain, or that your level ground is sloped enough to drain the rainwater off. My hammock gets set up at chair height, and indeed can be sat in like a chair, and a swinging chair at that. With the tarp stretched overhead I could sit in my hammock-chair very comfortably even in a rain, nice and dry, off the ground. And sleeping in a hammock is unbelievably comfortable. Most people don't realize it, but if you lie on the diagonal in a hammock you are nearly flat, not the banana-shape usually associated with a hammock. So you can sleep on your back, or on your side, or even (almost) on your stomach. The main advantage though, is comfort. With no pressure points underneath you feel like you are floating. I don't usually move much during the night in a hammock, I just get into a comfortable position and fall asleep, and remain in that position until morning. I believe it is pressure points that cause you to need to roll over in your sleep, which do not exist in a hammock. Their big disadvantage is that they are colder than a tent. Without the ground below you, the wind is free to blow underneath. A sleeping bag isn't the answer because the weight of your body compresses the down under you, rendering it nearly useless. A foam pad inside the hammock will work, but it is generally accepted that the most comfortable and warmest option is an underquilt, a square of down-stuffed silnylon that is suspended on the *outside* of the hammock, to cover the hiker's backside. Then on the inside of the hammock you have a topquilt, which is like a smaller version of a sleeping bag, except that you don't get inside it, you just put your feet into the "footbox" and pull the rest of it up over your shoulders. I had a good topquilt and underquilt, but I am also a cold sleeper. I would have loved to have carried a pad as well as an underquilt, but I just didn't want to add the extra weight and bulk to my pack. My daughter had made me a fleece sleeping bag liner that I hoped would provide the extra five or ten degrees I needed to stay warm on the coldest nights. I believed that between my wool long underwear and wool socks, fleece jacket and gloves, the bag liner, top- and underquilts, I would be able to stay warm on the coldest nights April could throw at me. I also had a down jacket and wool hat I was willing to sleep in, if needed.

After hanging my hammock I rather self-consciously set about the usual evening chores, the ones that everyone else at the shelter had been doing every night for a week, while this was my first night on the trail. I walked down to the creek to get my water. There were four or five people there, and introductions were made. A woman roughly my own age was sitting on the creek bank downstream from the little pool where we were collecting our water, with her bare feet in the stream. "Come on down!" she called to me in a friendly voice. "Let's have a foot-washin'." I walked over and happily pulled off my boots and socks. Happily, at least, until I stuck my feet into the icy stream, at which point it didn't seem like such a good idea, after all. We joked around for a bit. It turned out that she, like me, was an RN. Her trailname was Songbird, and she was from North Carolina. I met another couple of hikers my age, a married couple called Lewis and Clark. The rest of the hikers were in their twenties and mostly male. But they were all very friendly, and I walked back to the shelter area with clean, if cold, feet, and a feeling of shared purpose and freedom. I made supper and ate it although I still had very little appetite, then hooked my food bag to the big hook on the bear cables and pulled it high up into the air, where it joined the ten or so other bags already there, looking like a collection of small, colorful, hot air balloons. I visited the privy, washed my face and hands, and changed under the privacy of my tarp into what I considered my "camp clothes": the wool long johns (covered for modesty's sake by a pair of nylon basketball shorts), clean socks, clean top, and a pair of Crocs to replace my hiking shoes. I put the down jacket on, as the setting sun was lending a definite chill to the air. The other hikers had a fire going by this time, and the warmth of the blaze felt heavenly as I sat down on a log and listened to the camp talk swirl around me.

A young hiker named Busted whom I had met down at the creek was now lying down inside the shelter, with several people gathered around him. After warming up by the fire, I wandered over to see what was going on. He had the worst blisters on his feet that I could imagine: big deep, raw open wounds, angry and red. There were actual craters between each of his toes and on the balls of his feet and at the back of the heels. The group was discussing treatment options, but one hiker who seemed to have some expertise in this area had assumed the mantle of medical practitioner (later I found out that Busted had paid him in cigarettes for his medical treatment). He was advocating cutting off the loose skin with a knife and filling the holes with Super Glue. Songbird had joined the group by this time and, being less reticent than I am to give advice, was instructing him (and rightly so) that as the body's first line of defense, skin should not be cut off. She recommended wrapping the affected parts in clean gauze and reducing the walking time, distance, and the wearing of the boots. This was all good advice. She looked to me for backup, and I concurred. So the two actual medical people on the scene were in agreement as to the treatment plan, but Busted went with plan A, and then commenced to groan and squeal as his skin was indeed cut off with a camping knife, and the resulting craters filled with Super Glue. I couldn't watch. Once the glue dried, he found that his toes were all glued together, and he couldn't walk. His helpful friend then took the handy knife and cut through the dried glue between the toes. The sharp edges were then filed down, and voila, he declared himself pain free and able to walk. I regret to say I never found out how this plan of care worked out for him in the days to come. I did ask Busted later, around the fire, how he came by his trail name, and found out that this incident with the blisters was only the latest in a series of hiking misadventures. He had already burned a pair of boots and several pairs of socks by leaving them too close to the fire to dry out.

Eventually the excitement died down, the talk dwindled, and people started drifting off-- to their sleeping bags in the shelter, to their tents, and me to my hammock. I climbed in and realized that I was spectacularly tired, even though it was before nine o'clock and I had only hiked five and a half miles. They were a strenuous few miles though. I had started with the 1.4 mile climb up Rocky Mountain, which was followed by the 1.3 mile descent. And then came the very long two and a half mile hike up Tray Mountain, and finally the half mile descent down to the shelter. None of those five and a half miles had been easy, but I had walked every step of them, and with the Green Monster on my back. I had set up my camp, taken care of myself, and made some friends. It had been a good day on the trail. I took my Vitamin I and went to sleep.

Tray Mountain Shelter to Deep Gap Shelter
April 8, 2013

My first night on the trail in my hammock had proven to be a cold one. Situated as it was near the top of Tray Mountain, the shelter area was at the mercy of the early spring winds, which had blown all night long, from seemingly twelve different directions at the same time. As I hastily packed the Green Monster in the morning for another day of hiking, I was hopeful that the name of the next shelter was promising--I planned to go to Deep Gap Shelter, and surely being down in a gap (a sort of valley between mountains) would be warmer than being up on the mountaintop itself. I also felt that my underquilt hadn't been hung properly and had leaked cold wind into the space between it and my body. I vowed to spend more time at night inspecting and testing the underquilt before I climbed into the hammock.

My goal for the day's hike was another modest one. It was only 7.4 miles to Deep Gap Shelter, with just one mountain to climb, the encouragingly named Kelly Knob. My guidebook and elevation profile showed that there was a gain of only 867 feet in the climb up Kelly Knob, and the ascent was only a mile in length. And something called a knob instead of a mountain couldn't be too hard, could it? So I set off in good spirits, optimistic about the hike ahead of me. The day warmed quickly as dawn turned into mid-morning, and the exertion of hiking meant that the chill of the night before was soon forgotten, and I took off my jacket and tied it around my waist.

This was the day to begin the program of prayers I had planned for my hike. As a convert to Catholicism from an evangelical church I found the concept of redemptive suffering to be novel and intriguing, yes, but also deeply meaningful. As a Protestant I had believed suffering to be either a punishment from God, the natural consequence of some action, or else just purely incidental. But having been a Catholic for nearly nine years by this time, I was coming to understand the Church's teaching that suffering was often actually a blessing from God, a chance to share in the suffering of Christ, to grow spiritually, or even to offer that suffering for someone else. While I don't pretend to be a biblical scholar, I found rich meaning in these scriptures:

2 Corinthians 1:5-7
For just as we share abundantly in the sufferings of Christ, so also our comfort abounds through Christ. If we are distressed, it is for your comfort and salvation; if we are

comforted, it is for your comfort, which produces in you patient endurance of the same sufferings we suffer. And our hope for you is firm, because we know that just as you share in our sufferings, so also you share in our comfort.

Romans 8:16-18

For the Spirit Himself giveth testimony to our spirit that we are the sons of God. And if sons, heirs also; heirs indeed of God and joint heirs with Christ: yet so, if we suffer with Him, that we may be also glorified with Him. For I reckon that the sufferings of this time are not worthy to be compared with the glory to come that shall be revealed in us.

As a general principle, I don't like to cherry-pick individual verses out of the context of the chapter in which they lie, as that often leads to misunderstanding and misapplication of Holy Scripture. And I obviously don't mean these two verses to represent an exhaustive study of the idea of redemptive suffering. But while researching the scriptures pertaining to this concept and reading the verses above in context, along with a great many others, these were the two that spoke most fully to me. I was gratified that suffering could have meaning, and that good could even come of it, but like most converts from Protestantism, I wasn't entirely sure how to apply this in a practical manner. And to be honest, I have been blessed in that I had not had all that much real suffering in my life. But I knew that there would be actual physical suffering while hiking the Trail, and I had determined to offer that suffering up every day for a specific person in my life. My plan was to begin each morning's hike by praying for that person specifically, to offer up to God any sufferings that might come my way that day for that person, to think about that person periodically during the day while I hiked and to be grateful to have that person in my life. I would also pray one Divine Mercy Chaplet every day, for the "Person of the Day".

This day was to be Day One of my prayer plan, and the person I chose to start with was.....myself. In retrospect it sounds selfish to have put myself first, but at the time it seemed like the right thing to do. So as I hiked along I crossed myself (awkwardly difficult to do with a hiking pole in each hand!), set myself before God, and asked Him to bless my hike and protect me from harm. I asked that He give me the strength and energy to complete the day's hike. And I told Him that I willingly offered up any suffering I might encounter during the day--sore feet, aching knees, tired back, hunger, thirst, cold, heat, and any other problems I might encounter--as an offering for my soul, and for His will to be done. And then I began the process of working out how to pray the divine mercy chaplet. It is five sets of ten prayers, usually prayed on a rosary to help you keep count of where you are in the chaplet. But I couldn't handle a rosary while hiking with my poles, and I wanted to pray while walking, not while stopped for a rest. So I figured out a complicated system of counting on my fingers the groups of ten, while counting the groups of five on my knuckles. Somehow it worked, and I was able to complete the chaplet. I discovered that it worked best to pray while climbing uphill, rather than on the way down. I prayed it out loud, although it was actually more like murmuring or whispering. And while going uphill I had to gasp for breath often enough that it kept the prayer from being too rushed. It went something like this: "For the sake (huff, puff), of His sorrowful passion (huff, puff), have mercy on us (huff, puff), and on the whole world (gasp, gasp)." Going downhill it sounded like this: "ForthesakeofHissorrowfulpassionhavemercyonusandonthe wholeworld." Definitely better on the uphill climbs, and I prayed it while walking uphill every day for the rest of my hike.

I hiked throughout the afternoon thinking that this hike was really much harder than I had anticipated. I cruised into the shelter area late in the afternoon, chagrined that seven miles of moderate terrain could reduce me to a whimpering shell of a woman. There weren't as many hikers at this shelter as there had been the night before at Tray Mountain, and none of the same people. Where had they all gone? I realized though, that they were all hiking greater daily distances than I was, and had gone on, not content with the 7.4 miles that nearly wiped me out. I hung my hammock (carefully checking my underquilt for gaps), did my other camp chores, and went to the shelter to eat my supper and meet the other hikers who were just starting to trickle in. There were two hikers from Germany, the first of many I was to meet over the next few weeks. There had been a German documentary about the AT that had been repeatedly aired on their televisions, and so there was a great influx of German hikers on the trail. I enjoyed meeting them and hearing their stories, as I enjoyed every hiker that I met.

As the night grew darker and the fire burned low, I retired to my hammock and considered my plan for the next day. I was 3.6 miles from Dick's Creek Gap, where there was a road crossing from which I could get to the

Blueberry Patch Hostel, where I had intended to take my first zero day. I didn't need the zero now, since I had zeroed only three days before at the Hiker Hostel, but I still wanted to stop there. The Blueberry Patch was one of the places that I had read a lot about, pre-hike, in all the trail journals I had read. I felt like I knew it already, having seen so many pictures of it, and I couldn't imagine walking past it without stopping to see it for myself. So I decided to go for it, but to hike to it one day and away from it the next, no zeros. Gary Poteat, the owner, came to Dick's Creek every day to return the previous night's hikers to the trail and pick up another batch to bring home for the night. He made this shuttle run at 9:30, which put some pressure on me, a slow hiker, a (Blue) Tortoise. Could I pack up and hike 3.6 miles by 9:30 in the morning? I was averaging just under a mile and a half an hour, which meant the distance would take me approximately two and a half hours. Never one to pass up a challenge (or a hostel), I set the alarm on my phone for five AM and went to sleep.

Deep Gap Shelter to Dick's Creek Gap
April 9, 2013

I woke up in the dark when the alarm went off. I had slept well, it was definitely warmer in the gaps, or maybe the adjustments I had made to the underquilt had paid off. I packed up by the light of my headlamp, being careful not to shine it into the shelter or the tents of the other hikers, still blissfully snoring. I was on the trail by 6:00, enjoying the novelty of hiking in the dark and watching the sunrise over the mountains to the east. I was glad that the trees were bare of leaves, affording me the beautiful view. I moved as quickly as I dared in the dark and was glad when it became light enough for me to turn the headlamp off. I really pushed myself, glancing frequently at my watch, determined to make it to Dick's Creek in time for the shuttle. I chose my husband Mike as my person for the day, and offered up all my sufferings of the day for him. I thanked God for him and said my divine mercy chaplet.

I arrived at the road crossing at 9:15, and with a huge sigh of relief shrugged the Green Monster off my shoulders. There were already nine or ten people there, but only one other person besides me was waiting for the Blueberry Patch shuttle. The rest of them were going into the town of Hiawassee for the morning to eat town food and resupply, and would return to the trail in the afternoon. An old Jeep pulled off the road into the small parking area, with hikers in every seat and in the back hatch, and bulging backpacks tied to the roof. They all cheerfully peeled themselves out of the car, reminding me of circus clowns coming out of a Beetle. The driver was a pleasant-looking gray-haired man whom I assumed must be Gary. Each passenger gave him a big warm hug and thanked him, and he wished them all well as he lifted the packs off the roof of the Jeep. He called out "Who's going to the Blueberry Patch?" and I stepped forward and introduced myself. "Nice to meet you Blue Tortoise," he said. "Climb on in there." Since there were just the two of us, our packs were put into the back of the Jeep, and off we went to the hostel. The other passenger was a young hiker named Left Hand. He was an electrical engineer in-between jobs; so he had decided that the time was right for hiking the trail, something he had always wanted to do. He did have another job lined up for the fall, giving him time to complete the hike.

We pulled into the driveway of the Blueberry Patch, and I recognized it instantly from the photos I had seen. Gary, a former thru-hiker, and his wife Lonnie lived in a modest frame house, painted pale green. The hostel was in a converted garage and consisted of two rooms. The front room had a long rough table running down the center, surrounded by benches and mismatched chairs. Along the wall were a refrigerator, stove, cabinets and countertops, and bookshelves full of books. It all had a cluttered, homey feeling. There was a woodstove in the corner but the day was shaping up to be warm and sunny, and I knew we were not going to need a fire that night. The room in the back had bunks stacked three high on all sides. Gary showed us around, assigned us bunks, and took us out the back door onto a small deck to point out the shower house in the back yard, a free-standing building with a single bathroom. Then he gave us each a laundry basket and said if we would give him our dirty clothes he would wash them and return them to us. He invited us to use the basket of loaner clothes if we needed them while our own clothes were being laundered, and showed us the huge "hiker boxes," where hikers deposit their unwanted but still usable food, clothes, and other hiking paraphernalia, and other hikers are free to take what they want. Almost every place of business that caters to hikers along the entire length of the trail has some version of a hiker box. I had only been on the trail for two days since my slackpack, but this concrete-floored largesse seemed very luxuriously decadent to me. I took a hot shower and gave Gary all my dirty hiking clothes, asking him to return them to me wet so I could hang them on his clothesline to dry. He said he would be driving into Hiawasee in the afternoon if I wanted to go. Throughout the morning other hikers came drifting in. Songbird came, whom I had met two nights earlier at Tray Mountain Shelter. There was a young German girl named Laura who was badly sunburned and had deep, painful blisters on both feet. There was a pair of octogenarian hikers, Rock Solid and Greybeard. Rock Solid was making his third thru-hike, having completed previous hikes in 1993 and 2003. Evidently he hiked the trail every ten years. Greybeard was taking a zero for an ankle injury but would be getting back on the trail in two more days. I told him about Laura, who was sitting on her bunk looking very sad. She didn't speak quite enough English to make for easy communication, but she had expressed to me that she just hadn't researched quite as well as she might have, and didn't realize there was a possibility of sunburn, and was totally unprepared for foot blisters. It turned out that Greybeard's real name was Ernst, and, though he was an American, he was fluent in German. He went in to talk to Laura and they became fast friends, with him taking her under his wing as a grandfather-figure and mentor. I found out later that they both stayed at the Blueberry Patch for another day or two and then hiked on together. Gary was also wonderful to Laura, bringing aloe for her burns and moleskin for her blisters from his house. I was beginning to understand the generosity and unselfishness of the hiking community, something I would see over and over again for the next few months.

I called Mike on the phone, something I hadn't been able to do while out in the woods without cell service. I hung my clean clothes in the warm sunshine to dry, then stood on the deck watching a small community of mice in the tall grass. They would stick their noses and whiskers out of their holes and sniff nervously. Not sensing danger, and oblivious to me hanging over the deck rail watching them, they would dart out and chew through the stem of some plant that must have been particularly tasty. The whole plant would disappear down into one of the holes as it was dragged down by the little mouse, who would then re-emerge and start on the next one. I was completely enchanted by this little scene, and realized that it would be so easy to overlook this activity, taking place as it was in total silence, and entirely in the small patch of weeds between the driveway and the deck. Although it was no more than four feet from my nose, in my usual, busy life, I would never have seen any of it. As it was I stood there for probably 15 or 20 minutes, only because I was a hiker and had nowhere else to be at that moment, and wondered what else I might be missing in my life back home because I was too busy to see what was happening right under my nose. The mice all disappeared into their holes when Gary started the Jeep up and called for those wanting to ride into town.

Left Hand, Songbird, and I were the only takers. Gary dropped us off in Hiawasee and arranged to pick us up two hours later in the grocery store parking lot. We debated about which restaurant to go to, and decided on a typical southern family restaurant that Gary had recommended when I asked him where the best cheeseburgers were found. He was right. The cheeseburger was hot and greasy with melted American cheese and crisp lettuce, my favorite food in the whole world. I had an icy cold Mello Yello with it and good conversation as I got to know Songbird better. (Left Hand had opted for pizza, and had seen some hikers he recognized at the pizza joint). We all met up at the grocery store where I bought more ibuprofen and some cheese and hard rolls. There was a long stretch coming up, probably six hiking days until the next town day, so I needed to be well-supplied. Gary picked us up as scheduled and drove us back to the hostel. I took my now-dry clothes down from the line and visited with the other hikers until bedtime: hiker midnight, nine PM.

Dick's Creek Gap to Unnamed Campsite
April 10, 2013

Breakfast at the hostel more than lived up to the great reputation the Blueberry Patch has among hikers. When the bell rang we all filed into the back room of the house, a lovely, rustic room with sunny windows, quilts, and a real wood cookstove. We took seats around the long farmhouse table which had been beautifully set with china and glasses of orange juice and jars of fresh wildflowers. It was a scene from a home, garden, and decorating magazine of artfully casual elegant dining, the kind that you just know was staged for the magazine but doesn't exist in reality. But here it was, come to life, and I was sitting at the beautiful table with a motley assortment of fresh-scrubbed but hairy male hikers, and female hikers devoid of makeup and jewelry. I thought they were as beautifully, rustically elegant as the setting. But soon the food started appearing at the table, borne in by Gary and his wife Lonnie in great bowls. There were fresh hot biscuits, and sausage, and scrambled eggs. But the piece de resistance was the blueberry pancakes, made with the berries that give the hostel its name. All talk ceased as the hikers, who knew that it was ramen noodles and protein bars from here on out, tucked into the repast. Evidently the phenomenon of the missing appetite was disappearing, to be replaced by the famous hiker appetite. The Blueberry Patch is operated as a ministry, not a business, so there is no set fee charged for the services we had enjoyed for the past 24 hours. Instead, there was an envelope under each plate, and Gary told us that we were welcome to make a donation to help keep the hostel running. I put a 20 dollar bill into my envelope and hoped he didn't get stiffed too often, as I remembered his humble way of washing all of our dirty hiker clothes, driving us into town, and sharing his knowledge and humor with us. As I got out of the Jeep at Dick's Creek Gap a little later I hugged him warmly and thanked him and suddenly understood why I had seen yesterday's hikers do the same. What a blessing he is to hikers!

Well, back to work. I started the climb up the steep hill out of the Gap. Days almost always began with a steep climb. I found myself walking with Songbird, and the morning went by quickly as we talked and joked and enjoyed each other's company. She made me laugh, and laughter is a lovely gift to find on the trail. We had a lot in common: I am from Tennessee, and she was from our neighboring state, North Carolina. We were nearly the same age, and both of us were RNs. We both had husbands supportive of our hikes and grown children. Physically, she was several inches shorter than my five feet seven inches, and just a bit rounder, although her arms and legs were slim and she was in good hiking shape. She wore her shoulder-length strawberry blonde hair in a tight ponytail while hiking, had twinkling blue eyes, and a mouth that always looked to be on the verge of either a smile or a smart comment. She was much more out-going and self-confident than I, which was a nice complement to my natural reticence. I hadn't planned on having a hiking partner, but just like that, I had one, and her natural friendliness and sociability meant that I was to meet many more people than I would have on my own.

We came to the first shelter but it was too early to stop, having walked only four and a half miles, so we decided to keep going. We knew there were storms forecast for the next afternoon, and we wanted to be sure to make it to the next shelter early enough to avoid the rain. So on we walked. The sun came out and the day was warm, and I was soon sweating. When I took my bandana to wipe the sweat from my neck I found that it was lightly sunburned. We were tired when we found a nice spot to set up our camp, but it was nice to busy ourselves with the typical camp chores: setting up my hammock (and Songbird's tent), collecting and filtering water, gathering wood for a fire, and making our suppers. In the course of this activity a young couple came, Freefall and Footloose, and I will admit I was glad for the company in our lonely campsite. They set up their tent just up the hill from us, and then another man came limping—no, lurching—into our little camp. His name was Glen, no trail name, and he looked and acted quite ill. Songbird and I went into professional mode and peppered him with questions: when did you last eat? have you been drinking water today? are you diabetic? do you have any underlying cardiac problems? are you on any medications? He was pale and sweaty, and looked like he might keel over at any moment. His answers were vague, but eventually we were able to piece his story together. He lived close to the trail, but had never really hiked before, and was overweight and out of shape. For some reason he suddenly decided he needed to start hiking and felt that he should be able to do 20 miles a day, because he had read that "that's what hikers do." So he had loaded up a (probably too heavy) pack and set out on a hot day, with a plan to walk 20 miles. No wonder he was dehydrated, fatigued, and feeling like he might die any second. I got him some water and he set up his tent and stumbled into it to lie down. We heard him retching a bit later and called out to ask if he needed help, which he denied. I sponged the worst of the sweat from my own body with a bandana, and called it a day. The hammock felt great as I stretched out in it, and it rocked gently as I eased off into sleep.

Unnamed Campsite to Muskrat Creek Shelter
April 11, 2013

The weather was cool and overcast as I took down my hammock in the morning and repacked the Green Monster. Not a big breakfast eater under the best of circumstances (meaning with access to a stove, oven, running water, utensils, and a refrigerator full of food), I had opted to keep things simple on the trail by eating protein bars for the morning meal. Even though my missing appetite had returned, this, along with my ever-present water bottle, sufficed until my mid-morning snack. Songbird and I set off on the day's hike and were soon laboring up mountainsides that had me gritting my teeth while sweating in the cool morning air. Grrr. Was this ever going to get easier? Where were my trail legs that everyone promised I would get?

A bright spot came midmorning, however. Our first state line! There was no big billboard alerting us of our move from Georgia into North Carolina, such as would be seen on a highway. Instead, just an inconspicuous wooden sign, nailed to a tree, with GA/NC carved into it. This was cause for much rejoicing, however. Somehow it just felt more real, having hiked all the way through a state. One down, thirteen more to go! We took the obligatory photos with the little sign and continued walking. We very shortly came to what is arguably the most famous tree on the trail. At Bly Gap there is a gnarled old oak tree that curves in the most absurdly sinuous fashion, running parallel to the ground to start with before curling up and into shapes that Songbird somehow found sexual. We laughed and took some obligatory photos (every hiker gets a picture with this tree), but it was truly a beautiful sight, and had I been alone I would have been thinking a great deal more about the age and history of the tree than the sensuality of its curves!

I had never thought about having a hiking partner, but

found I was enjoying spending time with Songbird. I hadn't imagined that there would be anyone compatible with both my slow hiking speed and my personality, and I assumed that if such a creature existed, I would still weary of spending so much time with him or her. But we were getting along famously. She made me laugh and take everything just a bit less seriously than I was inclined to do, and that was a wonderful benefit. For the most part we did not actually hike together, meaning walk along with each other. Most of the actual hiking was done solo, each at our own pace, and we would wait for each other at rest breaks or places of interest. I actually walked faster than she did going uphill and she walked faster than me going downhill, and it all seemed to even out. On the few level stretches we did occasionally walk together, swapping gross or funny nursing stories, or singing (which of us was worse it would be hard to say), or talking about our families. At other times I would hear her somewhere ahead of me, singing along with her MP3 player, loudly and off-key, and I would laugh and admire her lack of self-consciousness.

After the joy of the state line and the beauty of the Bly Gap oak, the trail got hard, and the hiking got more serious. I prayed my divine mercy chaplet as I walked, and offered up the trials of the day for my second daughter. "Plenty of them, too," I thought, gasping for breath. Coming out on the top of a high ridge with views that went on seemingly forever, I came across Songbird on the phone with her husband. We seldom had phone reception, but she had been trying to reach him all day and had finally gotten through. She had only a few brief moments before the signal faded again, but he was able to tell her that there was a bad storm coming our way, with rain starting at four PM, thunderstorms by seven with the potential for hail, high winds, and maybe even tornadoes.

There was a shelter just a mile and a half further down the trail, and we knew we should stop there for the night, even though it was still early afternoon. The next shelter after that was another five miles, and given our slow pace, we might not make it before the storm hit. So we headed for Muskrat Creek Shelter. It was a small one (capacity of eight according to my guidebook), and we hoped it wouldn't be full of hikers already, gathered to wait out the storm. We hadn't seen any other hikers all day. I assumed that most of them had been smart enough to stay at the last shelter or even at the Blueberry Patch until this front passed.

As luck would have it, we ended up as a group of eight. Besides Songbird and myself there was a young couple,

Shockarone and Andrea; a father and son team; a young man from Asheville; and an older hiker named Pacer, on his second thruhike. We all had plenty of time through the afternoon and evening to get to know one another, and it was a congenial group. All hikers have a story to tell, and the time passed very pleasantly indeed as we built a fire and each did our little homey tasks. I didn't have a sleeping pad, as a hammock camper who had never intended to sleep in a shelter, so I would be sleeping on the hard wooden shelter floor. It seemed a better alternative than facing the weather that was coming in my hammock. So I set up my sleeping bag liner on the floor, staking out my space. I was able to use my underquilt as a pillow and my topquilt as a blanket, and told myself that people all over the world routinely slept on wooden floors without pillow-top queen-sized inner-spring mattresses. It would be good for my back, I told myself. Then I went to rejoin the rest of the group around the fire and eat my mashed potatoes (with a foil packet of chicken added).

I gave someone a trail name. Petite Andrea was the only one paying any attention to the fire, and she kept wandering off into the woods and returning dragging tree branches as big as she was. "What a lumberjack!" I quipped in appreciation of her efforts, and the name stuck,

Lumberjack she was. The son of the father and son pair was a great big guy, a new hiker who wasn't altogether enthusiastic about hiking, but he was good-naturedly going along with his dad who was living out his dream of hiking the AT. It was a good thing the son was so big and hopefully strong, because his pack was massive and had to weigh 50 pounds. Shockarone, another big guy, was carrying a pack that weighed 25 pounds, which the son seemed to find incomprehensible. He seemed quite devoted to all his stuff, however, and not really amenable to suggestions or helpful advice on how to lighten his pack weight. Pacer, seeing himself as the voice of wisdom and experience in this group of newbie hikers, commenced to giving advice right and left, and I began to realize how the son had felt. Hike Your Own Hike, dude, as they say.

But for the most part it was a very enjoyable afternoon/evening, and when the rain started in earnest we abandoned our fire and retreated into the shelter. We lay side by side, and I was roughly in the middle, with Songbird on one side and Lumberjack on the other. The camaraderie continued as the rain and wind picked up, until it became just too difficult to talk. Shockarone took a set of battery-operated Christmas tree lights out of his pack and wrapped them around a beam in the ceiling of the shelter.

The shelter was quite small and already seemed a bit cozy, but with the colorful lights twinkling in the darkness it all seemed very homey and somehow cheering. Son made us all laugh when he said, in a very deadpan voice, "Dude. You've got a twenty five pound pack. AND you've got Christmas lights." I laughed further when I thought about the incongruity of the whole situation: I was sleeping way out in the woods, in an open shelter during a fierce storm with seven strangers and a string of Christmas lights twinkling merrily overhead.

The storm raged for quite a while, living up to its billing with roaring wind, thunder and lightning and pounding rain. Being in the middle of the line of bodies I stayed dry, but the guys on the ends had to sleep in their rain gear because they got wet as the rain blew in on them. No one complained. Hikers rock.

Muskrat Creek Shelter to Beech Gap Campsite
April 12, 2013

Nine and a half tough miles of hiking the next day brought us to a campsite named Beech Gap. The term "campsite," when used on the AT, doesn't mean "campground," with picnic tables, bath houses, maybe even a camp store. "Campsite" means a spot in the woods level enough to set up a few tents, with evidence of where the last inhabitants' campfire had been. Beech Gap Campsite was actually a pretty big area, and when we arrived there were already 15 or 20 people there, a veritable crowd by AT hiking standards. I was absolutely worn out; it had been a tough day which included a two and a half mile ascent of Standing Indian Mountain. I hadn't slept well at the shelter the previous night; it turns out that cold hard wooden floors are just about as comfortable to sleep on as they sound. The evening air was cold, the kind of cold that promised much colder temps before morning. I was, perhaps, a bit cranky. This condition was not improved when I attempted to cook my supper. Lacking a picnic table or other flat surface, I tried to light my little alcohol stove on a rock that was maybe six inches off the ground but had a reasonably level top surface. I got it lit and had the water boiling and was just about ready to drop in the Ramen noodles when I somehow jostled the rock. Stove, pot, alcohol, and water went flying. From this I learned that alcohol spilled all over the ground will continue to burn in an alarming fashion, and the water from one's pot will not put it out.

I put the fire out and cleaned up my mess. I was too cold, tired, and disheartened to try it again, so I ate a protein bar and made my way down to a small creek to collect my drinking water. It had a muddy bank after the previous night's rain so the hikers were lined up and taking turns getting down to the only dry spot. Thinking that my trail name should have been "Grace," I slipped and ended up with one foot in the mud up to my ankle. There was a good sized group behind me that was hiking together, probably about five or six people, and they were all speaking what I assumed to be German. They were extraordinarily cheerful, not recognizing my pity party which was fully in progress. On top of that, the girls all had thick, shiny, clean hair! I pulled my foot out of the mud and slunk off, back up the bank to the campsite.

We had already determined that I would sleep in Songbird's tent with her for the night. I was just too tired to find trees to hang my hammock, and we were hoping that it would be warmer with two of us in the one-man tent. The temperature was dropping quickly, and it looked to be our coldest night yet. Shockarone and Lumberjack had arrived and set up their tent near ours, right under a tree with a sign identifying the area as a protected bear sanctuary! We shared a campfire until it was fully dark with them and a few other hikers, including a young man who identified himself as a "trail chaplain," evidently a self-appointed title. I thought he might have a few words of wisdom or encouragement for us around the fire, but he was too busy trying to get his water filter to work. We could hear coyotes from somewhere out in the night and I was surprised that they didn't sound like I expected them to. They sounded like monkeys more than anything else, chattering and giggling.

Finally we retired for the night to Songbird's tent, where I spent my second cold, uncomfortable, sleepless night in a row, and decided I simply had to rethink my sleeping gear. The lack of a pad left me lying on the cold ground (next to Songbird on her big fluffy inflatable pad). The ground felt just as hard as the shelter floor the night before but was much colder. The cold seemed to seep into my bones all night long. I was wearing my usual sleeping ensemble, consisting of: wool long johns, wool socks, wool short-sleeved shirt, synthetic long-sleeved shirt, down jacket, stocking cap and gloves. I was sleeping in a fleece sleeping bag liner and covered with a down top quilt, and I was cold enough that my teeth chattered all night long. The decision not to bring a sleeping pad had been a deliberate one, made to save weight and bulk. Now however, listening to Songbird snore while I shivered and waited for dawn, I was beginning to see the value of a good pad.

Beech Gap Campsite to Betty Creek Campsite
April 13, 2013

Morning dawned, and I stumbled out of the tent, resolved to sleep in my hammock from then on, no matter how tired I felt at the end of the day. Hammocks are infinitely more comfortable for 50 year old bones than the ground and certainly no colder than what I had experienced the last two nights. But once the Green Monster was packed and on my back and the day's hike commenced, my body warmed up and my mood improved as the sun shone. The scenery was spectacular, soaring vistas from every vantage point on the mountaintops. I could see beautiful rhododendron thickets down in the valleys, their shiny, dark green foliage a welcome relief from the relentless browns and grays of the still-winter forest floor. My priority was to try to make a phone call to my husband, St. Mike, to arrange our next rendezvous. We had planned a get-together in Franklin, North Carolina, which was now less than two days hike away. I hadn't had cell service for days, but I continued trying as we hiked throughout the day, checking my phone on every mountaintop, only to stuff it back into my pocket each time, wondering if it was better to have a phone you couldn't use, or not to have one at all. Finally, on one windy ledge, Songbird called out excitedly "I've got two bars!" My phone was still playing possum, but we each were able to place a call on hers before the signal faded. St. Mike was still planning to come to Franklin, so we made arrangements to meet at Wallace Gap the next evening, for a ride to town, a motel room, a shower, and town food! This sounded quite unbelievable. Did such luxuries still exist?

We hiked on with new pep in our steps and stopped for the night to camp at a very pretty campsite ringed with rhododendron bushes. We had hiked less than seven miles, making it a short day, but it was only nine more miles to Wallace Gap so there was no reason to push on much farther. We wanted to tackle the upcoming Albert Mountain in the morning when we were fresh, and not try to deal with it later in the afternoon when we were bedraggled. We had been hearing about Albert Mountain and its grueling hand-over-hand climbs for days, and we were both a little leery of it.

I went to bed in my hammock after hanging my food bag and cooking my supper (without incident this time) wearing an extra pair of socks and my hiking pants over my long johns. I don't know if it was actually warmer than the previous two nights, if it was due to the extra clothes, or if I was just heartened by the idea of getting to town the next day, but I slept reasonably warmly and cozy, dreaming about greasy cheeseburgers, ice cold beverages, and a warm hug from my husband.

Betty Creek Gap Campsite to Wallace Gap
April 14, 2013

Well, this was the day. Albert Mountain day. Songbird was inordinately worried about it, and looking through her guide book she found an alternate trail that went *around* the mountain, rather than up and over, and then rejoined the AT on the other side. She was convinced that this is what we should do, but the suggestion made me uneasy. The AT is marked for its entire length by the white rectangular blazes painted on trees (and occasionally on rocks, bridges, and even small town streets!), and the alternate or side trails are marked with blue blazes. Hikers who divert from the AT to the blue-blazed trails to save miles, take an easier route, or avoid obstacles are called, derisively, "blue-blazers." I had no desire to be a blue-blazer and believed that if everyone else could climb Albert Mountain, I could too, even if I would be a little slower and a lot less graceful than most of them.

I had another reason, which I did not discuss with Songbird, why I didn't want to make it easier for myself today of all days. My person of the day to pray for was my mother. I wasn't looking for shortcuts when it came to offering everything I had to offer for her. Mom was 89 years old and very much in her right mind, lived in her own home and took care of herself. She was spry and strong and looked younger than her age, a fact in which she took great pride. And she had been diagnosed with pancreatic cancer the previous November. Her prognosis at the time had been that she had six months left, but now five months later she was still completely symptom-free and I was beginning to doubt the diagnosis. I was a hospice nurse and she didn't look like someone with a serious cancer to me. The diagnosis had been made on the basis of an abdominal ultrasound, not by CT, MRI, or biopsy. She lived 500 miles from me, and when she had gotten sick and gone to the hospital the previous fall, I had gone to care for her after her discharge. She was quite ill at that time. When the doctor came back with the ultrasound results, and gave the sad news to my three sisters, two brothers, and me, I asked if he was sure. He said, "If it waddles like a duck and quacks like a duck, it's a duck." I asked him what he would do if she was his own mother, and he said he would take her home and keep her comfortable for the six months she had left. So we decided as a family not to subject her to any more testing, and certainly not to any devastating treatments for an untreatable cancer. She was sleeping a lot at the time and not completely alert when she was awake, so we found ourselves for the first time in our lives having to make decisions for our strong mother. The world seemed to have shifted on its axis.

We took her back to her home, and as the nurse in the family, I prepared to stay until the end, to care for her physically for what would surely not be six months, but only a week or two, as weak and sick as she seemed at the time. We got a hospital bed for her room and a wheelchair for when she felt well enough to sit up, and I managed her medications, took her to the restroom, helped her with her bath, and tried to find things she was willing and able to eat. She then proceeded to surprise all of us by getting better. Every day she was stronger and sharper until our familiar and much-loved mother was back, laughing and joking, sneaking out to the yard to rake leaves when no one was looking. I had seen many hospice patients have a rally, when they felt better for a little while before eventually succumbing to their disease. These rallies were generally short-lived though, only a few days at the most, and Mom just kept getting better. I was so grateful for this period of respite, for however long it might last, but it went on for so long that eventually I had to make arrangements to go back home to Tennessee. We signed her up with the local hospice agency so she would have a nurse and a social worker come to the house several times a week, and an aide to help her with her toilette when that became necessary. She completely balked and nearly threw the poor aide out of the house, so I knew Mom was back, and went home confident she was in good hands. My widowed sister had actually moved in with her some months before, so Mom wouldn't be alone. My other two sisters lived close by in the same small town, and I was only a phone call away. I kept close tabs on her throughout January, February, and March, ready to go up and resume care of her when she needed me and fully prepared to delay the start of my hike as necessary. I made a couple of trips during this time to see her, and each time she was her old self, shopping online and buying clothes she would never wear (except around the house, strutting like a little banty rooster. She was so cute, in her love for new clothes, her "finery" she called them.) Whatever illness she had had in November showed no signs of recurrence.

So I started my hike on April first. I called her as often as I could with the little bit of phone service I occasionally had, and I communicated with my sisters by phone or email, and our arrangement was that if or when she became incapacitated again, I would leave the trail and return to care for her. But she continued to feel well, other than some normal aches and pains, and she even tried to shovel snow during the Indiana winter. "Irrepressible" is a good word for her. So by this time I had come to strongly suspect that she had never had pancreatic cancer, that the original illness was something else entirely, and that whatever was seen on the ultrasound was not a cancer. She just wasn't sick enough to have pancreatic cancer. But the doubt and concern remained. She was my person to pray for as I climbed Albert Mountain and I did not want to take any shortcuts. I wanted to grunt and sweat and struggle up and over the summit, because my sweet mother was 700 miles away from me and there was nothing else I could do for her on this lonely mountain ridge. I remembered teenage rolling of my blue eyes—the same as hers--and I remembered cutting remarks I had made to her, and stomping feet and slamming doors, and I wanted to climb Albert Mountain on my hands and knees if it would make her well. I would have slithered up Albert Mountain on my belly if it would prove how much I loved her. I wanted to have something to offer God for her health, for her life, for her soul, for her happiness. I asked my Mother in Heaven to keep a special eye on my mother on earth, and I shouldered the Green Monster, determined to ignore any blue-blazed trails I passed on the way to Albert Mountain.

In my guidebook, the elevation profile shows the trail to the top of Albert Mountain as nearly a vertical line. For most of the morning, as we went up (and up, and up) it wasn't any worse than any of the other mountains we had climbed, and we enjoyed a few minutes of bravado—"This isn't so bad!" "I thought Albert Mountain was supposed to be steep!" But then—there it was. The trail appeared to stop, dead-ending into a wall of rock. But no, there were the white blazes, on the rocks, over our heads, and continuing up. My head fell back as I looked up into the sky and asked Songbird, "Do you think we're supposed to go up there?"

"How did we miss that side trail?" she fumed. "The map showed it as going off to the right about a half mile back. Did you see it?"

"No, no," I replied, thinking that it really wasn't even a white lie if I didn't see a trail I had refused to look for. "But look, we can go around that big rock right there, it's really not exactly straight up."

"Oh, brother," she sighed as she grabbed a branch of a scrubby trailside shrub and pulled herself up.

And so our rather ridiculous and ungainly assault on Albert Mountain commenced. My hiking poles, usually so helpful on uneven terrain, now dangled uselessly from my wrists as I took hold of branches, rocks, roots, handfuls of mud, whatever I could grab to use to pull myself up a few more feet. Songbird and I kept up a running conversation, advising each other of potential handholds and good rocks for foot placement. We found ourselves surprisingly cheerful and buoyed as we made what we considered pretty good progress up the mountainside. We stopped and scooted a little bit off the "trail" when we heard voices coming up from behind us. A small group of long-legged and extremely youthful appearing hikers showed up walking—yes, walking!—along the trail we had just been crawling up.

"How are you all doing that?" Songbird demanded. "Are you part mountain goat?"

They chuckled and made what I'm sure were meant to be encouraging remarks as they strode confidently past the two middle–aged women clinging with both hands to the rocks they blithely scampered over. We looked at one another, shrugged, and resumed our painstaking climb. A short time later, Songbird, who was in the lead, called back to me, "This is it! The top! Pull yourself up over that next big rock and we're here!"

The summit of Albert Mountain was a barren, rocky, windswept place, bereft of vegetation. At that moment, it was the most beautiful place I'd ever seen. Besides representing victory over the challenges presented by the climb, to an Appalachian Trail hiker it also represents a milestone: 100 miles walked. Songbird and I laughed, hugged, celebrated, and took a variety of silly pictures with the number "100" spelled out with rocks, sticks, and dirt. What we did not do was climb the fire tower located on the summit. We didn't even consider it. Much later, after the hike ended, I occasionally had people ask me in surprise, "You mean you didn't climb the tower on Albert Mountain?" No, actually we didn't. The view was quite lovely from the ground. I still don't regret it! (This did set a precedent for my hike. There were to be other towers along the way. I didn't climb them, either.)

"One hundred miles down, only 2,080 left to go!" we crowed as we started down the other side of the mountain, intent now on getting to Wallace Gap to meet Mike and ride into Franklin, NC. We arrived just before five PM, more than an hour early for our scheduled rendezvous time of six. The hiker's enemy, rain, was falling again, so we pulled our raincoats out of our packs and hunkered down to wait. Soon two more hikers joined us, a pair of Germans trailnamed, charmingly enough, Hansel and Gretel. They were not quite fluent in English, but enough to tell us that they were hoping to get a ride into town from this gap also, and they gratefully accepted my offer to ride with us if they didn't mind waiting. So now there were four of us huddling under the trees and looking hopefully up and down the quiet country road, listening for the sound of a motor. Two different sets of locals in pickup trucks came along and stopped to talk to us. The first offered us a ride into town, which we of course declined (I told Hansel and Gretel they could go with him if they'd rather not wait, but they declined politely also.) The second just wanted to talk, but he had a cooler in the back of his truck and handed out beers. I would rather have seen a steaming cup of tea or hot chocolate, but I did appreciate the friendliness and generosity that is a hallmark of trail life.

Soon enough I saw our Jeep Cherokee coming down the road, a welcome sight indeed! It was tight quarters, with Mike, our two dogs, their kennel, Mike's bags and the blue sleeping pad he had brought for me, and now with four hikers and four huge backpacks, but we all squeezed in, glad to get out of the rain, and drove to Franklin. The quaint small town was boiling with hikers, this being right smack in the middle of hiker season. Hansel and Gretel saw some friends walking down the street and happily disengaged themselves from the sardine can of a Jeep and joined them. I felt a strong sense of solidarity, that these were my people, that I was part of this community, when I saw the tarps and tents and sleeping bags hanging from the rails of the two motels to dry in the warm air. Why is it that it was always raining on the trail and sunny in town? We secured two rooms in one of the motels and dinner in a Mexican restaurant, and then I enjoyed a long, hot, shower, my first since Blueberry Patch Hostel. It was lovely, and I decided that nothing smells as good as soap and shampoo. I thanked God for my blessings, for my husband, asked Him again to watch over my mother, and switched off the light.

Franklin, North Carolina
April 15, 2013

In my pre-trail prep period, I had somehow imagined that a zero day in town would be restful and peaceful, and would consist mostly of laying in the motel bed resting my bones, watching television and eating large quantities of food that were brought to my door by a steady stream of delivery people. But in actuality, there are a lot of chores to be done. After the obligatory shower and first big meal, the pack gets emptied out and the contents spread all over the motel room for assessment. You can be sure that every single item in the pack needs to be either washed, dried, repaired, replaced, or just aired out. My tarp, hammock, and quilts joined the others on the railing. Then the stinky clothes go to the laundry. We don't carry very many clothes, so the question is what do you wear while they are in the washer? You could do two loads, but that seems rather excessive (and expensive) when they already constitute such a small load. It's considered quite normal to see hikers on warm sunny days wearing their rain jackets and rain pants while doing laundry. It was easier for me on this stop, Mike had brought the overnight bag I had prepacked before the hike, so I had "civilian" or non-hiker clothes to wear, and I felt like an imposter in jeans and flip flops. I filled the bathroom sink up with hot water and lots of soap and added my water filter and bottles, my spork, knife and cooking pot. Mike, Songbird, and I went to the grocery store to resupply for the next leg of the trip with food and ibuprofen, the magic "vitamin I," that I took twice every hiking day to keep my knees happy. The last stop was the outfitter, that fabulous store full of all the things hikers dream of buying someday. I bought a few more of the little chemical handwarmers that heat up when the packet is broken. I had found them very comforting on cold nights, even though they did only warm up a three square inch portion of my body at a time.

Then it was time for Mike to leave and we said our sweet goodbyes, and he and the dogs got back in the Jeep and headed home. Songbird moved into the extra bed in my room. I thought briefly about taking a walk around Franklin, it was a lovely small town, historic and scenic, but honestly hikers just don't want to walk on their days off. So instead I lay on the bed in my bland motel room with ice bags on my knees and watched television. Then we ordered a pizza and ate it all. Finally, this was how I had pictured zero days!

As I drifted off to sleep I pondered about the two very different worlds I inhabited. Here in town, everything was easy. You want hot water? No problem, just turn the knob! Are you just a bit chilly? There's another magic knob for that. Let alone the wonders of indoor plumbing, and the scrumptious food that just appears at your door if you call for it. It was hard to believe that just a couple of days ago I was exposed to all the elements and lumbering up the sides of mountains with everything I owned on my back, my biggest, all consuming consideration how far it was to the next water source. And although I was really enjoying all the creature comforts of town life, I could honestly say that I was eager to get back out on the trail, and that town life seemed somewhat bland and colorless. We had a shuttle scheduled to pick us up at the motel in the morning and deliver us back to Wallace Gap, and I was ready. But for tonight, I had a nice firm mattress and a pillow!

Wallace Gap to Wayah Gap
April 16, 2013

Songbird had a surprising proposition for me in the

morning. She suggested that we reserve our room for another night, and arrange for a shuttle to pick us up in the afternoon at Wayah Gap, and bring us back to the motel for another night. That way we could slackpack, leaving most of our gear in the room, and arrange for yet another shuttle to drive us back to Wayah Gap the next morning, to resume our hike in earnest. I didn't really like the idea of paying for another night in the motel, another restaurant meal, and a couple of extra shuttles, but she could be very convincing, and in spite of my yearning for the wilderness the night before, the pull of town can be very strong, and I succumbed. As I was to come to see in the weeks ahead, Songbird was the queen of the blue blaze, the shortcut, the slackpack, the hostel, the motel, and the zero day. And I came also to realize that I don't have much of a backbone when someone dangles a cheeseburger in front of me.

The hike was lovely though, nine miles without the Green Monster on my back. The weather was warm and sunny, so I was able to unzip the legs off my hiking pants and wear shorts for the first time. The air and the sun felt good on my pasty white legs. We were in pretty good hiking shape by this time, and even the five mile ascent of Siler Bald didn't faze us. We were hiking machines.

It was a day of mysteries, as if I were being reminded

rather forcefully of my impression the night before of town life being bland and colorless. The trail was so full of mystery that I really had no desire to return to the dreary motel room at the end of the day. The first mystery I encountered was the bald itself. I've read several theories on how these balds came to exist, but no definitive explanation. For some mysterious reason, certain mountains in the southern Appalachians have no trees on the tops, even though they're not tall enough to be above treeline. Siler Bald was my first bald, and it was magical to suddenly emerge from the cool, dark, ubiquitous forest into a sunny grassy field. We lay on the grass until it got uncomfortably warm, and then continued on.

At the far edge of the bald, just before re-entering the woods, we came upon the day's second mystery. An entirely normal, harmless looking tree sat there, half in the sun and half in the shade of the forest. As I walked under it, appreciative of the shade it offered, a big drop of water dripped on my nose. "Oh, no, not more rain," I thought, looking up. No rain, no clouds, just a bright sunny sky. Another drop hit me on the forehead, and then a third. "Hey, Songbird, come look at this," I called to her. We walked around and around the tree, trying to find the source of the dripping water that had created a twelve inch round puddle on the trail. The dripping was coming out of a branch that was probably twenty feet over my head, too small in diameter to house any source of liquid that made sense to me. The tree was crying, we decided. Songbird gave it a big hug, and I patted it and tried to reassure it that everything would be all right. Perhaps it was crying for the souls lost in Boston, in the tragedy of marathon proportions we had heard about on the television in Franklin.

We gave the crying tree a final pat and walked on. Then in the silence of the forest I heard the third mystery, the sound I had been hearing for days when the woods were quiet—a very soft sound of distant drumming. I had asked other hikers what the sound was, and had never found anyone else who had heard it. I was beginning to think that I was the only person who could hear it. In a fanciful mood after the crying tree, I began to wonder if the drums were the echoes of the Cherokee who used to rule these woods, and who were my ancestors. I asked Songbird if she heard them, and was quite surprised that she did indeed. *(Not to spoil your own sense of mystery, but I was later told that the sound was likely that of a ruffed grouse beating his wings in an avian display of his awesomeness, and that many people are unable to hear them.)*

We walked on, and the trail had a final mystery for me.

Songbird got quite far ahead of me, as was usual, so far that she was completely out of sight, and I seemed to be alone in this vast, beautiful, and silent world. The trail was winding around the side of a mountain, so that the mountain rose up quite sharply on my right side, and the trail dropped off equally sharply on the left, stretching away down into a valley far below. Across from the valley were more trees, more mountains, more silence, and no people. Suddenly I heard a loud POP! that sounded like a gunshot. It seemed to come from somewhere ahead of me, and down in the valley. It startled me, as I knew that there was no road crossing anywhere near, no source of people capable of making such a loud noise. I thought about Songbird walking somewhere ahead of me, and wondered if I should call out to her, or if I should stop, or go on and just wait to see if anything else happened. Then there was a second POP!, and a third. Then silence. I resumed walking, keeping my eyes and ears open, scanning the woods for anything out of the ordinary. It was silent for several more moments. Then there was a huge noise, not like the pop of a gunshot this time, more like the bang you would hear if someone hit a car with a sledgehammer. Then another one. Then a sound like a machine gun—bang-bang-bang-bang-bang, real quick. Then finally the big CRA-ACK of wood splitting, and an enormous tree down in the valley below began to fall. I was able to watch it fall, almost in slow motion, until it finally landed with an enormous thud on the forest floor. I felt very blessed to have seen it happen, and I felt like the wilderness was putting on quite a show for me today. First, a sunny bald appeared out of the depths of the forest, then an ancient crying tree allowed me to see its tears, and my Cherokee ancestors played drums for me until a giant tree put on its own fireworks show, tumbling through the trees to fall with great violence to a peaceful place on the forest floor, perhaps to become a home for mushrooms and timid animals. Thank you, God, for letting me experience all this. The television back at the motel seemed not just bland and colorless, but also petty and superficial. This natural world was a new world, and I was an adult-sized child, experiencing things for the first time, alternately delighted and charmed and surprised by things I had never seen nor imagined. I had gotten used to living in a world where all knowledge was available 24/7 through Google on my phone if I could be bothered to look it up. Where everything was explainable and nothing was surprising. Now I was in a new world, a world of wonders and surprises, and I was a child again, sitting at God's feet, laughing and clapping my hands in delight.

This was the day I discovered I could still skip, even on a rough trail, with a child-weight slackpack on my back.

I walked on to the road crossing at Wayah Gap where Songbird was waiting for me. The shuttle arrived shortly after and drove us through a fast food window on our way back to the motel. I was more than ready to get out of civilization and back to the woods the next day.

Wayah Gap to Wayah Bald Shelter
April 17, 2013

The Green Monster was on my back again with the new addition of the blue, closed-cell foam pad that Mike had brought from home. It wasn't terribly thick, but I knew that it would make sleeping much more comfortable, because it would serve both as padding on the hard shelter floors, and as insulation in my hammock. It wouldn't fit inside my pack, but rolled up and attached by Velcro straps, it hung from the bottom of my pack, where I could feel it bouncing off my backside as I walked. It was a little bulky, but light enough that I didn't even notice the added weight. The day warmed up quickly as I hiked along, becoming almost hot.

I came upon my first group of trail maintainers, one of the many beautiful things about the Appalachian Trail. Although the trail itself falls under the jurisdiction of the National Park Service and has an office in Harpers Ferry, West Virginia with a small paid staff, the actual trail itself, all 2,180 miles of it, is maintained strictly by volunteers. Each area has a local club or group who take it upon themselves to keep the trail in good hiking shape. This group had three men and two women walking along carrying a chain saw, axes, rakes, shovels, and other tools. They were good-natured and friendly, and stopped to talk and ask about trail conditions behind me. They told me they came out each Wednesday morning to hike their section of the trail, to do whatever was needed to keep it safe and passable for hikers. I thanked them for their service and hiked on, thinking about all the many behind-the-scenes people in my real life who labor, usually unacknowledged, to make my life easier. I resolved to seek them out when I returned home after my hike ended and thank them as well.

As I climbed Wayah Bald I broke into a sweat as the day became not just warm and humid, but cloying and still, the kind of stillness that precedes a storm. And, sure enough, as I looked at the horizon I saw dark clouds rolling and boiling all over each other in their race to claim the sky. Near the top of the bald was a road crossing, and a local gentleman was there with his pickup truck. He was sitting behind the truck on a lawn chair, and on the tailgate was a cooler and a large plastic storage bin. Trail magic!

"Would you like some ice water?" he called out to me. I hurried over to him.

"Would I!" I exclaimed. "I'm nearly out, and the water I have left is as warm as bath water!" He handed me an ice cold bottle of water. I tipped my head back and nearly drained the entire bottle in one attempt. "Oh, that's so good. Thank you." I realized that in 20 minutes time I had had occasion to thank two different sets of complete strangers for kindnesses done for me.

He handed me a second bottle and offered me some trail mix from the plastic bin. I sat and talked with him for a short while before moving on. He shared that there was going to be rain this afternoon, starting very shortly, and it would rain steadily for a few hours, with a break in the rain from approximately four to seven PM, after which it would start in earnest, and would rain and storm the rest of the night.

"Well isn't that special," I thought to myself in the spirit of Dana Carvey's Church Lady, from a few years back. I was feeling a bit out of sorts actually, bristly and chagrined at the thought of the extra money I had spent in Franklin on the third motel night and two rather expensive (and rather unnecessary) shuttle rides. Songbird didn't seem to mind spending money in town, but I did. I had saved money for my hike before leaving home, several thousand dollars in fact, but 2,180 miles is a long way, and the six months I estimated it would take me to finish is a long time. And while hiking is technically free and the cost of the food I was eating on the trail quite minimal, the town stops were proving to be very costly, and I really couldn't afford to spend much time or money on them. Mike was at home, working every day at his own job, and keeping our home business, making soap and herbal bath products, going as well. He was doing all our usual spring craft shows alone and making products and shipping them out as the orders came in. He was doing all this willingly and had actually encouraged me to embark on this adventure and was cheering me on, which is how I came to give him his own off-trail trailname, St. Mike. I have heard other hikers talk about guilt trips laid on them by their families back home, and some hikes have ended early for this very reason. Maybe sometimes the guilt trips are warranted. Maybe some hikers don't take care of their responsibilities at home and rush off to adventures on the trail leaving others to unwillingly take up the slack their absence creates. I didn't think this was the case for my hike, and Mike absolutely never offered anything but support and encouragement. In fact, my solo hike of the Appalachian Trail not only had his blessing, but was his idea. My original idea was for the two of us to hike it together. He demurred but gave me the great gift of offering to be my support person if I wanted to hike it alone. I was very fortunate, among all the hikers I met during my entire hike, to have a cheerleader as devoted and resourceful as St. Mike.

But abundant finances weren't one of our resources, and I thought about him toiling at home in solitude while I was out living my dream. I knew I couldn't afford to waste time and money as I had in Franklin. And so it was with the uncomfortable feelings of guilt, unaccustomed heat, and the ominous feeling of the approaching storm that I started down the mountain from Wayah Bald. The rain started shortly after, and it felt so cool and refreshing that I didn't even stop to put on my rain jacket. I walked down the trail immersed momentarily in my own little pity party and had to remind myself to offer up these little discomforts for my grandson.

It was only another mile from the top of the bald to Wayah Bald Shelter and all downhill, so I arrived there in the early afternoon. Although I hadn't seen any hikers on the trail all day, there was a pretty good sized group already there, planning to spend the night to wait out the coming storm. Songbird was there, and had already staked out her spot in the shelter. The rain stopped shortly after I arrived, and I wanted to walk on, my feelings of guilt over three nights in Franklin still fresh in my mind. The storm wasn't due for another few hours, and there was another shelter 4.8 miles further on. I felt confident that we could make it to the next shelter before the storm arrived, and well before dark. Songbird wasn't budging, however. She had a spot in the shelter (the last spot, it was now full for the night) and she did not share my rather cavalier attitude towards storms. The truth is, I kind of like storms. I'm not afraid of them, and I do enjoy sitting under a roof, whether that roof is a house, a shelter, or even my own tarp, and watching a good thunderstorm. I believed we could beat the rain to the next shelter, and even if we couldn't I didn't expect to melt if I got wet. But Songbird couldn't be convinced to give up her sure-thing spot in this shelter for a possible spot in a shelter nearly five miles away with a thunderstorm on the way. I could have gone on, of course.

She was leaving the trail for an indefinite period for a job interview from the Nantahala Outdoor Center (NOC) which was just 17 miles away, so we would be splitting up in the next couple of days anyway. I would be going solo after that, and she was unsure when or even if she would be coming back to the trail after her interview. If she got the job and they wanted her to start right away, she would not be coming back. I wanted to stick with our plan to hike into the NOC together, so I acquiesced and went in search of two trees to hang my hammock.

After gathering and filtering my water, cooking and eating my supper (instant couscous with bacon bits), cleaning out my cookpot, hanging my food bag to keep it from the bears, and performing my modest toilette, I joined the group around the campfire. Generally this is a bright spot in the day. Usually several of the hikers in the group would be familiar, people we had met on the trail and camped with on other evenings. It was fun to reconnect and hear everyone's adventures since we last met, and meet new people and learn their stories. There was always a lot to talk about: how did you get your trail name, what do you do in your real life, when did you start your hike, and have you seen any bears yet? Stories and jokes abound, and all ages and social classes enjoy each other's company without prejudice (social classes off the trail just don't compute to hikers on the trail, who are all generally in the same social class for this brief season of their lives. Except that some people can spend multiple days in motels and some settle for a single night in a hostel on town stops.) Hikers are hikers, a single social class of our own, who often proudly own up to the epithet "hiker trash."

This group skewed younger as a whole than any group I'd been in yet, though. The conversation started out quite pleasant, but soon veered into subject matter I found to be just a bit too risque, although I'm not a prude. That is, I wasn't shocked, or offended, or even uncomfortable. I was just about 30 years past being interested, as it was juvenile as well as graphic. One of the young men lit a joint and it started making its way around the circle. It came to me, and I passed it along. Marijuana is not uncommon on the trail, and it didn't really bother me, any more than the flasks which frequently come out at campfire time. At most shelters, while the pot-smoking is not hidden or secret, neither is it this bold, taking place around the main campfire. Generally the smokers will sit a bit separate, off to themselves or behind the shelter, and then rejoin the main group later. On this night, the smokers *were* the main group, and I felt suddenly old, tired, and out of step. I excused myself, although it was still a bit early, and retired to my hammock. The rain had just started to sprinkle again as I walked away from the fire, and I saw a woman who had just arrived putting up her tent. I went over to say hello and see if she needed any help, since it was nearly dark and the rain was starting to pick up. She was about my age, and about eight inches shorter, with the appropriate trail name of Little Janie. She was pleasant, and we spoke for a few minutes until the first rumble of thunder when we both retired to our silnylon shelters.

I zipped myself into my cozy hammock nest and found that I just wasn't ready to sleep. I had had such a good night's sleep the last three nights in a motel bed, and it was still quite early, even for hikers. I rarely turned my phone on, trying to conserve the battery, but I splurged and turned it on to read a book on my Kindle. I could hear the group still at the campfire in spite of the cold drizzle and the approaching storm, and I found the sound of the distant talk and laughter comforting. My book was interesting, but I was starting to get sleepy, so I turned it off and pulled my rosary out of its pouch. I was only a couple of decades in when someone at the firepit started playing a tinwhistle. The turmoil of earlier in the day slipped from my mind as easily as my rosary slipped through my fingers. The sweet sounds of *Ashokan Farewell* mingled with the plop plop of raindrops on my tarp were the last sounds I heard as I drifted off to sleep, rocked gently in my hammock by the wind.

Wayah Bald Shelter to Tellico Gap
April 18, 2013

I emerged from my hammock cocoon into a world utterly changed by a beautiful fog. I was completely delighted as I packed the Green Monster for the day's hike. The dense fog lay heavy on the ground, softening the edges of trees and rocks, mischievously moving in wisps everywhere I looked, and completely obscuring any objects more than 15 feet away. It was charming and ethereally beautiful. I ate my small breakfast with Songbird and we took to the trail. We separated, as was usual, and I found myself walking alone through the fog, and it was easy to say my divine mercy chaplet as I walked and prayed for the person of the day, my sweet little granddaughter.
After walking mostly downhill through dense forest for about four miles, I came out on a sunny clearing at Burningtown Gap and found Songbird sitting on a log

eating lunch. I joined her, shucking the heavy pack from my pack. I was looking forward to my lunch. I had bought hard rolls and cheese in Franklin and planned to make little cheese sandwiches. Something was up with Songbird though, she wasn't her usual cheerful self, and I made small talk while I waited for her to say what was on her mind.

"Well, I guess this is where we part ways," she said eventually.

"Wait—what? I thought you were leaving from the NOC! That's another 13 miles. We won't be there until tomorrow. How are you leaving from....here?" I said, indicating the rather underused appearing dirt road that came into the gap.

"There's another storm coming tonight, and I've come to realize that I'm a fair weather hiker. I just don't want to spend another night in the rain, and I'll be leaving tomorrow anyway."

"How are you going to get out of here? Your husband's picking you up at the NOC. I wouldn't even know how to tell him how to get here from there."

"There's a hostel at Tellico Gap, about another five miles down the trail. I've got phone service here. I'm going to call for a shuttle and have someone meet me there and take me to the hostel and spend the night in comfort, not out in the woods in the cold rain, again. Then I'll either hike on into the NOC from the hostel or stay and have Joe pick me up there."

Songbird, queen of the hostels, struck again. I was sorry to part ways with her, but it was only one day ahead of our planned separation. I was beginning to sense that she was mentally checked out of the hike by this time. Her mind was on home, her husband, and her upcoming job interview for her dream nursing job, and I understood. I had enjoyed having a hiking partner, something I had never expected to have, but by this time I had confidence in my ability to go it alone, so I finished my lunch as we said our goodbyes.

"Good luck on your interview! Let me know how it goes—call me or email or call Mike. If you have some time before the job starts and you want to hike some more, just let me know and I'll wait for you somewhere up the trail. Wish me luck in the Smokies!" I said as I heaved my pack up on my shoulders.

"Why don't you come with me?" she asked. "If we get off at Tellico Gap and go to the hostel that will be almost nine miles for today, and that's not too bad. Then tomorrow we can walk to the NOC together, it'll be about eight more miles. We can get a room there, and Joe will come to get me the next day. Come on, it'll be fun. Won't it be good to be out of the rain tonight?"

Still stinging from the money spent in Franklin, I declined. I told her that I really don't mind stormy nights, and I couldn't justify another hostel stop at this point. She encouraged me and offered to pay for my bunk at the hostel if I would come with her. "I can't ask you to do that!" I said in surprise.

"You didn't ask. I offered. Come on, I really don't want to go alone. You have to stay somewhere tonight, might as well be there, right? Won't cost you a penny. My treat. I insist."

And so it was that I found myself back on the trail with the goal of Tellico Gap and Aquone Hostel in mind. Songbird, the queen of the hostels and her lily-livered sidekick, Blue Tortoise, started up Copper Ridge Bald. She outpaced me, and I walked alone up the trail, equal parts chagrined and pleased. I had heard a lot of good things about Aquone Hostel, reputed to be one of the nicest on the trail, and I was glad to be able to see it. I hadn't expected to, with it falling right in the middle between Franklin and the NOC, both planned stops. I came across Little Janie sitting on a log having a break, and we walked on together. She was good company, and we got to know each other as we hiked along. The weather was nice and the walk was

pleasant, at least until I started the two mile descent into
Tellico Gap. It was long and steep, steep enough to bruise
my toes again as they jammed into the ends of my boots
with every step. I stopped and retied the laces tighter,
which helped some, but it was still a relief to walk down
into the level ground of the gap.

Songbird was waiting there, on the phone talking to
Wiggy, owner of Aquone Hostel. I invited Little Janie to
stop for the night with us, but she declined and walked on.
Soon enough Wiggy arrived to take us to the hostel. He
picked up the Green Monster and slung it into the back of
his car, and then reached for Songbird's pack and grunted
as he picked it up. "What have you got in there?" he asked.
"You should have a pack like that," he said, gesturing at
my pack. I had never lifted Songbird's pack and didn't
realize it was heavy. She never complained of its weight.

We climbed into the car and then commenced on a hair-
raising trip on a steep and narrow dirt road, barreling down
the mountainside and flying around sharp curves. I was to
later come to realize that all shuttle drivers drove like this,
being thoroughly familiar with the roads and their quirks.
Wiggy was completely calm and in control and noticeably
amused by our white-knuckled grips on the upholstery. He
was English and had hiked the AT years before, returning

to the United States to open the hostel after retirement from the British army. I joked with him about at least trying to stay on the right side of the road. I'm sure he'd heard that one a few hundred times before, but he was good-natured and laughed along with us. After a few more hairpin curves taken on what seemed to be two wheels, we pulled in to Aquone Hostel.

It was absolutely lovely, nestled into the woods and backed with a charming creek. The building itself looked like a Swiss chalet. Wiggy asked us to leave our packs, poles, and boots on the back porch, and we entered the hostel. It was high-ceilinged with wood walls and floor and a huge stone fireplace on the long wall, a cheery fire dancing merrily on the grate. A deep, comfy, sectional sofa faced the fire, with a large screen television off to the side. One corner of the large room had an elegant kitchen area, and the other corner had a game table and cushioned benches. Everywhere I looked there were shelves of books or board games or charming antiques. Prominently placed on the mantle was a discreet, hand-lettered sign reading "All hikers must shower on arrival." I chuckled and took a picture of it, but I got the point--the place was immaculate. Wiggy showed us the bunk rooms and bathrooms next, and the overall effect continued to be that of a spa or retreat.

The closet in the bathroom was full of track suits of various sizes, loaners we could wear while Wiggy and his wife Maggie did our laundry. Songbird and I took showers, donned the track suits, left our dirty laundry in the baskets provided, and went downstairs for supper.

There were only two other hikers in the dining room, older gentlemen from the Gulf Coast, Bill and the Mississippi Mule. They were section hikers, or at least George (the Mississippi Mule) was. Bill was his supportive, non-hiking friend who went with George on vacation. George hiked during the day, and Bill found beautiful places like Aquone. Bill had a hard time remembering "Blue Tortoise" and called me Purple Turtle, which I quite liked the sound of. The four of us were served a home-cooked meal on real plates, meat loaf and potatoes and broccoli. It was delicious. Many moments on the trail seemed surreal, and this was one of them. One night you're sleeping outside in a cold rain after eating couscous and going to the bathroom outside, and the next night you're in a resort. "Wiggy," I said, "This place is gorgeous!"

"When I was hiking the trail I appreciated every hostel I stopped at, but after a while I got tired of the dreariness and the dirt and the worn out furniture. I didn't see why a hostel couldn't be clean and nice, and I resolved that if I was ever to own a hostel it would be beautiful. Hikers aren't really trash after all." He was referring to the epithet "hiker trash" that may have started as a derogatory term for dirty, smelly, hikers, but that now many hikers claimed proud ownership of.

"Well, it definitely is beautiful," Songbird said, and Bill and the Mississippi Mule added their assents.

After supper we went back upstairs and spent a pleasant evening around the fire swapping stories and getting to know each other. I couldn't help comparing it to the campfire of the evening before. There's something to be said for a good sectional and mature company.

Aquone Hostel, Tellico Gap
April 19. 2013

I awoke in what I assumed was the dreary pre-dawn, judging by the dimness of the light in the bunkroom. I was about to roll over and try to go back to sleep when I noticed that Songbird's bed was empty and there was light and the sound of voices from the next room. What time was it?

Why was everyone up so early?

"Blue, you'd better come look at this," Songbird's voice called out. I joined the group in the next room, gathered around the television. It was tuned to the Weather Channel, and local radar showed us right in the middle of a giant orange-red blob. Worse yet was the temperature which was forecast to drop dramatically throughout the day, especially in the higher elevations (namely the Appalachian Trail). I looked out the window. It wasn't pre-dawn, it was nearly eight o'clock, there was just no sun to be seen through the dark clouds obscuring the sky and the fat raindrops which fell from them.

I was utterly frustrated. All I wanted to do was hike. I was a mere eight miles from the Nantahala Outdoor Center, less than a full day's walk. As beautiful as Aquone was and as jovial the company, I hated the thought of spending another day and night inside, my progress stalled, and more money spent. I was perfectly willing to don my rain jacket and rain pants and start hiking. I didn't mind walking in the rain, as long as there was no lightning. I was ready to go and said so.

Songbird, of course, disagreed. And although she really was the queen of the hostels, in this case she was also the voice of reason.

"Look," she said. "It's nearly freezing now, and you know it's worse up on the trail. And it's only going to get colder as the day goes on. We might make it to the NOC tonight, but it doesn't make sense to get out in this weather. It's going to be sixty degrees tomorrow! It would be much smarter to wait until then to hike out."

"I just spent three nights in a motel in Franklin! And now two nights here? This isn't a hike, it's a vacation!"

"But we only took one zero day in Franklin. We hiked the other two. And we hiked yesterday, and we can hike tomorrow. So it's really only one unplanned zero day. And the weather certainly justifies it."

She had a point. But I still felt that I could hike eight cold wet miles easily, and rest at the NOC just as well as at Aquone . We compromised by agreeing to wait a while and watch the weather, and if we saw a break before noon, we would go for it. Much as I wanted to go on, it was very hard to saddle up and head out into the cold wet day, leaving behind a lovely warm hostel and three hikers telling me I was nuts to even consider it.

Of course there was no break in the weather, and as the day wore on hikers came down the mountain and staggered into the hostel in various states of cold, wet, and frozen, telling about a bad night on the trail, and waking up to boots frozen solid. One by one they arrived throughout the day, showered, and joined us on the couch as we watched the manhunt for the Boston Marathon bombers unfold live before our eyes. We were riveted. My thoughts of hiking fled as the day never warmed up and each new hiker arrived with a fresh story of a cold and miserable night on the trail. For breakfast and lunch I snacked on what was in my bag, but when suppertime rolled around Bill and George decided to drive into the town of Andrews, North Carolina, and eat at a restaurant. Feeling a bit claustrophobic, I accepted their invitation to join them, as did Songbird and a young hiker named Hard Drive. (The home-cooked hostel meal was ten dollars. I reasoned that a restaurant meal would be about the same cost.) We went to a Mexican restaurant and had a great meal to go with the great company.

I slipped into my bunk that night with a fierce resolve to hike the next day, in rain, sleet, hail, storms, or tornados. But I prayed for good weather and patience.

Telllico Gap to the Nantahala Outdoor Center
April 20, 2013

I awakened to lovely, filtered light on my bunk. The sun was back! With a much lighter heart and a prayer of gratitude to God I packed the Green Monster and joined Songbird in Wiggy's car for the return trip from the hostel to Tellico Gap. We found the drive to be equally exciting going up the mountain. At the top we said goodbye to Wiggy, thanked him, and turned and started up the trail. It felt good to be hiking again. The air was cool but the sun was warm on my arms. My pack felt light, but maybe that was because I had eaten most of the food in my food bag. Oh well, by the end of the day we would be at the NOC, where I could do a resupply. Songbird's husband Joe was meeting us this evening, and she would be leaving the trail to go home for her job interview. She might rejoin me further down the trail if she didn't get the job, or if she did but it didn't start for another few weeks. Or she might not. Either way, I felt good about it. I was strong, and confident, and ready to hike on, with or without a hiking partner.

The climb out of the gap was not bad, and as we got to the higher elevations we began to see ice in the vegetation, and realized anew that it had indeed been a cold night up on the mountain. We kept hiking and, unlike most days, we stayed together most of the day, cognizant that it was our last day to hike together. At the top we were treated to glorious view after glorious view of the surrounding valleys and woods. At one point we walked on a high narrow ridge of land that afforded us 360 degree views. We felt that we were on the very top of the world and I had a strong sense of well-being, that the world was a good place. This was so different from what I had been so strongly reminded of by the television coverage of the day before, and I believed that it was the voice of God Himself whispering, "It is good." At that moment I would have been happy to stay up there forever and never venture back into the world of people down below where anger and animosity live. There was no hatred up on the mountain where I stood. But God whispered again in my soul that He had pronounced the sixth day's creation to be good, too, and I felt that it was my obligation to look for that good, and believe it was there. It was easy to love Him in the middle of such peace and beauty, a little harder to love people. But they are His creation, too, as much as the mountains and trees. In fact, they are the climax of creation week, and if I didn't see their beauty and goodness, well, that was my problem, and

I needed to learn how to look for it. "Help me Lord," I prayed, my feet crunching on the icy path. I pondered these things as I walked along, and although I couldn't have known it at the time, I now believe that God used this time to prepare me, to soften my heart, for the big lesson He had in store for me the next day.

Eventually we started back downhill, for it was a long, five mile descent to the NOC. As usual, I found hiking downhill to be harder than walking uphill. Going uphill only stressed my lungs, which was easily remedied by stopping to catch my breath. Walking downhill, though, especially if it was long or steep (and this stretch was both) crunched my toes painfully, bruising them, and put a lot of stress on my knees. As a former sprained ankle recipient, I was always worried about turning an ankle on rocky downhill stretches. So I picked my way carefully down the trail. Songbird was slightly ahead of me and out of sight around a switchback when I heard her shriek. I hurried ahead and found her picking herself up off the ground. She had been trying to go around a downed tree that was lying across the trail, and stepped into some steep slick mud, sending her sprawling.

"Oh my goodness! Are you okay?" I cried, rushing to her side. She was already up on her feet by then, assessing the damage.

"I think so. Oh, but I'm all muddy now! And I think I bruised my bottom."

"Well, I'm not checking it for injuries!" I joked. "But you'll be seeing Joe soon enough. He can treat your wounds. And after today, you won't have to wear those pants anymore, at least not for a while." Like most hikers, Songbird only had one pair of pants, which she wore every day.

She laughed, and after a few minutes to pull herself together, we hiked on. It was then that she noticed that her hiking pole was bent. "Better your pole than your leg," I said after we ascertained that the pole was sound enough to continue. Hiking poles are tremendously important. It wasn't all that long ago that no one carried a pole, but then the older hikers started using them, and now I would estimate that probably 90 percent of all hikers, young and old, carry at least one pole, usually two. I would not have been able to hike without them, for the amount of stress that they took off my knees. I used them to pull myself up the steep trail, and to support myself on steep downhills. They steadied me on numerous near-falls and told me how deep many water and mud puddles were. They were made of lightweight titanium and had a strap or loop of leather that went around the back of each hand. I already had a "strap line" on the tan that had developed on my hands after many days in the leafless woods. Once as I sat down to rest on a handy log and set my poles to the side, I smelled the distinct scent of dirty feet. I of course still had my socks and boots on, although I did occasionally remove them for longer breaks. It was a couple of days later, after getting that aroma at odd moments, that I realized it came from the straps on my hiking poles. It turns out that hands smell just like feet, under the right circumstances. I resolved to clean my straps at each town stop after that.

But Songbird's pole was sound, bent but able to support weight, so we continued down the long descent to the NOC. We stayed together now as the trail became steeper. We found the bookend to the hand over hand climb up Albert Mountain at a point called the Jumpoff. It was equally steep, except that we were going downhill this time. We advised each other all the way down, and once when I asked Songbird if there was a place under me to put my foot while sliding on my tummy over a rock, she mumbled, "Can't talk. Holding a root in my teeth." At another point I was sliding again, this time on my bottom, across a large smooth rock, when I heard the telltale rrr-ippp as the seat of my pants tore. Once we were safely down Jumpoff I tied my fleece jacket around my waist to hide the gaping hole in the back of my pants.

We continued down the trail, Songbird's excitement at seeing her husband growing as we drew closer and closer to the bottom of the mountain. She pulled away from me, as usual, and I made no effort to keep up, wanting her to have the luxury of a brief time alone with Joe before I joined them. Down, down, down I walked, through the quiet of the woods. Eventually I started to hear road noise off in the distance and knew I was nearly there. Then I started to see little splashes of color through the trees. I quickened my pace and came upon a tall man in civilian (non-hiker) clothes standing at the side of the trail, a cold bottle of Mello Yello in his hand. Before my mind could comprehend this vision he reached it out to me, saying "You must be Blue Tortoise. This is for you."

"Oh, Joe! Nice to meet you!" I exclaimed, and managed to shake his hand before opening the bottle for a long drink. We walked together the short distance to the road, and then the whole spectacle of the Nantahala Outdoor Center unfolded before me. In all its hustle, bustle, and bright colors it was a great contrast to the silence and stillness and muted colors of the trail. The NOC is a complex of buildings surrounding the swiftly moving Nantahala River.

It is essentially a kayaking center, and as a kayaker myself the boldly colored little boats darting among the rapids made me happy just to see them. There were people everywhere, lounging on benches, eating ice cream as they strolled across the pedestrian bridge, watching the kayaks, enjoying the warm spring day. A road race was just coming in at the same time, and the people erupted in cheers as each new runner came into view. It was overall a scene of such busyness and liveliness that it gave me one of those "Is this for real?" moments that I had so often while hiking the trail.

We went in to the restaurant that overlooked the river for an early dinner and I had a great cheeseburger. Then it was time for Songbird to go, so we said our goodbyes and she climbed into their car, and just like that, I was a solo hiker again. I found that I was actually kind of excited for the challenge, and I liked the idea of calling my own shots again and believed that I would make better time now, maybe walk greater distances or take fewer days off. I would miss her company in the evenings, though. Her outgoing personality made it easy for us to make friends along the way. "Oh well," I thought. "I'm a big girl. Time to step up."

I went into the little market to check into the hostel and

got a bunk for 17 dollars. I walked across the complex to
the bunkhouse and unlocked the door to my room. It was
very basic, two sets of bunkbeds being the only furniture in
the grim little room. Quite a contrast to the relative luxury
of Aquone Hostel! It appeared I didn't have any
roommates in the other bunks, at least not yet. I left my
pack on the bunk and went downstairs to the communal
restroom/shower room. After showering I went to the
equally dreary common room where I sat at a long table
and sewed up the rip in my pants. There were a few other
hikers around, but no one I knew. I was tired, a bit bored
and listless, and decided to go to bed early. My plan for the
next day was to go through my guidebook and determine
my hiking itinerary from this point to the Smokies. I was
going to meet St. Mike at Clingman's Dome on April 29,
and he was going to hike the second half of the Smokies
with me. I also needed to resupply and while I knew there
was a market and an outfitter on the premises, I presumed I
would still need a shuttle to town. With a long section
without towns coming up I needed to have a full food bag
before leaving the NOC. It was very cold outside again
tonight, even down in the gorge, as the NOC was called. I
turned up the heat in my room, laid my pad on the bunk,
and covered up with my top quilt. I could figure out the

logistics in the morning.

Nantahala Outdoor Center
April 21, 2013

It was Sunday, and there was a Catholic Church in Bryson City, the nearest town, which was 13 miles away. I got the phone numbers for a couple of local shuttle drivers from my guidebook, but there was no answer when I called them. I walked across the complex to the market and then to the outfitter for assistance in getting a ride to town, but neither was open for the day yet. I wasn't worried. It was still early, and I could try the shuttle drivers and check in at the market a bit later. So I turned my attention to the rather daunting logistics of the next leg of my hike.

The problem was the Great Smoky Mountains National Park, which was looming only 30 miles ahead. The Appalachian Trail through the Smokies is 70 miles long, and in every trail journal I had read in preparation for my hike, there was always some type of trouble in the Smokies, frequently weather related. Weather can be brutal in the Smokies at any time of year, and to make matters more complicated, it isn't easy to get off the trail once you enter the national park. To this point on my hike there had been a road crossing, and thus an opportunity to get off the trail, nearly every day. Often the road was a dirt road, or a forest service road, or just sparsely traveled, but it still represented access to leave the trail and get into civilization, if it was needed. The 70 mile stretch of trail in the Smokies crossed roads exactly twice: at Clingman's Dome and at Newfound Gap. Before beginning my hike a common question I was asked was if I was afraid. I always truthfully replied that no, I wasn't afraid. Not of being in the woods alone or bears or maniacs or any of the other frightful things that were brought up. The only thing I was actually afraid of was the weather, specifically cold and wet weather, and more specifically, the weather in the Smoky Mountains.

In addition, there were other rules and restrictions to take into consideration before entering the park. As a national park, a camping permit had to be obtained before entering. I planned to get my permit at the NOC outfitter when they opened for the day. The permit has to specify the date the hiker enters the park, after which they have a specified number of days to hike through the park and exit. Access is not unlimited. Hikers anywhere else on the AT can set up camp anyplace they decide to stop for the night.

The shelters do have some advantages, and the previously established campsites will offer at least a level spot for a tent and a log to sit on, but you really can stop and set up camp wherever you want to. But in the Smokies there is no camping allowed *except* at the shelters, to avoid overuse of the land. Hikers are obliged to stay at the shelters, and actually *inside* the shelters, at least until they fill up, after which they have to stay just outside of the shelter.

With all this in mind, I had to take my preparations for this next leg of my hike very seriously. Mike was going to meet me at Clingman's Dome on April 29, and hike the rest of the Smokies with me, a 38 mile stretch. Our original plan had been for him to hike the entire 70 miles of the park with me because of my fears about the weather, which he shared. That wasn't feasible because of his job, so we had reached a compromise. He now planned to meet me at Clingman's Dome with fresh supplies and walk the last half of the park with me. I had 30 miles to hike to get to the park entrance and then 32 miles of park to our rendezvous spot for a total of only 62 miles, and I had eight days to do it if I left the next morning. That meant I was no longer in such a rush to put some miles behind me, as it would be of no benefit for me to get to Clingman's Dome ahead of Mike. I felt a weight roll off my shoulders. I could easily make this next section, even at my usual tortoise pace. In fact, I had plenty of time and could take time to actually enjoy the beautiful Smoky Mountains. I did, however, need eight days of food. I normally started off with four or five days worth of food in my pack, food being the second heaviest item to carry, next to water. Eight days would be a heavy load, but I comforted myself with the knowledge that at least it would get lighter with every meal that I ate!

Feeling better with a plan to work from, I walked back to the market which was now open, and realized that I would not be able to buy eight days worth of hiking food from the snack-laden shelves. The clerk also did not know of any shuttle drivers or even have any friends willing to pick up a few dollars by driving me to Bryson City. I again called the phone numbers for the shuttle drivers listed in my guidebook, again with no answer. I crossed the street to the outfitter where there was a good selection of hiking-specific food (much too expensive to pack for eight days), but still no leads on any shuttle drivers. So I found myself in serious need of a ride to town to go to mass and to find a grocery store, and apparently no shuttles were available. "Well," I told myself, "It's time to try hitchhiking."

Hitchhiking is common along the length of the AT and is considered safe. The residents of the small towns near the road crossings of the trail are used to hikers, and many of them are happy to pick up the hikers and take them into town. I, of course, being a fairly conservative 54 year old woman, had never hitchhiked before and wouldn't even consider it in my real life. But I had known that I would attempt it at some time during my hike, and it looked like that time had come. Since I had just over an hour to make the 13 mile trip before mass started, I walked out to the road and stuck out my thumb. It was a paved, two-lane road, the main road into Bryson City, but traffic was light on this Sunday morning. I heard a car coming up behind me and tensed up, but it passed me without stopping. So did another one a few moments later. And then a third and a fourth. Hmm, this might not be as easy as I expected it to be, as the minutes ticked rapidly by.

Later, I was to realize that the probable reason for my difficulty in getting a ride was that without my pack on my back and my poles in my hands, I didn't look like a hiker. I just looked like a slightly scruffy woman. The people who would normally stop for a hiker didn't even slow down for me. Or maybe it was that God had His own timing and a specific driver in mind for me. I was praying as I walked, both for a ride and for safety on that ride. I was confident that God wanted me to go to mass and that He would make it possible for me to get there. But as a few more minutes ticked away I started to become less confident and maybe even a little annoyed. "God," I explained to Him, "I know that You want me to go to mass. *I* want me to go to mass, and I have done everything I can to get there. Now it's up to You. Please send me a ride to church."

A few more cars zoomed past, and I was becoming bewildered, wondering why God wouldn't send me some form of transportation to church. (Yes, I do realize how arrogant that sounds. But that was how I felt at the time.) I walked on, thumb out, checking my watch frequently, until it was 20 minutes before mass started, and I realized that if I didn't get a ride in the next couple of moments I would have to turn around and go back to the NOC, as I would have no hope of making it in time. By this time my feelings were hurt, as I wondered if God wasn't getting involved because He didn't care and if I was being presumptuous in assuming He took notice of me. "Okay," I thought. "One more minute, and then I'll just go back to the NOC." A last car passed me.....and kept on going. I dropped my hand and started to turn back. Just at that moment the car pulled over to the side of the road, some distance ahead of me. In astonishment I raced up to the car and opened the passenger door. "Can you take me to

Bryson City?" I asked.

"Sure!" the driver said cheerily. "Hop in. I'm not going all the way in to Bryson though. Is it okay if I let you off on the bypass outside of town?"

"That would be great," I answered, resolving to cross that bridge when I came to it, by either getting a second ride or maybe, if I was lucky, the church itself would be on the outskirts of town, close enough that I could walk the rest of the way and still make it in time.

I climbed in, buckled my seat belt, and turned to face my new hero, the driver. "Thank you so much for stopping. I really appreciate it. I was about to give up," I said as my mind started to click along trying to figure out if the driver was male or female. "My name's Kathleen," I offered, under the assumption that introductions would settle the question.

"I'm Chris," was the answer, which wasn't much help. "Are you a hiker?"

"Oh, yeah," I laughed, realizing the problem the lack of my pack caused as to my identity. Our conversation flowed smoothly, as Chris was a former thru-hiker and so we had a great deal in common. But not being able to ascertain Chris's gender made me uncomfortable. I looked for clues while we talked. Chris was younger than me,

shorter and thinner, but wiry, with a sense of strength. He
wore (I will default to the male pronoun, but I didn't have a
greater impression of masculinity than I did of femininity)
a very loose synthetic tee shirt, long, equally loose
basketball-style shorts, gym shoes and short white socks.
Nothing screamed male or female. His hair was probably
short, but was brushed back under a baseball cap and hard
to see, and he wore big sunglasses which obscured his eyes.
I studied him as closely as was polite, but didn't see an
adam's apple, breasts, hints of facial hair, or any other
obvious sign of gender. Even his voice fell exactly halfway
between soft male voice and deep female voice, leaning
neither way.

Our conversation continued merrily, and I found that I
enjoyed Chris's company very much. He was smart, and
funny, and kind. But it continued to disturb me that I didn't
know if he was male or female. I looked around the
interior of the car, which gave me no clues either. At one
point he mentioned his partner, who hadn't wanted to go
hiking with him, and I pursued that line of thought, hoping
for a pronoun for the partner to help me make a distinction
as to Chris's gender. I realized that wouldn't necessarily
help, though, as he could be a male with either a male or
female partner, or a female with either a male or female

partner.

Our conversation came to an end as Chris pulled to a stop on Main Street in the middle of Bryson City. "I thought you weren't going into town?" I asked, surprised to see where we were when I looked through the windshield.

"I wasn't, but that's ok. This way you don't have to try to get another ride, and it's not that far out of my way."

"Thank you so much! Can I give you something for your time?" I asked, reaching for my money belt.

"Oh, no, absolutely not!" Chris laughed. "Just enjoy your hike."

We said our goodbyes. and I closed the door. Chris pulled away, and I looked around. There, on a small hill just across the street, was St. Joseph's Catholic Church. Chris had unknowingly delivered me to the front door of my destination! It was two minutes before mass started so I bounded up the hill, through the door, and into a pew in the back. I knelt and thanked God for helping me get to mass on time, and asked forgiveness for my earlier doubts and petulance. I sat back on the smooth wooden pew and breathed deep, taking in the peace and quiet that I always perceive in church. My tangled thoughts smoothed out as I realized anew that God is in charge, and He is bigger than me, and it's not up to me to figure everything out. I could rest in His love.

I looked down at my hiking pants, newly mended up the back and dirty around the cuffs, at my brightly colored wool socks and the Crocs that I wore when not hiking to rest my feet. I always dress for church, believing that it is disrespectful for me to come to worship the Creator of the universe wearing the same types of clothing I wear to the grocery store. I wear a dress or skirt. They're more likely to be a long full skirt with a peasant top or sweater than a fashionable ensemble with heels and hose, but they are, for me, dressing up. I was slightly ashamed to wear dirty hiking clothes to mass, but there really was no way around it. I listened to the readings for the day and then the homily, and I stopped worrying. God is love, every part of the mass said to me. Perfect love casts out fear, I knew, and I also felt it cast out doubts, self-centeredness, and the critical, judgmental nature I so often find myself inhabiting. I recited the ancient responses and was lifted up as I worshipped with not just the good people of St. Joseph's parish, but with the universal Church, the communion of saints, and the very angels in Heaven as we all proclaimed "Holy, holy, holy" together.

Eventually, of course, the priest said "The mass is ended, go in peace."

I murmured "Thanks be to God," and found myself walking out the front door, back into the bright sunlight of a spring day, and down the steps to the sidewalk. Now I needed to find a grocery store to buy my eight days worth of food, and a ride back to the NOC. I sat down on the steps and pulled out my phone. I called the shuttle drivers again—still no answer. Where *were* these people? I mulled over my options, which seemed to include only hoping to hitchhike back to the gorge, and I still had no idea where a grocery store was. I stood up and was about to start walking when I felt a hand on my shoulder. I turned around to find an attractive, well-dressed woman.

"Would you like a ride back to the gorge?" she asked.

I was astonished. Where had she come from? How did she know where I was going? I was thrilled to have a ride, but realized that I wouldn't be able to ask her to make a detour and wait while I bought my resupply. Beggars can't be choosers, though, so I quickly reconsidered the possibilities for resupply available at the NOC and blurted out, "Oh, that would be great! Thank you!"

My questions were answered when she said, "I sat behind you in mass and thought you must be a hiker. I'll be glad to drive you back to the gorge if you don't mind waiting while I buy some groceries."

I couldn't help giggling as I said, "Well actually....that would be great because I sort of need to pick up a few things myself." We introduced ourselves as we walked down the sidewalk. Her name was Mary, appropriate I thought for a Catholic appearing out of thin air in answer to prayer. Arriving at her car, I was caught up short as I looked at the rear bumper. It was covered in bumper stickers from the other side of the great political divide that engulfed our country. From the side that supported abortion and politicians that promoted it.

"Hop in," she said as she walked around to the driver's side. "Just move that stuff out of the seat," she added, gesturing at a neat stack of papers in the passenger seat. I climbed in and got to know the driver as we made small talk on the ride to the grocery store. Her husband was a former thru-hiker and currently worked at the NOC. "He told me to never pick up hitchhikers, even hikers. But you look pretty harmless," she laughed.

"Well, technically, I wasn't hitchhiking. At least not yet." We laughed together and I found that I enjoyed her company. We arrived at the Ingles market, and I did the fastest resupply ever, not wanting to keep my trail angel waiting while I agonized over the monumental decisions of resupply: instant mashed potatoes vs. Ramen? Knorr's sides vs. instant couscous? How many Little Debbies can you put in a food bag without crushing them? We met back at her car and she drove the long 13 miles back to the gorge, completely out of her way, and when we got there she, like Chris, refused to accept any money from me.

I thanked her profusely and carried the bag of groceries up to my room and dumped it out on my bunk to begin the process of repackaging—removing all extraneous packaging so that it would fit into my food bag. It all did fit, but just barely, and it felt good knowing I had enough food to get me all the way to Clingman's Dome. With that task done I had the rest of the afternoon ahead of me, and it was another beautiful warm spring day. I wandered down to the riverbank and watched the kayaks frolicking in the swift current and a couple of young men with a little boy, teaching him to fly fish. Their joy when he finally landed a fish was heart-warming. I wasn't hiking out until the next morning. Another cold night was forecast, and now I was actually in no hurry, as I had more than enough time to get to Clingman's Dome to meet Mike.

I went into the restaurant for lunch, then returned to the river bank to consider the events of the morning.

I had needed a ride into town, and I had presumptuously assumed God would meet that need. Was that presumption or was that faith? It had gotten until the very last possible moment, and then a ride had appeared. I could see the hand of God in that, which could be interpreted as either His sense of humor, as a test of my faith that He would provide (did my faith falter in those last few moments?), or even as chastisement for my presumption. I wasn't sure exactly which interpretation I bought into the most. Regardless, my response was the same: gratitude and renewed humility at Divine Providence and His concern for this little sparrow. He had also given me a ride back to the NOC and even a grocery stop, with no effort on my part other than asking Him and having faith.

I was grateful and humbled, but my musings now brought me to the point that lay heavy on my heart. What about the particular people that had stopped to help me, at their own time and expense, out of the depths of the goodness in their own hearts? Chris was a person of indeterminate sexuality, and Mary was a Catholic who violated the church's teachings on the sanctity of life. Both were lovely, thoughtful, intelligent, warm-hearted, and generous. God had chosen both of them to work through, to minister to me. And both were people who, I am ashamed to admit, I would not have expected to be on "God's radar." Presumption? Indeed! I would have assumed that their sins had distanced them from God. I remembered Mother Teresa who, in conversation with an atheist who performed charitable works, said "Where love is, there God is." God is love, and there is no doubt that in making their small sacrifices these two people were showing love. It was also sure that God worked through them on that day. Mother Teresa also said, "If you judge people, you have no time to love them." She also said that we are to see all people as "Jesus in disguise."

Utterly shaken and ashamed, I fell to my knees on the riverbank and sobbed as I asked God for forgiveness. I had at first thought that my sin of presumption was only in assuming that God would answer my prayers. But I now realized that it was much worse than that. I had presumed that people who sin differently than I do were somehow further from God than I was. I was surprised that He would use them to minister to me.

Chris and Mary were children of God, loved by Him. I have no idea of the relationship each has with Him, and I don't need to. He was telling me not to judge, but He was telling me more than that. There is still a certain spirit of judgmentalism in the very proclamation that I would not judge others or in the statement to "hate the sin, love the sinner." It still emphasizes my awareness of the sin itself.

I was casting first stones, right and left, indiscriminately, it seemed to me. I was ignoring the beam in my own eye while I focused on the speck in others'. I was St. Peter and God was lowering a sheet with people of all types on it and telling me not to call unclean what He was calling clean.

I sat on a bench and composed myself, and begged forgiveness. I had indeed been presumptuous, but it was an entirely different presumption than what I had first understood. I thanked Him for this lesson in love.

I still believe homosexual activity to be a sin and I struggle to understand the concept of same sex attraction, and how it fits into my (admittedly meager) understanding of human nature, sin, and God. I also know abortion to be a great sin, the murder of innocents. But we are all sinners struggling here together, and my sins-- presumption, judging, ego, and pride, among others, are not looked upon by God with any less distaste than others. I felt like He told me a great big "None of your business" as I considered Chris and Mary and their differences from me. "They are mine," He said, "I can deal with them. Worry about your own little old self, and leave them to me. I love them."

Chris and Mary, my trail angels. Thank you for being more charitable to me than I was to you.

Summer 2016

Even now, three years after that day in Bryson City, I remember it as if it were yesterday, and the lessons I learned from my confrontation with my own small-mindedness continue to be reinforced. While sitting in my home church this morning making a holy hour, looking at the monstrance with the host sitting on the altar, I remembered the story of the old man who was asked what he did during a whole hour of adoration.

"I look at Him, and He looks at me," he answered humbly.

I looked at the altar. What do I see, when I look at Him? With my human eyes I see a brass instrument in the shape of a cross, maybe a Celtic cross, with a circle around the center. I find its shape very pleasing to look upon, straight lines and curved lines gleaming in front of the candles. In the center is the host, perfectly round and pale, hard to see, actually, because of the glare on the surface caused by the same candlelight reflecting on the glass window covering the host. My human eyes do not see Jesus, but my heart and my mind, my faith, tell me He is there. I know there are some saints, St. Faustina comes to mind because I am reading her diary, who actually saw Jesus in human form in the host, but this gift is not given to me. So I see a brass ornament and a wheaten wafer. I do not see all that is really there. I am blinded by the veil of humanity.

And what does He see when He looks back at me? If He looked only with His human eyes He would see a normal, rather plain woman, neither beautiful nor striking in appearance. He would see occasional expressions of boredom and even annoyance on my face. He would see me fidget and grimace in my pew as my knees hurt on the kneeler. If He looked at me with only human eyes, He would not be impressed.

But He sees more than that, because He is more than human, He is God. He sees the real me, the whole me. For that I am grateful, but also ashamed, because I know that my heart isn't always pure and my mind, even in adoration, isn't always clean. He sees that underneath my boredom and annoyance and fidgeting and grimacing is a heart that loves Him and prays to be able to love Him more. He sees that I strive for holiness. My intentions are good, even though my execution of those intentions is sloppy, lazy, even lukewarm at times.

When I looked at Chris and at Mary, it was with the same veiled human eyes with which I look on the monstrance. I did not see all that was there. I did not see what God sees when He looks at them.

And worse yet, I categorized and judged them based on the veiled, limited view I had of them.

And worst of all, I took the limited amount of information I knew about Chris, and drew inferences from it, and then categorized him, and then judged him, based on those assumptions. I do not know Chris' gender, but neither do I know his sexual or gender orientation. I do not even really know Mary's political stance. I just know what the bumper stickers on her car proclaimed. So I took a limited amount of information, seen through the veil of my own human ignorance, and formed impressions about these dear people based on it.

I don't see Jesus as He really is. I know that people don't see who I am when they look at me. Yet somehow I thought I could see who Chris and Mary really were. I couldn't see them as Jesus sees them, which is the only perspective that really counts.

Thank you, Jesus, for teaching me to look with eyes of love.

I blew my nose and walked over to the outfitter to buy my hiking pass for the Smokies before they closed for the day. I had just walked through the door when a young man approached me and excitedly asked, "Are you a thru-hiker?" When I affirmed that I was he practically giggled and asked, "Can I give you some trail magic?"

"Well, sure," I said, wondering how much more trail magic I could stand for one day. He excused himself, went out to his car, and came back in with a full box of Little Debbies, which he handed to me and wished me good luck on the rest of my hike. I thanked him sincerely, honoring his compulsion to give, and not acknowledging the whole box of Debbies I had back in my room. An older couple browsing nearby heard our exchange and came up to me after my newest trail angel had gone.

"Are you really hiking the Appalachian Trail? Oh, that sounds so exciting! We would love to try it, but I'm sure we could never actually do it. Still, we'd love to get out there for maybe a short section. What do you think? Can we do it? At our age? You must be having a blast!"

This was another case of the extreme opposites that I had encountered so often on the trail: from freezing nights to sweating days, from squalor on the trail to luxury in the hostels, from ravenous hunger to a stomach bursting with cheeseburgers. Now I had gone from debasement and recognition of myself as a sinner to rock star in five minutes. The sweet older couple thanked me profusely for the advice I had given them ("Just do it. Prepare and practice, but go for it.") and wandered off to look at hammocks. I went up the stairs on the instructions of the clerk to find the computer I could use to register for the Smokies hiking permit. I finally got it all figured out and paid for, then turned around—and there they were, waiting for me. "We're so sorry, we don't mean to be pesty! But what about stoves and water filters? What do you carry? Would you mind awfully to come look at the stoves over here? There are just so many different kinds!" They chattered on as we walked over to the stove display. "I know you must be so busy and we're so sorry to take up so much of your time! But it's just so great having an actual hiker here to help us! Now what do you think about this model here?"

I assured them that I had plenty of time and answered all their questions. Actually, I had absolutely nothing else to do that day, and it wasn't even suppertime yet. This was an unusual feeling, but no more unusual than being treated like a celebrity or being a witness to the tender love of God or any of the other remarkable things I had experienced that day.

I went back to the common room, the room I had sat in while I sewed up my hiking pants the day before. There was a group of hikers there now, all saying that they had come in for the night because of the cold. I shared my trail magic box of cakes and was popular again (hikers love snack cakes.) I met a hiker named G-Ma, a lady who was in her seventies at least and had just the slightest trace of a fading English accent. She was lovely and gracious, and I was to find out over the next few days that she could outhike people half her age. I was to hear stories about her for the next month or so, as her wisdom, generosity, and cheerfulness impacted every hiker she met, as well as her tough as rocks demeanor.

I then went to my room to find out that I now had roommates, the other three bunks having filled up with hikers fleeing the cold on the mountain. A young woman showed me a better way to tie my shoes to keep them from loosening up or sliding around. I repacked the Green Monster and made ready for the next leg of my hike, what I was considering my epic eight day trek through the wilderness without town stops. Then I got into my bunk, pulled my top quilt up over my shoulders, and started a conversation with God. I had a lot I needed to say.

"The greatest destroyer of peace is abortion because if a mother can kill her own child, what is left for me to kill you

and you to kill me? There is nothing between." Mother Teresa

"We need to find God, and He cannot be found in noise and restlessness. God is the friend of silence. See how nature—trees, flowers, grass—grows in silence; see the stars, the moon and the sun, how they move in silence...We need silence to be able to touch souls." Mother Teresa

Nantahala Outdoor Center to Sassafras Gap Shelter
April 22, 2013

I heaved the Green Monster up onto my shoulders and said goodbye to the NOC with a feeling of real excitement. The pack was heavy on my back with the unaccustomed weight of eight days worth of food, and I still hadn't gotten used to the pad hanging from the bottom, although I was sure I would appreciate its comfort at night whether in a shelter or in my hammock. My legs, too, seemed to have gotten lazy over the long interval of relatively light hiking that I had been enjoying. "Time to toughen up," I muttered to myself. "Suck it up and hike."

My saving grace was that I could hike at my own pace and not feel pressured to put in any big-mile days. I had some rough terrain coming up, but my scheduled rendezvous for April 29 meant that I had plenty of time to cover the 62 miles. There was a long, six mile ascent out of the NOC, and I had heard horror stories about it, but I was resolved to just motor on up, however long it might take. I was hiking along at what I felt was a pretty good pace, when G-Ma came up from behind and easily overtook me. I made my usual, self-deprecating jokes about my slow pace, and she was gracious in her response as she disappeared up the trail.

The six miles up to the top of Swim Bald weren't always steep, but there were plenty of steep sections. The worst parts were the boulder fields, long stretches of huge rocks which I painstakingly made my way across. I took my time, stopped for breaks whenever I felt like it, and ate the heaviest food in my pack for lunch. There were fabulous views back down into the gorge I had just left, the Nantahala River twisting among the trees and rocks and growing progressively smaller as I climbed the mountain. I didn't see any other hikers through the day, so I had plenty of time to think as I walked along and to pray for my person of the day, my son-in-law. I also went back over the lesson I sensed God had taught me on my trip into Bryson City and thanked Him again for His tender compassion, and asked Him to shower me with as many other lessons as He thought I needed and could handle.

It was mid-afternoon when I reached the top of the bald and started down the other side, grateful to finally be walking downhill. Off to the left I could see a roof through the trees—the shelter. Although I had walked less than seven miles and it was still quite early, I decided to stop for the night. The next shelter was nine miles away, which would make for a good hiking day. With so few other hikers on the trail I felt more comfortable staying at a shelter than stopping at a random campsite, and I liked that shelters also had tables, privies, and bear cables. I was getting better at throwing the rope to hang my food bag from trees, but cables were definitely easier. It would be nice to have some company for the night, too, and that was more likely to happen at a shelter.

So I took off down the blue-blazed trail to the shelter, and of course, this early in the day I was the only hiker there. I took off my shoes and put on my Crocs, and did my usual chores: collected my water and filtered it, gathered wood for a fire, got my supper and stove out of

my pack. This particular shelter didn't have bear cables, so
I went looking for a good branch to hang my food bag. In
order to keep a food bag safe from bears it has to dangle at
least 20 feet up in the air from the branch of a tree, and at
least ten feet from the trunk of the tree. Bears have been
known to climb trees to get food bags that are close enough
to the trunk for them to reach. To hang a food bag you start
with an empty bag (or stuff sack). I used the bag I kept my
water filter in. I would add a rock or two for weight to the
sack and then clip it by a carabiner to a length of paracord.
Then came the tricky part: finding the appropriate branch.
Although there were always roughly a million trees at any
campsite, finding branches that were horizontal to the
ground and ten feet from the trunk was a hard job. The
branches were mostly vertical, or nearly so, in the thick
forest. But eventually I would find one that fit most of the
criteria, and then I simply had to throw the decoy bag up
and over the branch. (A decoy bag was used because if I
were to throw my actual food bag, there would have been
nothing left in it but crumbs, as I often missed and the bag
fell repeatedly to the forest floor.) Early in my hike I had
tried to use an overhand throw, but I'm not strong enough
to get the bag over the branch that way. I had accuracy
with that method, but not distance. Through trial and error

I had discovered that if I swung the rope at my side a few times and then gave it a mighty toss into the air, it went far enough to go over the branch. Except that it usually didn't, at least not on the first couple of dozen tries. I had distance, but not accuracy. But of course, eventually it always did, and then I would replace the decoy bag with my actual food bag, hoist it up into the air, and tie off the other end of the rope to a nearby tree. As a rule I usually attempted to hang my food bag when there were no other hikers around. We were all safer that way, and I was spared some embarrassment!

A couple of other hikers drifted in, a man roughly my age named Old New Yorker and a young fellow named Brick and his dog Mika. I hadn't had any real opportunities to talk to a hiker with a dog yet, and I enjoyed getting to know Brick and learning about canine hikers. Mika, like most hiking dogs, was just above medium sized, strong, young, and well-trained. She was devoted to Brick. I hadn't yet found the perfect branch to hang my food bag, and I decided not to bother with it with Mika present. Surely she would announce the presence of any bears before they could snatch my food and run away with it. I also decided to sleep in the shelter instead of hanging my hammock. I had the blue pad now, so the floor wouldn't be so hard.

Sleeping in shelters instead of in my hammock was a mistake I made consistently along the trail. I loved my hammock, and was well aware that it was warmer and more comfortable than the shelter floors. I somehow seemed to forget those facts in the evenings while sitting in a shelter enjoying the company of other hikers. I always managed to convince myself that it would be warmer than previous nights (and indeed it usually was reasonably warm before the sun went down, and I just never seemed to believe that it would get that cold again.) I was also tired in the evenings, and getting the hammock out of the pack and putting it up, which was actually easy to do, was still harder than putting my pad and quilts on the floor of the shelter. In addition, I was frequently reluctant to leave the camaraderie in the shelter, which continued after everyone was lying down and the headlamps were turned off. And finally, I told myself how nice it would be not to have to pack up the hammock in the morning, and that I could get off to an earlier start.

So for all those reasons I left my hammock in my pack and lay down on the shelter floor to sleep, and then endured what was one of my hardest nights on the trail thus far. It was insanely cold, and the wooden floor felt hard as concrete under me, blue pad notwithstanding. I could not get comfortable, could not get warm, and did not sleep throughout the night that seemed to last twelve hours. I lifted all these small sufferings up to God for my son-in-law and felt that he was really getting his money's worth.

Sassafras Gap Shelter to Brown Fork Gap Shelter
April 23, 2013

I was happy to see the sun rise, and I got up and packed early. I wished I was a coffee drinker for the comfort that coffee seems to offer its fans. I ate a cold protein bar and washed it down with water, said my goodbyes to Brick, Mika, and Old New Yorker (knowing they would be passing me up at some point during the morning), saddled up, and set off down the trail. My goal for the day was nine miles to the next shelter. The guidebook showed it as mostly downhill, but with a one-mile ascent first thing in the morning to the top of Cheoah Bald and another one at the very end of the day that looked short but quite steep, charmingly named "Jacob's Ladder."

I had a headache from the lack of sleep, which came and

went throughout the morning. It was a beautiful, warm, spring mountain day, and I was gratified to see the dogwoods blooming. It's easy to forget the miseries of the night before on a beautiful day, but I was resolved to remember it and to sleep in my hammock that night, no matter how congenial the company at the shelter. I was conscious of feeling very dirty. The floor at Sassafras Gap shelter had been filthy, and I had crawled around on it setting up my spot. As the day grew warmer and I started to sweat, it all felt much worse, and I wet my bandana in a creek to wash my face, hands, and neck. The headache grew worse as I started the steep downhill into Stecoah Gap and heard the traffic on the busy highway that passes through the gap. A plan formed itself in my head, almost without my knowledge or consent, and when I reached the bottom I walked right past the picnic table where some hikers sat and toward the road. Several of the hikers were people I had met previously, and they called out a greeting to me and invited me to sit at the table with them for a break. "Nope," I called. "I'm going to town."

I heard some mild scoffing from the group, evidently skeptical of my ability to just head on into town that easily, but I walked out to the road, stuck out my thumb, and five seconds later was climbing into the cab of a pickup truck. I smiled back at the hikers at the picnic table, now staring at me with mouths open. "Can you take me to Robbinsville?" I asked the driver.

He was a middle-aged man, a supervisor on a road crew, who didn't live in the area, so he wasn't used to seeing hikers. He was on his way into Robbinsville to meet his crew and do some work on an intersection right in town. He had a lot of questions about hiking and hikers, and we enjoyed some good conversation on the trip to town. It was against company policy for him to pick up hitchhikers, but he was too much of a gentleman to leave me standing on the side of the road. He drove me the seven miles into town, and I found a place that looked like it might serve a good cheeseburger. I was right, and very much enjoyed a hot burger with a stack of fries, an ice cold Mello Yello, and a candy bar. I felt like a new woman afterward, my headache a thing of the past, floating away on a dose of my old friend, caffeine. A young female customer struck up a conversation with me over lunch. She had a lot of questions about my hike, and after talking a while she offered to drive me back to Stecoah Gap.

From there it was two and half miles to Brown Fork Gap Shelter, which included the challenging bit of steep trail called Jacob's Ladder. But I was refreshed and up to the task and arrived at the shelter in the early evening. It was a small shelter, capacity of six according to my guidebook, and there were already a few hikers there, but it didn't matter because I remembered my earlier resolve to sleep in the hammock. I found a good couple of trees and hung the hammock, washed up, ate the other candy bar I had purchased in town, and zipped myself into my hammock to do a couple of Sudoku puzzles before it got too dark to see. Then I pulled out my rosary and thanked God for many things, not the least of which were cheeseburgers, caffeine, and chocolate.

Brown Fork Gap Shelter to Fontana Dam
April 24, 2013

It was an uneventful day, with the terrain being some of the easiest I had yet experienced, without any big elevations changes going either uphill or down. The weather continued to cooperate, too, and it was sunny and mild, great hiking weather. And so it was that I walked twelve miles to get to the fabled Fontana Dam Shelter, fondly called the "Fontana Hilton" by hikers. After having read so much about it in other hikers' journals, I looked forward to seeing it for myself. The last four miles were a reasonably gentle downhill hike. I was able to see glimpses of the dam from quite far back on the trail, tantalizing me with visions of shelter at the end of a long, though not difficult, day of hiking.

As I walked that last long four miles down the mountain, it was as though spring was coming to life in the woods surrounding me. I gradually started to see more and more greenery as the forest floor slowly turned from brown to green, resplendent with abundant plant life. As I rounded each bend in the trail steadily making my way downhill, I was amazed to see more and more plants, until finally the woods were a sea of wildflowers, sweet heads gently bobbing in the light breeze. It was as if they were welcoming me into the valley. My eyes filled with tears at the sheer beauty of creation, and I thanked God once again for His bounty.

I was starting to see more hikers, too. I came upon a rest stop (a log) and there were Father and Son, with whom I had spent a stormy night back at Muskrat Creek Shelter, which seemed like a long time ago! It was good to see them again. They had another son with them now, and the three of them were headed down into Fontana Village where they had wives waiting. They were going to spend the night at the Fontana Lodge and asked if they would see me there later. "Not me," I said. "I'll be staying at the Hilton." They laughed, knowing that to be the shelter, wished me well, and got up to continue hiking. I sat down on the now vacant log and drank some water, then got up to finish the day's hike.

A short while later, almost within sight of the road, I came across the three of them again. That was strange, as at my slow hiking speed I wasn't used to catching up with people who were ahead of me. I would have thought that they would be enjoying a hot tub at the lodge by now. Instead, they were standing in a little clearing, worried looks on their faces. It turned out that the younger son, the one who had only recently joined them, had turned an ankle, maybe spraining it. They were trying to figure out how to get him the short distance down to the road, where they could call their wives to pick them up. There wasn't much I could do to help. Finally the middle son took up both packs, his own and his brother's, and put one on his back and one on his front. The father got on the injured son's bad side, and with his son's arm over his shoulder, they hobbled on down to the road.

I got to the road, crossed it, and finally came to the fabled Fontana Hilton. It was indeed a lovely shelter, big and clean and altogether more civilized looking than any other shelter I had seen. It was a two level shelter, with upstairs and downstairs sleeping platforms on either side of a central breezeway. It had a capacity of twenty according to the guidebook, but it looked even bigger than that to me. The grounds were landscaped and the grass mown, with a gravel picnic area beside the shelter, and a pretty lake right behind it. Perhaps best of all, there were real restrooms, and each one had a shower! It wasn't in the woods, but I didn't intend to look for trees for my hammock anyway. I wasn't going to pass up the opportunity to spend a night at this iconic trail shelter. I staked out my spot and placed my pad and quilts, then called for a shuttle for the short drive to Fontana Village. There was a post office there, and Mike had mailed me a package. I rode with a couple of other hikers to the post office and retrieved my package. Surprise! I had two. Mike had sent me a few resupplies I had asked for, batteries for my headlamp and some food to supplement my food bag, and my friend Leslye had sent me a box of luxury items—fresh oranges, homemade cookies, chewing gum, and hair conditioner. It was just like Christmas, sitting on the floor of the post office porch opening my packages. I rode back to the Hilton and gathered the supplies for my much-needed shower, including my new hair conditioner, and walked over to the bath house. I thought I would have to wait my turn, as the little bathroom with a shower was built for only one person at a time, but there was no one ahead of me. I enjoyed my shower very much as I watched the dirty water roll off my body and down the drain. I didn't realize I had a problem until I came out of the shower—there was no towel. Hikers don't carry towels, and none were provided. I did the best I could with a couple of bandanas, which it turns out are not very absorbent. I then used a couple of paper towels, but didn't think it was right to use more than a few. Then I spied the hot air hand drier, and inspiration struck. I was grateful for years of yoga as I assumed heretofore unknown poses trying to get different areas of my body up under the hot air stream. Eventually I decided I was dry enough, put on my least dirty clothes, and rejoined the cheerful group of hikers at the shelter.

I saw hikers I had met earlier and made new friends as well. It was a friendly group and everyone seemed to be in a great mood. One fellow had bought a dozen eggs in the village, saying he just couldn't resist the lure of fresh food. He was boiling them two at a time in his little stove and giving them away, with plans to reserve the last six for himself. I saw a young hiker named Fresh Step, with whom I had camped a few nights earlier, and I met three middle aged men who had met on the trail and were now hiking together. They were: Johnnie Walker, a soft-spoken man of few words whom the other two seemed to acknowledge as a leader because he had a lot of hiking experience; Highlander, who was Scottish and so possessed a charming brogue; and Phoenix, a fellow Tennesseean who seemed to be just happy to be there. Another hiker at the shelter said he called them the Johnnie Walker Express because they always walked together, single file, like a train, with Johnnie Walker in the lead.

I took a seat on a bench right against the front of the shelter and opened my food bag, anticipating a nice supper to be supplemented by oranges and cookies from my package. I laid a round, wax-wrapped Baby Bel cheese on the bench beside me while I reached back into my bag for some crackers. Just at that moment, Brick and Mika came around the corner of the shelter, and with a single big GULP, my cheese was gone. To be fair, the bench was just at the height of Mika's head. I wasn't sure how well a dog's digestive juices would process sealing wax, but I warned Brick anyway, in case he was to see the blob of bright red again, somewhere up the trail.

It was getting dark, which in the hiker world means

bedtime. I went inside the shelter and to my sleeping pad. The conversation was lively and everyone agreed that this was the best-smelling group of hikers we had ever seen in a shelter, as people came drifting back, one by one, from the shower. I wasn't the only person who had gotten a mail drop at the post office, and no one wants to carry extra weight into the Smokies, which we were all set to enter the next day, so food was being traded, given away, or consumed. I would call out "Who wants a pack of spearmint gum?" and someone else would call "I'll take it" and I would toss it across the shelter. Or another hiker would say, "I've got Skittles!" and a voice from the top tier would be heard, "I want 'em. Thanks." It was fun. The oranges and cookies I ate myself or put in my food bag for later.

Eventually the trading was done, the eggs eaten, the stories told, and darkness fell, bringing quiet. I was the second from the wall, and the young hiker lying by the wall turned to me with a question. "What kind of spider do you think this is?" he asked, shining the beam from his headlamp onto a long legged brown spider on the wall near his feet.

I looked closely. "I'm not sure, but it could be a brown recluse," I said. I had looked them up after caring for a patient in the hospital who had lost an arm to a spider bite, and this one looked suspiciously like the one I had seen in the article.

"I thought so too," he said, and fell silent for a minute. "What do you think I should do?" he asked.

"I think you should kill it," I said, without hesitation.

He didn't answer, evidently wrestling with his conscience. Eventually he got up, scooped up the spider onto a page of his guidebook, carried it out of the shelter to place it gently on the grass, and came back to his sleeping bag. I wondered how long it would take the spider to get back into the shelter, and how many cousins he had living in the shadows. I didn't wonder long though, as sleep overtook me quickly after my long day of hiking.

Fontana Dam Shelter to Mollie's Ridge Shelter
April 25, 2013

I was one of the first to wake up and leave the shelter, my excitement about entering the Smokies palpable. I packed quietly so as not to disturb the sleeping hikers around me and walked out of the Fontana Hilton, following the white blazes which led to a road that crossed the top of the famed Fontana Dam, the highest dam in the eastern US. I stopped to call Mike while I still had cell service, knowing that once I re-entered the mountains I would not be able to contact him until our meeting at Clingman's Dome in four days. It was early, but St. Mike is an early riser, so I knew I wouldn't be waking him. He was glad to hear from me because he had good news, and bad news, and more good news. The first good news was that our soap and herbal products business had just been accepted into an herb market in Asheville, North Carolina, that I had been trying to get into for years. The market was a week and a half away, and they had a last minute cancellation and wanted to know if we could come on short notice. The bad news was that if Mike was to go to Asheville to do the market he wouldn't be able to hike the last 38 miles of the Smokies with me, as we had long planned. The last piece of good news was that he would be in Asheville for the weekend, and if I could get all the way through the Smokies in that amount of time, he would pick me up at the other end, and I could spend the weekend in Asheville with him, doing the market.

I was devastated at the idea of having to hike the entire park by myself, as suspicious as I was about the likelihood

of bad weather and bad conditions, and I had really wanted
to hike *with* him, bad weather or not. It would have been a
chance not only to spend time together but to share my
hiking lifestyle with him. But, on the whole, I had to admit
it was a good tradeoff—doing the Asheville market would
be great for the business, I would still get to spend a couple
of days with my husband, and I had a motel waiting for me
after I ran the 70 mile gauntlet of the Great Smoky
Mountain National Park. As we lamented our missed
opportunity to hike together, which we had both been
looking forward to, we came up with a compromise of
sorts. Mike didn't mind making the four hour trip from our
home to the mountains on two consecutive weekends, so if
I could get to Clingman's Dome by April 27, or even by the
28, he could come spend a day, maybe a night, in
Gatlinburg, and hike a short dayhike with me. The section
between Clingman's and Newfound Gap is about seven
miles long, so perfect for our purposes. This was close to
our original rendezvous date, so not much was changed for
me as far as my hiking itinerary for the next few days,
except that I had one less day to hike the first 32 miles.
Two, or at the most three days to hike 32 miles was a
challenge for me. Having to stay only at shelters was
limiting also. On top of that, I wouldn't be able to

communicate with him by phone for the next few days to keep him apprised of my progress. We agreed that he would keep the weekend open and I would call him when I got to Gatlinburg. With a new sense of urgency, I donned the Green Monster and started down the road across the dam.

There was a low-lying early morning fog that still hadn't burned off when I got to the dam, lending the area the mysterious, misty, peaceful quality that I find so enchanting. I was the only person on the dam at that time of the morning. It was magnificent, but I couldn't help wishing St. Mike was there to see it with me, knowing that engineering marvels mean more to him than they do to me. I was most impressed knowing that one of my favorite actors, Tommy Lee Jones, had been here, filming *The Fugitive* with Harrison Ford.

I walked across the top of the dam itself, which was actually sprinkled with AT white blazes, then down a quiet road, and finally into the park. I was taking a picture of the iconic sign announcing the Great Smoky Mountain National Park, when hikers came up behind me. It was the Johnnie Walker Express, and they offered to take my picture with the sign. So we swapped photography skills and then turned off the road and onto an unassuming little trail that led off into the woods and immediately started a steep uphill climb. There was an unmanned wooden box right on the trail to put the top section of our hiking permits into, retaining the bottom section which we were to have on our person at all times while in the park. We were now officially commenced on our hike into the Smokies.

It was a long, steep climb, roughly 2,902 feet in elevation gain in the eleven miles I would hike to the first shelter. But I knew that once I made it up to the top, the rest of the trail through the Smokies follows a high ridge, so there was actually not a lot more climbing to be done for the rest of the trip. It is the high elevation of the trail through the park that contributes to the unpredictable, often bad, weather.

This day was shaping up to be beautiful, though, and as the Johnnie Walker Express motored up the mountain I became the caboose on the train for a while, hiking right behind them, and I enjoyed their good-natured teasing and joking with each other. We stopped for a snack and rest break midmorning and sat on rocks munching on granola and getting to know each other better. We were joined by Fresh Step and a few other hikers from the Fontana Hilton the night before, and we were all in good spirits and cheerful. The climb was not unreasonably steep after all, and somehow just having entered the Smokies felt like having accomplished a milestone, and we all looked forward to the next week hiking the "high road" as we took to calling it.

I was quite surprised by an unusual sound approaching from around a bend on the trail, which sounded like…. horses? On the AT? Sure enough, three beautiful horses rounded the bend and joined us, their riders explaining that horses are allowed on some sections of the trail in the Smokies. The trail always seems to have surprises for me, something new around every curve. I admired the horses and talked to the riders and after a few moments they departed and headed on down the trail. Eventually we got up and continued on as well. I was still behind the Express, but they had pulled far enough ahead of me that they were nearly out of sight, but not out of earshot, when I heard an excited exclamation from them. "Trail magic!"

I was excited at the thought of trail magic, but also baffled. Who would have left trail magic way out here in the wilderness, so far from any road crossing? I raced ahead, wondering what it might be, hoping for fresh fruit and cold drinks. When I reached the spot where the Express had been there was no cooler, though. Instead, there was a big pile of fresh steaming horse manure, right smack in the middle of the trail. "Is this what you call trail magic?" I yelled. I couldn't see them, but the sound of their laughter drifted back easily to me in the still morning.

It was late afternoon when I finally arrived at Mollie's Ridge Shelter and heaved a sigh of relief as I dropped the Green Monster from my back. It was a medium sized shelter, with room for twelve hikers according to my guidebook. There were eight or nine other hikers there before me, and there was also a ridge-runner, an employee of the Appalachian Trail Conservancy. Their job is to advise and educate hikers on the trail, provide assistance when necessary, compile reports on the number of hikers, etc. Generally, they are the eyes and ears of the ATC on the trail. This ridge-runner spoke to each hiker as we arrived, getting our names and what state we were from. He then went on to advise hikers to continue on to one of the next two shelters, which were 2.8 and 5.7 miles further on. He explained that those few miles were relatively easy, while the seven or so miles after that were the hardest in the entire park. I believed he was trying to prevent a big hiker traffic jam, as everyone stopped at the first shelter they came to. Many people took his advice and continued on, but I told him that I was tired and was going to stay put for the night.

There was a huge tarp covering the entire open side of the shelter, the first I had seen. It had been a beautiful and very pleasant day, but as the sun went down it started to become cold alarmingly fast, so I was grateful for the tarp. I was to see one of these tarps on every shelter in the Smokies. I cooked my supper and cleaned up, visited with the other hikers, and was on my pad, covered up and ready to sleep by eight o'clock.

Mollie's Ridge Shelter to Derrick Knob Shelter
April 26, 2013

My goal for the day was to hike the twelve miles to Derrick Knob Shelter. That seemed rather ambitious for a tortoise, as I kept hearing that this was the most difficult section of the Smokies. But if I could accomplish it, that would leave only a ten mile section between me and Clingman's Dome, and I was still hopeful that I could salvage a day of hiking with St. Mike. Phoenix, from the Johnnie Walker Express, offered me a ride into Gatlinburg with his wife, who was meeting the Express at Clingman's Dome on Sunday morning, April 28.

This seemed to be a great plan. If we got to Gatlinburg

early enough, I could make it to mass there, and Mike would have time to drive over for our visit, stay Sunday night, and hike with me on Monday.

I changed my approach to hiking for the day. Ordinarily, knowing I had twelve miles to hike over difficult terrain, I would push myself relentlessly, trying only to get the miles under my belt, with a constant sense of worry that I wasn't going to make it. It would be the hiker version of stress. I decided that I just wasn't going to stress over it. I was going to walk even slower than usual, to pace myself. I resolved to take long breaks frequently, to stroll, to linger, to literally stop and smell any roses I might encounter. I had twelve miles to walk and all day to do it and nothing to be gained by rolling into the shelter early (except a spot in the shelter itself. As a late arrival, I would need to put up my hammock. So be it. I loved my hammock, anyway, and usually regretted the nights I left it in the pack to sleep in the shelters.)

I sauntered off, quite enjoying this new approach to hiking. My fears about the weather were proving groundless as the day bloomed warm and sunny. I climbed a mountain called the Devil's Tater Patch and then walked through a series of balds, each golden meadow sweeter than the one before. It was definitely the prettiest scenery I had seen yet. I stopped under a tree to recline in the soft, sweet-smelling grass and eat my lunch. I took off my shoes and socks and stretched my toes. This gift of time I had given myself felt decadent and luxurious.

Lunch over and shoes back on my feet, I strolled on and came to a rocky outcropping that, according to my guidebook, was called Rocky Top! I climbed to the summit and looked around at the sweeping vistas before me. I could see for miles in all directions. I had been singing about *"Old Rocky Top"* all my life, and now I was standing on it, looking at the gorgeous views it provided, all trees and surrounding mountains. There were no roads or manmade structures to be seen. If Songbird had been there I know we would have sung Rocky Top together at the tops of our lungs. I was alone but I sang it anyway, though perhaps not as loudly or with as much gusto as if she had been there egging me on. A father and son came along, interrupting my impromptu concert, and offered to take my picture (maybe to get me to stop singing?). Afterwards we looked through their binoculars and were able to see Fontana Dam way off in the distance. I couldn't believe that I had been there just two days ago, and that I had walked all that way! Then we turned the other way and were able to see the Clingman's Dome observation tower, just a speck in the trees on a distant peak. Equally hard to believe that I would be there in another two days, and that I would walk that entire distance. I would not have thought myself capable of it, if I wasn't actually already doing it.

Reluctantly I left Rocky Top and sauntered on down the trail. Toward the end of the day I encountered the longest steepest downhill section I had seen yet. It was full of loose, brick-sized rocks that wanted to turn as I stepped on them. I picked my way very carefully down the rocky trail, my toes and ankles screaming at me in protest. Nearing the end I heard steps behind me, and then beside me, as a young man came running—*running!*—down the steep rocky trail. "Hi," he said breathlessly as he zoomed past. "Ow, ow, ouch, hi," I answered.

He was still sitting at the bottom when I finally got there, water bottle in hand. We introduced ourselves, and he said his name was Wolf.

"Wolf, how in the world are you able to just run down the trail like that? I would sprain my ankle for sure if I tried that," I asked him. He explained that it was actually easier for him to run than walk on a section like that.

"As my foot makes contact with each rock it might start to turn, but I have pushed off of it and am gone before it actually turns. I'm on each rock for only a fraction of a second, so no sprained ankles."

I understood how it could work, in theory, and I was fascinated by it. I visualized myself blithely skimming along the trail, daintily skipping from rock to rock, like a water spider never breaking the surface of the lake. I knew if I tried it, however, I would end up with not only two sprained ankles, but likely a broken nose as well. I was doomed to carefully pick my way through every rock field I encountered. Wolf and I walked through Starkey Gap together, then he bounced off ahead of me on the next downhill section to Sugar Hill Gap. Eventually I started the last one mile uphill to Derrick Knob Shelter, my destination for the night. It was starting to rain when I arrived, so I quickly hung my hammock because, as I had anticipated, the shelter was full. I sat in the protection of the shelter to eat my supper and visit with the Johnnie Walker Express who had spots in the shelter, and with Little Janie, who set up her tent near my hammock. Many of the hikers in the shelter were calling this day their hardest day yet on the trail. I had enjoyed it, except for the steep descent into Starkey Gap, and hadn't found the rest of it to be all that hard. I could only guess that my more relaxed attitude and leisurely pace had helped. The rain started to pick up, so I retired to my hammock and was all snuggled in before the sun went completely down.

I wondered why I had ever been so frightened of the Smokies. Just because I had read a few trail journals of other hikers who had had bad experiences while in the park didn't mean every hiker had such a hard time. The weather had been just lovely for me so far, the best of my hike in fact. The scenery was equally beautiful, and the terrain was challenging enough to be interesting, but no more difficult than several other sections I had hiked. There were only eleven miles between me and Clingman's Dome, and I had hiked twelve miles that day with minimal difficulty. I had a leisurely day planned for the next day, a Saturday, only 7.2 miles to Double Springs Gap Shelter, the last shelter before the Dome. Then on Sunday morning I would get up early and hike the remaining three miles to the Dome to meet Phoenix's wife and ride down to Gatlinburg. I had hopes of getting there early enough to make it to mass, and also that Mike could make it on such short notice to come to Gatlinburg for a visit. Maybe he could even stay over and hike the seven mile section of the trail between road crossings with me on Monday.

It was a great plan, a comfortable plan, even an elegant plan. I may have been a bit too smug in my comfort as I fell asleep, listening to the raindrops gently tattooing my tarp. I should have known. The Smokies will not be mocked.

Derrick Knob Shelter to Silers Bald Shelter
April 27, 2013

The rain was still falling when I awoke. It felt like it might be cooler outside than it had been the night before, but I was warm and comfortable inside my hammock. I made no effort to get up. With only seven miles to hike for the day there was no reason to rush out into the cold wet morning. I could take my time, wait a bit for the rain to stop, wait for it to warm up. It was a luxurious feeling, like sleeping in, like staying under the covers when the outside world is calling.

But wait, the world *was* calling. And it had a Scottish accent. "Tortoise! Tortoise," the world called, trilling the rrrrs.

I realized the voice of the world was actually Highlander, and I unzipped my bug net and stuck my head out of my hammock to see the three members of the Johnnie Walker Express lined up in their usual single-file hiking fashion, packs on their backs already, obviously prepared to hike. They explained that the plan had changed, because terrible weather was coming in, at least three days worth. They were going to walk all the way to Clingman's Dome, to try to get down off the mountain and into Gatlinburg before the worst of the weather hit. They hoped to have phone reception at the Dome to call Phoenix's wife to tell her of the change in plans. If she couldn't get there, they would call a shuttle.

I was grateful to be included in their plans. Segregated from the group at the shelter, I wouldn't have known of the upcoming storm if they hadn't stopped to tell me, and I was glad to have a ride into Gatlinburg. I told them I would get up and pack and join them at the Dome later in the afternoon, and they hiked off. I roused myself and sprang into action. First I went to Little Janie's tent to tell her about the bad weather moving in. We had talked about sharing a room in Gatlinburg, and I offered her a seat in Mrs. Phoenix's van. We busied ourselves taking down our shelters and packing our backpacks. It was difficult because it was still raining, harder now, and my tarp and hammock suspension was wet. I didn't like to pack up while my gear was wet, and tried to dry it with my chamois cloth, with moderate success. I told myself it didn't really matter though, because I would be in a warm dry motel room by evening, and take a zero day tomorrow, and everything would have time to dry out.

With our packs loaded and our raincoats on, Little Janie and I started off down the trail. The weather conditions were quickly deteriorating. The rain was harder and colder and the wind started to blow. Before long conversation was impossible, and we were walking with our heads down and backs bent into the wind. We trudged on into the howling wind, with visibility so poor that I could only make out the trail under my feet and Little Janie a few feet in front of me. My rain coat and rain pants tried valiantly to keep me dry for the first couple of hours but eventually they gave up the effort and the cold rain soaked through to my hiking clothes and then to my skin. My fingers inside my wool gloves and "waterproof" mittens were wet and soon grew numb. It became increasingly difficult to grip my hiking poles, which were slippery from the icy rain.

And yet we pushed on, because really, what else could we do? There was no choice but to keep going. Visions of cheeseburgers danced in my head, hot and greasy, with melted cheese running down the sides and crisp lettuce and juicy tomatoes. Somewhere there was a world with dry motel rooms with heaters you could turn up to high, and soft warm dry beds. All we had to do to get to that world was to keep walking through this one, the only real one, the one with a fierce wind whipping cold rain right into my face, with a pack on my back that was getting heavier by the minute as it, like everything else, was taking on water.

It was too cold and wet to get my guidebook out to consult it, but I remembered that there was a shelter five and a half miles from Derrick Knob Shelter, or halfway through the day's hike to Clingman's Dome. I had to get right into Little Janie's face and yell for her to be able to hear me over the howling wind, but I reminded her of the shelter and asked her to help me keep an eye out for it. It would be a good stop for the middle of the day, to get out of the weather for a few minutes and rest and eat some lunch. Then we'd be able to tackle the last half of the day.

The shelter appeared before us, squat and dark, but an offer of relief from the relentless wind and rain. Janie pointed to it, I nodded, and we sloshed through the mud to the tarp covering the open side. Pulling back the tarp we stumbled in. It took my eyes a few seconds to adjust to the darkness inside, but when they did I was astonished by what I saw. I expected there might be another hiker or two, like us seeking shelter from the storm. Instead there was a row of eyes, solemnly blinking back at me from the sleeping platform. Silers Bald Shelter had a capacity of twelve, and there were almost that many hikers there now, at two o'clock in the afternoon, all laid out in a row in their sleeping bags, looking like it was time for bed. It took my mind longer to adjust than it had taken my eyes. Evidently they had all stopped hiking for the day and planned on waiting out the storm here. And the three gentlemen of the Express were there, so the plan to hike out today was apparently cancelled. I had been so intent on getting to Clingman's Dome that I had become single-minded on that purpose and had a wrenching time switching gears. There was to be no motel room, no hot bath, dry heat, warm bed. No cheeseburger. Instead it was to be a long afternoon, evening, and night in a cold, damp shelter. I was more than disappointed, but the thought occurred to me that maybe I had been foolhardy to consider walking on. Everyone else seemed to think that stopping for the night was the prudent thing to do. I was clearly outnumbered, so I shrugged the Green Monster off and it hit the ground with a damp *splat.*

Little Janie and I found places on the sleeping platform, and I began to take stock of my belongings. I peeled the rain jacket and rain pants off my body and found a nail on the shelter wall to hang them. Hopefully they would drip dry, or nearly dry, by morning. My hiking pants were just as wet as the rain pants, so I peeled them off as well and hung them, dripping, from the same nail. Unfortunately, in my haste to break camp that morning I had not taken off the wool long underwear bottoms that I slept in, so they were also saturated. I had nothing else dry to put on the lower half of my body. Fortunately the bottom of my pack was still dry, including my meager bag of clothes, so I had a dry shirt and, praise God, my down jacket was dry, as well as my "sleeping socks", a pair of socks I kept just for nighttime and didn't hike in. I lamented to Janie my lack of pants, and Highlander, bless his heart, from across the shelter heard me and volunteered a dry pair of long johns for my use. They made their way across the shelter, handed from hiker to hiker, into my hands. I put them on. They felt heavenly and I thanked Highlander profusely and promised to give them back in the morning.

Now wearing dry clothing, I assessed my sleeping situation. My blue pad was carried rolled up and hanging from the back of my pack, on the outside of the pack, which meant that it was sopping wet and covered in mud. I wouldn't be able to sleep on it, so I was back to sleeping on a hard wooden floor. My fleece sleeping bag liner was dry, as were my topquilt and underquilt, so I spread them out on the shelter floor. I put my damp long johns under the liner so that I would be lying on top of them, hoping that my body heat would dry them enough to be bearable in the morning. I had no such hope for my pants, which were wet enough to wring water from.

The mood in the shelter was somber, and it was unusually quiet with only soft murmured conversations here and there. The rain pounding on the roof and the wind blowing were loud enough to make conversing across the shelter problematic. There was a rough fireplace in the shelter, but no one even considered the possibility of venturing out into the storm to scavenge firewood. It would have been too wet to burn anyway. With my clothing and bedding arranged as best as I could make them, my thoughts turned to food. It had been a long time since my protein bar that morning. No one was cooking, and I certainly didn't feel like fumbling with my alcohol stove with numb fingers either, so I got some cheese, tuna and crackers from my bag and shared them with Little Janie. No thought was given to hanging food bags to protect them from bears or even from mice. The consensus seemed to be that any bear or mouse strong enough to brave the elements could have what they found. I put my food wrappers back into my food bag and settled back to wait out the storm. I got out paper and pen to write a journal entry and a page from my Sudoku puzzle book to work on. I put my headlamp on my head and tried to get comfortable. The hard shelter floor dug into my bones, no matter what position I tried to sit or lay in. I had lost weight since starting my hike. In addition, I was cold. The situation seemed grim and morning couldn't come soon enough. I was sure that any hope I had of seeing St. Mike this weekend was flying out the window with this unexpected delay.

Suddenly I heard Phoenix's voice call out from across the shelter, "Hey y'all. Listen to this," and he turned the speaker up on his mp3 player. Music filled the shelter, a fun, determined, strident beat. The song was *"500 Miles"* by the Proclaimers, and the lyrics made perfect sense to the hikers shivering in the rough wooden shelter in the mountains in the rain.

"Well I would walk five hundred miles
And I would walk five hundred more
Just to be the man who walked a thousand miles
To fall down at your door."

Soon we were singing along, changing the lyrics to suit our situation:

"Well I would walk five hundred miles
And I would walk to Gatlinburg
Just to be the girl who walked all day and night
To get out of this damn storm."

Then the chorus started, and it was like popcorn as the *"La da lat da"* came from a different area of the shelter on each repetition.

The song ended, and there was a collective sigh from the group. The moment of communion and levity had helped, though, and we sank back into our individual pursuits with lighter hearts. I finished my journal entry and Sudoku puzzle, and then started naming all my blessings, all the things I was grateful for, and thanking God for them. There were so many, it was more than I could count, and I fell asleep in the middle of the task.

Silers Bald Shelter to Clingman's Dome
April 29, 2013

It was a Sunday morning, and I had no hope of getting to mass, but at the moment that didn't seem like the most pressing problem I had. It had been a very bad night, not just hard and uncomfortable, but very cold. I had shivered most of the night, in between short periods of dozing off, and this scared me. I knew that uncontrollable shivering is one of the early signs of hypothermia, and it looked like all the fears I had had of hiking in the Smokies were coming true after all. There had been some cold nights on the trail preceding this one, but I had never shivered all night long before. Sometime during the interminable night I made the decision that I was hiking out at daylight even if the storm didn't stop. I was no colder hiking than I was in the shelter, quite the opposite really as hiking generates a good amount of body heat and I was rarely cold while actually hiking. I believed I would be safer hiking in the elements than waiting in the shelter. It was about five miles to Clingman's Dome, an easily attainable distance. Perhaps if it had been ten miles I might have felt differently, but with only five miles to walk I was willing to go for it.

Morning came, and Little Janie woke up, and still the storm raged on. "Janie," I said, "I'm going on. It's too cold in here, I think I'll be warmer walking. I don't know how long this storm's going to last. Didn't someone say maybe three days? I just can't stay here. I don't blame you if you want to stay and wait it out, but I'm going on."

"I'm going with you. Let's go." Janie was a calm,

capable woman, not given to histrionics, and her confident demeanor gave me confidence as well. I was glad that she was going with me. None of the other hikers in the shelter gave any indication of budging from the spot. The thought crossed my mind that maybe we were crazy to be going out, but I couldn't stand the inertia anymore. I had to go.

I gave Highlander back his long underwear with much thanks and put my own back on. They were mostly dry, which is to say that they were still a bit damp. Then I took my pants down from the nail they were hanging on and found they were still drenching wet. I don't know what the temperature was, but I would guess that it was about thirty four degrees, because while it felt very, very cold, nothing that was wet actually froze. I put the wet pants on over my damp long johns because I had no other choice. I didn't bother with my rain pants. I had two pairs of dry socks, so I wore them both, then put my soaking wet, cold shoes back on. I made the decision to wear my down jacket under the rain jacket. It was at least dry, and warm. I never hiked in it, preserving it for nighttime use at camp, but if there was ever a time to make an exception this was it. I put the soggy gloves back on and tightened the hood of my rain jacket around my face. I didn't bother with my wet hat. Then I picked up the Green Monster. It felt like it weighed forty pounds with all the water-logged gear in it, but I heaved it up on my shoulders and we started off.

We walked out into conditions much the same as they had been when we had walked into the shelter the previous afternoon. We put our heads down and started up the trail. The five mile walk to Clingman's Dome was entirely uphill. Clingman's Dome is the highest point on the whole AT. We trudged up the trail, backs bent into the wind, which was howling around us, making conversation impossible. We made very slow progress, but we did progress. The trail in the Smokies is more heavily traveled than it is elsewhere, with the result that it is packed down. It is a rut in many places, with the ground rising up on either side of it five or six inches. In other places it is more like a trench, with the ground a good couple of feet higher on each side. With all the rainfall the trail had become a fast-moving stream. At first I endeavored to keep my feet as dry as possible by straddling the trail/creek where possible, by walking up on the edge, or by skipping from rock to rock. Eventually this became too difficult, requiring more energy than I had to give, so I gave up and trudged right through the middle of the stream. My boots had done a reasonable job of keeping my feet dry, but with the water up over my ankles they gave up in disgust and filled with cold, muddy water.

As the trail got higher, we were soon above treeline, and the modest protection from the wind we had gotten from the trees was gone. Now the wind really and truly whipped around our bodies. I felt like it probably would have lifted me from my feet if it weren't for the weight of the sodden pack on my back and the mud in my shoes.

Still we trudged on. At one point I fell while trying to step up a steep, slick, muddy bank. My left knee twisted painfully as I went down into the mud. I stayed down, seeing stars, wondering what I had done to my knee, envisioning a helicopter and an airlift rescue and trying to explain why we were out there in the first place when we should have been in a dry shelter. As my vision came back into focus I looked up into Janie's concerned face. I picked up my poles and tested my knee. Somewhat to my surprise I was able to get back up and continue on, the pain in my knee no more than a twinge. "I'm ok," I yelled over the wind. "Let's go."

We continued hiking, with a focus more single-minded than anything I had done since childbirth. And, like childbirth, there was a payoff in the end. Finally we saw the edges of a building up ahead. The Clingman's Dome tower! We had made it! We hurried ahead and reached the tower to find it totally deserted. Of course no one would be there on a day like this. We knew there was a visitor's center somewhere, so we located the road and walked down it. Oh glory, there ahead was a little building with lights on, and a chimney with smoke coming from it! And a parking lot full of cars! We reached the door of the building. We pulled hard to open it, and when it opened rather suddenly we fell in together and stood in the middle of a warm room with a fireplace and best of all, a blazing fire. Without a word we rushed to the fireplace and held out our hands to the warmth. Then we saw the two gentlemen in uniform—park rangers?—behind the counter, looking at us with a mixture of astonishment, sympathy, and humor. We must have looked like drowned rats with backpacks.

I apologized profusely for the amount of mud and water that had come in with us and was even then running in little streams across the clean floor from our packs and dripping from our clothes. They took it all in stride, though, and I realized that they had probably seen hikers in much worse shape than we were over the years. It was lovely standing in the warm, dry building, but I really wanted to get out of my wet clothes, and we still had a daunting problem: how were we going to get down to Gatlinburg 20 miles down the mountain? Neither of our phones had service, and to my surprise, the building had no land line. How did these rangers communicate with the outside world? I was unable to call for a shuttle. But there were cars in the parking lot, which meant there were people. Nothing to do but venture back out into the rain, walk to the parking lot, and try to wrangle a ride to Gatlinburg. Leaving my pack and poles in the visitor's center with Little Janie, I pulled my hood back over my head and, against my every instinct, headed back out into the storm. I walked down to the lot and the first vehicle I saw was a white van, maybe a twelve or even 15 passenger model. Maybe, if we were very lucky, this was a paid shuttle? I boldly walked up to the driver's window and knocked. The driver rolled it down. "Is this a shuttle to Gatlinburg?" I asked.

"No," he sounded amused. "This is a family."

"Oh, I'm sorry," I said. "I was hoping you were a shut..." but he was already rolling his window back up against the pounding rain. I walked on, wondering if I should have been more assertive and asked, begged, for a ride. Now was not the time for my innate shyness. He pulled away, and I resolved to be more emphatic and straightforward with the next motor vehicle owner I encountered. I heard a car door slam and looked across the lot to see a young couple loading backpacks into the trunk of a car. I hurried over to them, but my resolve wavered. I'm just not good at asking for favors or for people to go out of their way for me. Janie and I were sopping wet head to toe and muddy besides, and it seemed a huge imposition to ask to get into their spotless car. So instead, after brief introductions, I asked if they would please call a shuttle when they got to Gatlinburg and ask it to come pick us up. "Of course not!" the young man said. "Why don't you just ride down with us? We're going to Gatlinburg."

"I would really hate to get your car dirty. We're a mess. And we've got backpacks."

"Well, how many of you are there?" his wife asked.

"Just two of us, me and another lady," I replied.

"Nonsense, go get her and your stuff, and we'll take you."

That was all I needed to hear. I ran back to the visitor's center. "Come on, Janie, I got us a ride!" We grabbed our packs and poles and stuffed ourselves into the small backseat, holding our backpacks on our laps. I winced as I watched water roll off my pack and down the seat, and saw the muddy scuff marks my boots were leaving on the clean floor mats. On the ride into town I learned that my latest trail angels were a married couple from Maryland, Alan and Dana, who came to the Smokies for a week of backpacking every spring. They had been out in the same weather we had been in for the last two days, so they were sympathetic. They were very interested in our tales as thruhikers, and the ride went quickly. They took us right to the Grand Prix Motel, the little motel popular with hikers. We thanked them and again, like most trail angels, they refused payment.

It was much warmer down in town and sunny, the storm confined to the mountaintops. We went to the motel office to get a room....and the door was locked. A sign on the door notified us that the owners had gone to church and lunch and would return in the afternoon. I was by this time feeling rather desperate to get into a room and out of my wet clothes, but again I had no choice. While we stood dripping and shivering in the breezeway a hiker I had met earlier on the trail, Fresh Step, looked out the window of his room, saw us standing there, and took pity on us. He invited us into his room to wait for the motel owners to return. We left our packs outside his door and stood over his heater which he obligingly turned up to high. After half an hour of trail talk the office opened and Janie and I were finally able to get a room. She generously offered to do my laundry along with hers, an offer I gratefully accepted because I literally had nothing dry to put on. She carried the dripping laundry down the hall to the washing machine (all motels catering to hikers have laundry facilities), and I got into a hot shower. I am not a good enough writer to describe how amazing it felt, feeling the warmth creep slowly back into my bones, and watching the mud swirling away down the drain. I got out and combed my hair and wrapped up in a blanket. When Janie came back, my clothes were clean, dry, and folded! It was probably nearly eighty degrees in our room by that time. The dry clothes felt and smelled wonderful. Janie got into the shower, and I unpacked the Green Monster, hanging my wet tarp and hammock from the deck of our room and spreading everything else over every available surface. I ordered a pizza to be delivered and called St. Mike, who said he thought he still might be able to come for a day! Life was good.

While Little Janie and I settled into the luxury of hot food, clean clothes, and dry feet, I wondered about the other hikers we had shared the shelter with the night before. Had any of them decided to hike out, too, or were they all still waiting in the shelter? We had been the first hikers to leave the shelter, and in fact when we left everyone else seemed intent on staying put. We hadn't seen any other hikers all day on the trail. I especially wondered about the Johnnie Walker Express, who had been so kind to me. I hoped that they were somewhere warm and dry also.

Summer 2016 Three years later. I never saw any of them again, but much later I learned that all three members of the Johnnie Walker Express left the trail that week, for different reasons. Johnnie Walker got off with an injury, Phoenix's father died, and worst of all, dear Highlander had an apparent heart attack and died. Rest in peace, Highlander.

Gatlinburg, Tennessee
April 29, 2013

Little Janie and I really enjoyed our zero day in Gatlinburg. Our funky little hiker motel was situated at the very end of the town, so we were spared most of the over-hyped tourist area. There were no wax museums, fudge shops, or go-cart tracks at our end of town, and no crowds of tourists at the Grand Prix. Just a bunch of hikers who all spoke the same language. After less than a full month on the trail I was beginning to feel that we comprised a different race or tribe of people, that I had more in common with other hikers than I did with friends and family back home. There was a reasonable restaurant in walking distance from the motel, a gas station/convenience store, and, best of all, an outfitter. Little Janie and I made our way to the outfitter first thing after breakfast to admire the wares, but I also had some serious shopping to do.

First I had to address my stove situation. I had started the hike devoted to my homemade alcohol stove. It had every characteristic I required of my gear—it was very small, lightweight, and inexpensive. It was also, to me at least, a pain in the neck. I had never really learned to gauge correctly how much alcohol I needed in the stove. Too little, and it would go out before my food was done, and I would have to fill it up and start again. Too much, and it would continue burning long after I was done, wasting fuel. It was also slow. Many were the times that Songbird was enjoying her food, or even finished with it and cleaning out her pot, while I was still waiting for water to boil. In addition, I am leery of open flames, and lighting matches around the alcohol. I went against all my hiking gear priorities and bought a Jetboil stove in Gatlinburg. It was heavier, bigger and bulkier, and more expensive, but also much faster and easier to use than an alcohol stove. Then I went over to look at sleeping pads. I had the blue closed-cell foam Walmart pad, but it was big and bulky, while not adding much comfort. I would have liked to buy an inflatable pad, but I was being fiscally conservative after the splurge on the stove, so I bought a Therm-a-Rest Z-Lite pad. It was also a closed cell foam pad, like my blue one, and no thicker, but it was narrower, and it folded up accordion style, so it was much less bulky. In addition, one side was a shiny silver color, which it advertised as reflecting body heat, to keep you warmer. I saw a lot of them on the trail and no bulky blue roll–up types, so I took that as an endorsement and bought it. Then I looked for something for my muddy boots and bought two products, a cleaner and a waterproofer.

Back at the Grand Prix I went through the hiker box looking for treasure and found it: a long narrow waterproof stuff stack that was the perfect size for my new pad. The new pad in its sack would still hang from the back of my pack but it was much smaller, and with it now protected from the elements I would not have to sleep on a floor anymore because of a wet pad.

Next I tackled my boots, cleaning the mud off with the product I had bought at the outfitter, a brush borrowed from the motel office, and the sink. Then I propped them up on the room heater, and when they were thoroughly dry, I sprayed them with the waterproofer. I napped in the afternoon and ate. I called St. Mike and made plans for him to come in the morning and hike with me and spend the night. Janie was invited to come with us, but she was an independent hiker and wanted to keep going, so she was going to head out in the morning. We spent some time arranging shuttles for the next day (St. Mike was averse to the idea of hitchhiking).

Evening found me lying on the bed, more pizza in hand, Reese's cup and Mello Yello on the nightstand, a Braves game on the television, and a smile on my face.

Clingman's Dome to Newfound Gap
April 30, 2013

I awoke joyful, but restless. Joyful, to be warm, dry, and fed, and especially that St. Mike was on his way! But restless to get back on the trail at the same time. I was finding that although I very much enjoyed the initial decadent luxury of a hot shower, soft bed, and good food, by day two the appeal of town grew thin, and I wanted to be back out on the trail. Town seemed somehow superficial and artificial. Everything in town had a price, and everyone had an agenda. Life in the woods seemed somehow more pure, more real. All of the hikers on the trail have just one agenda, to keep walking north. And money is essentially worthless while hiking. The only things of value are the things on your back, and you definitely don't want to add any more to the pack. People, because they are rarer, have more value. You greet everyone you meet on the trail, you make real eye contact. Conversations (beyond greeting) don't *always* happen, but they often do, and when they do they are real and sincere.

I had hoped that Little Janie and St. Mike would be able to meet, but her shuttle pulled out of the parking lot just as his Jeep pulled in. I exchanged one roommate for another. I greeted him with a big hug, and it felt so good to be held. Hiking is such a solitary venture that it felt great to be part of a team again, to have someone to look out for me, even just for a day. We went for an early lunch and I ate nearly twice as much as he did, my hiker appetite on full display. I packed a slackpack for the day's hike, leaving most of my gear still sprawled around the room drying, and we caught our shuttle. The shuttle, a van full of hikers, was going to follow Mike and the Jeep to Newfound Gap, where we would leave the Jeep. The shuttle would then drive the hikers, St. Mike, and me to Clingman's Dome, where I had gotten off the trail just two days before. Mike and I would have only to hike the nearly eight miles to Newfound Gap where the Jeep would be waiting for us, and drive ourselves back to Gatlinburg.

We started our hike from the same visitor's center that Little Janie and I had stumbled into, wet and nearly frozen, just two days ago. Now, however, it was sunny and mild, and it was hard to describe the conditions we had hiked out in to St. Mike. It seemed dreamlike, unbelievable. It was a great hike, with only the lightweight slackpack on my back and my sweet husband by my side. Very early in the day's hike we passed my 200 mile milestone. We stopped to take pictures, and the fact that I had walked 200 miles seemed unreal. It didn't seem long since my 100 mile celebration atop Albert Mountain with Songbird. St. Mike then pointed out that the next day would mark one month on the trail. It was hard for these milestones to register in my mind. Two hundred miles didn't seem like much, since the entire trail is over 2,000 miles long. I was equal parts proud of having walked 200 miles and cognizant that it was just a drop in the bucket.

I couldn't think about how far it was to Maine. In fact, I

never really thought about it at all, because it sounded so far-fetched, like walking to Mars. In my mind my hike was a series of short hikes, sections, and I didn't think about the next section until I was nearly finished with the section I was on. Right now I was only concerned with getting out of the Smokies, and didn't look any further ahead than Davenport Gap, the end of the Smokies on the AT.

This day, however, I didn't even think about Davenport Gap. I had a short section to hike, with a very light pack, easy terrain, great weather, and a handsome hiking partner. We hiked slowly, even by tortoise standards, just enjoying each other's company. He caught me up with all the news from home, friends and family, and I described as well as I could my life and adventures on the trail. This section of the trail borders a highway for much of the distance, and I found the sight and sound of the road distressing. The proximity of civilization and non-hiking people felt wrong, as I felt the pull of the wilderness.

Soon enough we reached the parking lot at Newfound Gap, full of tourists, sightseers, and hikers. We drove back down the mountain to Gatlinburg, visited a grocery store for my resupply for the next 32 miles of trail to get me to Davenport Gap, and settled in at the motel for another Braves game, more food, and companionship.

Newfound Gap to Icewater Spring Shelter
May 1, 2013

I should have gotten an earlier start on the day, but it was hard to say goodbye to Mike. We were both reluctant to part, even knowing we would be together again for the weekend in Asheville. The terrible weather I had endured my last two days on the trail worried him on my behalf. For my part, as eager as I was to get out of town and back on the trail, that cold weather had scared me, too, and I was not eager for a repeat. The Smokies had become something to endure, to get through. But we eventually ran out of reasons to linger, and he drove me to Newfound Gap to resume my trek north. We stopped and picked up a hitchhiker just out of Gatlinburg, a hiker on his way to Newfound Gap. This was a new experience for St. Mike, as we don't generally make a habit of picking up hitchhikers. But this one's pack and trekking poles revealed him to be a hiker, and I had no qualms about it. He was very grateful for the ride and for the Gatorade powder I gave him. "My first trail magic!" he exclaimed.

Eventually we had to say our goodbyes, and I started back up the trail, and Mike turned the Jeep towards the four hour drive home, knowing that he would be coming back again in two days to do the herb market in Asheville. This was proof that he deserved his trailname of St. Mike.

It's always a climb out of a gap, and so I found myself huffing and puffing my way up the trail. I reached Icewater Spring Shelter early in my hike, only three miles from Newfound Gap. I stopped to consult my guidebook and plan the next few days. Because of the rule about only staying in shelters, I had a choice of either a three mile day or a ten mile day. I had gotten such a late start that I felt that going for a ten mile day was going to be pushing it, and I wished we hadn't lingered so long in Gatlinburg. If I had gotten an earlier start I could have made it to the next shelter. I was torn between my desire to get out of the park as soon as possible, and trepidation caused by my hike into Clingman's Dome. I decided to play it safe and stay put for the night. Looking ahead, I developed my itinerary for the rest of the distance to Davenport Gap.

The next day I could walk the twelve miles to Tri-Corner Knob Shelter. That left 14 miles remaining to Davenport Gap. I could do it in one long day, getting to the gap on Friday night, or break it into two seven mile days, because there was a shelter strategically placed at the midpoint, getting me to the gap Saturday afternoon. I liked having that flexibility. Mike would be arriving in Asheville on Friday morning to set up for the three day market. If I could get there Friday night, I would have two full days to run the booth, giving him free time. I felt bad that he had done all of my spring shows by himself (with help from our daughter), and I wanted to relieve him. If I couldn't get there until Saturday, though, I would still be there for the whole day Sunday and could help him take down.

I staked out my spot in the shelter. It was early in the afternoon, so I was the only one there, but I knew other hikers would soon start trickling in. I sat down to read the shelter log. All shelters along the trail have a shelter log, usually a spiral bound notebook, that hikers sign in when they stop for the night. It's a way to track hikers if, heaven forbid, one were to go missing, and it's also a way to pass on trail news, and even to express your creative side. Before my hike I had thought they would be great fun to read and I looked forward to them. In reality I found them mostly boring, and quite often didn't even pick them up to read or sign. I had plenty of time this afternoon though, so I opened it and found two quotes that I liked well enough to copy into my journal. One hiker had written on April 28, "Survived the culture shock of Gatlinburg, grateful to be back out here, even though I'm still slightly nauseous after experiencing such nasty tourism." Another entry from

April 26 read, "Lost faith in humanity while in Gatlinburg, found it again on the AT. God bless this strip of dirt," to which someone had added "Amen." Oh, I love hikers.

The warm, sunny weather held throughout the day, making me hopeful that it would last the rest of my time in the Smokies. Maybe that cold storm of a few days ago was over. Hikers did start coming in, and we soon ended up with a convivial group. After making and eating supper I went to put my leftovers and my trash back into my food bag. I picked it up from the picnic table, opened it, and stood looking into it in confusion. This was my bag, it was different and distinct from the other bags on the table, but this wasn't my food. It was all unfamiliar, and my mind hadn't grasped the fact that there might be another bag that looked like mine, when a harsh voice demanded, "What are you doing with my food bag? Put that down!"

I dropped it on the table and spun around. Harsh words were rare among hikers. A man about my own age stood there, with thick glasses and a scowl on his face. "You aren't supposed to get into other people's food bags," he spat out at me.

"I'm.....I'm sorry!" I blurted. "I thought it was my bag. Look, here's mine, it looks just like yours!" I belatedly saw my own bag and held it up, indeed identical to his.

"But it's not yours!" he declared. "It's mine, and you were getting into it!"

"I didn't get into it! I just looked in it. I hadn't yet realized it wasn't mine. I didn't touch any of your food, or take anything out. I'm sorry."

He snatched it up from the table, and snarled, "Just stay out of my food bag."

"I really am sorry. I'll be more careful now that I know we have similar bags," I said, trying to decide if I had done something heinous or if he was just irrational, and decided on the latter. "I'm Blue Tortoise. Here, let me make room on the table for your stove."

His name was Maple, and throughout the rest of the evening he shot me occasional sharp looks and even barbed comments from time to time about people who get into other people's stuff. No one else made any comment on the situation. I began to wonder if maybe he was kidding, but there was no evidence of that, no humor in his demeanor. Was he just touchy and territorial about his gear? Did he not see how I could have mistaken his bag for my own, since they were identical? I never found out, but I did make it a point to avoid him after that.

As the sun set the cold returned, and I retired to my bed in the shelter, bundled up as best I could, said my rosary under the underquilt, and tried to find something to like about Maple. I listened to the hikers who were still gathered outside the shelter while I tried to fall asleep and was saddened and surprised to hear that a hiker had died in this shelter about a month before, frozen to death. I prayed for his soul, for my physical body, and, reluctantly, for Maple.

Icewater Spring Shelter to Tri-Corner Knob Shelter
May 2, 2013

I got up and on the trail early, knowing that I had over twelve miles to hike and uncertain as to either the terrain or the weather. I had come to distrust both in the Smokies. Sure enough, the cold that had moved in overnight did not relent all day. The trail was at a high elevation, over 5,000 feet all day and over 6,000 at points. The weather was again bitterly cold and windy, with intermittent cold drizzle. The sun, so warm, golden, and mild the last few days, never made an appearance. Much of the walk was on exposed ridge lines, with the ground falling steeply off on both sides of me and the wind blowing. I don't like heights, and I can now admit that I was afraid. Once I realized that the misty rain wasn't letting up I got into my pack to find my waterproof mittens to put over my wool gloves, and there was only one. The other one must have been left at the shelter. I wasn't going to go back for it. "Maybe Maple has it," I uncharitably thought to myself. "He can keep it."

As if conjured into reality by my thoughts, Maple himself appeared from behind me. He started to pass me, then stopped to talk. The weather and wind weren't conducive to conversation, but I stopped and gave him an almost sincere smile. "Hey. You loving this weather?" I joked.

"Nasty," he said. "You still mad at me?"

"I was never mad," I said. "It just bothered me that you accused me of getting into your bag, when I only picked it up by accident, and I apologized."

"Well, you have to admit, it's wrong to get into people's food bags." He seemed stuck on that fact.

"But I didn't get into your food bag! I just picked it up, and when I looked into it I realized it wasn't mine. I never got into it!" I was getting mad. He just wouldn't let it go.

"Well, I'm sorry if I made you mad," he grudgingly admitted. Now I should have been the one to let it go. But I didn't.

"And then, you just wouldn't leave it alone. All night long you kept bringing it back up. And here you are, bringing it up again. Just let it go! I promise I will never, ever, ever, touch your food bag again!"

"I was joking," he said, unconvincingly.

"Fine. Apology accepted. Now can we forget the stupid food bags?"

"Ok. But I'm not wrong about it being inconsiderate to touch people's stuff."

I had nothing to say to that. I was tempted to think he just had a really dry, deadpan sense of humor, but I knew that wasn't the case. I just didn't get it, so I said goodbye to him and resumed my hike. I was hoping I wouldn't see him at the shelter that night, but knew that I probably would. The next shelter was another seven miles further, and I had a hard time imagining anyone hiking 19 miles on this terrain in this weather. He passed me, and I fervently hoped that he was a strong, resilient long-distance hiker, impervious to weather.

I hiked on and another hiker passed me. We said our greetings, and he looked at my hands. I had the one waterproof mitten on, and the sleeve of my rain jacket pulled over the other hand. "Oh, it's you!" he exclaimed cheerily. "I've got something you'll be happy to see," and he pulled my other mitten out of his pocket. "You left it back at the shelter. I was hoping to catch up with you."

"Everybody catches up with me. I'm a tortoise. Oh, thank you! It was so nice of you to bring it and look for me!" I pulled the mitten over my glove. He introduced himself as Willow, and I was glad that for every Maple there was a Willow.

I hiked on, Willow's back becoming smaller and smaller as did everyone's. I don't know how everyone was able to hike so much faster that I did. I didn't feel like I walked slowly. I would have liked to have hiked faster, especially that day in the foul weather, but the trail was covered with loose, fist-sized rocks, making it difficult to get up much speed. My ankles and feet ached. I didn't stop to eat lunch as there was no place to get out of the rain, so I nibbled trail mix as I walked. It was almost more trouble than it was worth, because I had to take off my gloves and mittens to be able to eat, and it was just too much trouble to take them off and on. The loose rocky trail required my constant attention anyway, so nibbling was kept to a bare minimum, just enough to stave off hunger.

Finally I reached Tri-Corner Knob Shelter. I felt that this had been my hardest day on the trail yet, excluding the Clingman's Dome fiasco, which I was sure would never be eclipsed. I was damp, but not thoroughly wet as I had been when I fell into the visitor's center at the dome. I was very cold, though, and my feet and ankles ached from walking on the loose rocks all day. My nerves were frayed from the high exposed ridges I had navigated, and I was grateful for the solid log shelter. I removed my shoes and socks and massaged my feet and ankles with the thick cream I carried and used so sparingly. I put dry socks on, and my Crocs in place of my boots, and made my way to the privy, where I found a moment of humor in the middle of an otherwise humorless day.

Many, but not all, shelters on the trail have privies, which are essentially outhouses. The privies in the Smokies are usually raised, composting privies. A ramp or steps leads up to the privy, which is surrounded by a chicken wire fenced area. The waste, instead of going into a hole dug into the ground, accumulates in the fenced area, which is aboveground. Inside the privy are a couple of five gallon buckets of mulch. Every time you use the privy, you are supposed to drop a handful or two of mulch down the hole. The idea is that the open air speeds the decomposition. In my real life I don't like port-a-potties and, with a nurse's twelve-hour bladder, can usually contrive to avoid them. On the trail I didn't like the privies either, and if privacy could be assured, would prefer to go out into the woods. On "town days" I could put my nurse's bladder to use and wait until I got to a porcelain receptacle. But in the Smokies I used the privies more often. There were stricter rules, more people, less privacy, and I was usually too tired to go off in search of secluded areas. This privy at Tri-Corner Knob Shelter, though, was interesting. It was handicapped accessible, in compliance (I guessed) with federal regulations, the Smokies being a national park. Situated at the end of a long rocky trail the privy had a wide, stable ramp with handrails. The privy itself was large, big enough inside to turn a wheelchair around in. There were metal handrails on all the walls, with signs demonstrating their use. There were two "thrones", a regular one and a wheelchair height one, surrounded by handrails. I was amused, astonished, and a bit aggravated by the foolishness of putting a wheelchair accessible privy in an area no wheelchair could ever reach. The only way to get a wheelchair in there would have been by airdrop. I had had enough difficulty navigating the steep rocky trail on two legs. "A fine example of bureaucratic waste and lack of common sense," I thought, as I documented the entire facility with photographs, sure that none of my friends would believe it without photographic evidence.

I returned to the shelter. It was incredibly cold. I had split the back of my pants again at some point during the day, but I was not going to be able to sew them back up, my hands too cold to even attempt to thread a needle. I decided I would just wear my long johns under them for the next two days to Davenport Gap. They were black, so anyone seeing the gaping hole in the back of my pants wouldn't be scandalized. It *was* going to be two days, I realized. As difficult as this twelve mile day had been, I knew I didn't have it in me to attempt a fourteen mile hike the next, so two seven milers it was. I put all my clothes on and it was still cold. I huddled in the shelter with the other hikers who had arrived, and we commiserated together. When one gentleman came around with a flask of peppermint schnapps I held out my mug of hot chocolate and he poured in a generous slug. It was good, reminding me of Thin Mint Girl Scout cookies.

I did a few jumping jacks to warm up and crawled into my spot on the shelter floor. It was dark, and the shelter grew quiet as the exhausted hikers fell asleep. I found it difficult to sleep, as usual, because of the cold, but I had just dozed off when there was a mighty BOOM! the loudest sound I thought I'd ever heard. I woke up, heart pounding, but it was pitch black, the kind of darkness you can only get in a place with no electricity. I had no sense of what could have made the sound. Instantly several headlamps clicked on, and a couple of men jumped out of their sleeping bags and down to the ground. After a quick glance around they ran out around the back of the shelter. Those of us who remained inside were murmuring, guessing what it might have been. Within minutes the men were back to report that there was a large tree branch on the roof, evidently broken off by the howling wind, and large enough to hit our fiberglass roof with a crash. *What next?* I thought, as I rolled back over and tried to go back to sleep. The hikers surrounding me started to drop off to sleep as well, the sounds of gentle breathing and light snoring a comforting counterpoint to the wind and rain.

Tri-Corner Knob Shelter to Cosby Knob Shelter
May 3, 2013

I was the last hiker out of the shelter in the morning. I knew that I had less than eight miles to hike and found it hard to get motivated and moving. I was so torn about the decision I had to make about getting out of the Smokies once and for all. One 14 mile day and I could be in Asheville that evening. Or two seven miles days and another night in a cold shelter.

Summer 2016

Now, in retrospect, I wonder why I didn't just go for it. As cold as I was and as much as I hated that section of the hike, I really should have just done it, hiked the 14 miles, and spared myself a day of misery. I can't explain my decision to split what would have been a long, miserable day into two shorter miserable days and a miserable night. I think it was fear—fear that I wouldn't be able to do it somehow, and that I would be making the last six mile descent into Davenport Gap in the dark, wind, and rain. I was playing it safe.

Finally I saddled up and walked out of the shelter. There was, thank God, no rain that day, but it was bitterly cold and windy. I could see my breath as I hiked. I scurried along through the open sections, the ridge walks and exposed areas, and lingered a bit longer in the few areas that had trees or rocks or some other protection from the wind. There were more of the ankle-crunching loose rock sections to navigate. I wanted a good photographic journal of my hike so I fumbled with my camera with numb fingers, and somehow accidentally discovered that my camera was capable of making videos. (I am functionally illiterate, technologically speaking, so it's no surprise that I didn't know all that my own phone could do. Much later, in the middle of some gorgeous vistas when things were green, I discovered the panorama feature!) I amused myself while walking by making a series of videos I called "Things I Hate About the Smokies." One featured the loose rocks, one featured the exposed ridges, and one consisted entirely of the tops of the trees whipping around in the wind.

I was still saying my daily divine mercy chaplet, of course, and offering up my pains for my person of the day, and the Smokies had given me a lot to offer. I had worked my way through my entire family by this time: myself, my mother, St. Mike, my four children, six grandchildren, three sons-in-law, five siblings (and their families), a couple of elderly aunts who were ill, and my dad's soul, who had died on Valentine's Day, 2002. I decided to offer this day for the souls in purgatory.

According to my guidebook I was about to come to a landmark called, simply, "Plane wreckage." I wasn't sure what I was looking for, but I found it—the remnants of an airplane that had evidently rammed into the spot where I stood. It wasn't hard to imagine how it might have happened as it was the top of a mountain. In the omnipresent clouds and fog which give the Smoky Mountains their name, this nearly 6,000 foot peak could hide from a small plane such as this one had been. There was no indication of when this tragedy had occurred, but judging by the weathering of the remaining pieces I would think it had been many years. I added the pilot and passengers on the plane to my prayer list, took some pictures, crossed myself, and hiked on.

There was no lunch again on this day. I was hungry, ravenously so, but as I walked on it seemed that in any spot where there was protection from the wind there was no place to sit, and where there was a rock or log that otherwise would have made a good seat, the wind was cold and brisk. It would have been too uncomfortable to stop, remove the Green Monster, and try to eat. I just kept sipping water and walking on. In retrospect, I suppose that the lack of food and the cold made me weak, which contributed to my inability to hike an otherwise reasonable distance, 14 miles. Perhaps if I had somehow found a way to keep myself better fed I would have had the energy to hike out in one day instead of two.

Regardless, I did eventually reach Cosby Knob Shelter, and took some comfort knowing that it was my last night in the Smokies. I had enough food left in my bag to justify a celebration of that fact so I made a double supper: one regular meal of Ramen noodles and tuna, followed immediately by a dessert of instant mashed potatoes and bacon bits. Washed down with a liter of cold spring water and then followed with what had become a nightly ritual for me, a large serving of hot chocolate, it was satisfying and improved my outlook tremendously. Other hikers drifted in, and the rest of the evening was spent in trail talk, comparing adventures and hardships. I did miss the peppermint schnapps guy, though.

Cosby Knob Shelter to Davenport Gap
May 4, 2013

Something was different, I knew as soon as I woke up, but it took my sleep-fuddled mind several minutes to figure out what it was. I was still in the shelter, still surrounded on both sides by sleeping or snoring hikers, although a few were up and about already. The floor was still hard beneath my thin pad. Gradually I realized that I could easily hear not only the soft snores of the hiker to my left, but also the murmurs of a couple who were boiling water for coffee, and even some birds on a branch just outside the shelter. That was it—I could hear even soft sounds easily—there was no whistling or moaning of the wind that I had heard incessantly for days. Prying open my eyes I saw the unaccustomed warm light of the sun, and coming out from under my topquilt, the air felt mild. The storm was over! *Hallelujah, thank God*, I thought, while at the same time being just a twinge put out that the weather improved just as I was leaving. "Couldn't have done this a day or two ago?" I muttered ungraciously.

I had no real urgency to get hiking early. Checking my guidebook, I saw that I had eight miles to go to get to Davenport Gap, and St. Mike wouldn't be there until about six o'clock. He couldn't leave Asheville until the herb market closed at five. If I was going to dawdle on the trail, at least it looked like I would have good weather to do so. There was a shelter seven miles away, one mile from the road crossing at the gap where Mike would meet me. I planned to take my time hiking to the shelter, which was called Davenport Gap shelter, and wait there until about five-thirty or so, then walk the remaining one mile to the road crossing. The shelter would be a more comfortable place to spend the afternoon waiting, since it would probably boast a picnic table. I wasn't really looking forward to the hike down to the shelter as it was a long, five mile downhill stretch, losing over 3,000 feet of elevation in those five miles. Ouch, my toes and ankles could feel it coming. Still, it would be warmer down there, and it was finally out of these mountains, so I packed the Green Monster, put a protein bar for breakfast into my hip belt pocket, and started off. I was the last to leave the shelter.

The day's hike started with a short, half mile descent into Low Gap, which was followed by a two mile climb up Mt. Cammerer, before the descent into Davenport Gap started in earnest. The name "Davenport Gap" had taken on mythic proportions to me by then. It was right up there with Shangri-La, Utopia, maybe even heaven itself. I walked on, munching my breakfast bar, with my heart light. The sun was warm, and I enjoyed the novelty of hiking in pleasant weather. Rounding a bend in the trail I came upon a park ranger, the first I'd seen. He looked impossibly clean to me, accustomed as I was to scruffy hikers. His shoes gleamed, his uniform was pressed. His blonde hair was combed neatly back, his blue eyes twinkled, and his teeth shone white. "He looks like Dudley Do-Right," I thought, becoming uncomfortably aware of the dirt under my nails and the lank hair tucked back under my buff. I smoothed back a stray strand and gave him a smile.

He smiled back, greeted me pleasantly, and asked to see my hiking permit, the park ranger version of license and registration. I pulled it out of my pocket and gave it to him. "Where you heading to today?" he asked pleasantly, handing it back to me.

"Down to Davenport Gap," I said, liking the sound of that. "My husband is picking me up there tonight. I'm going to Asheville for the weekend."

"Oh, that's nice," he said. "I just wanted to tell all the hikers I see today to find some shelter. There's a storm coming in, might be a bad one. Should start around two or so. You'll want to be off the mountain by then."

Oh my word, I thought to myself. If there was a storm coming, what do you call what I had been living in for the last few days? Well, no more lollygagging on my way down to the shelter. I would just have to pick up some speed and get there early, wait out the storm, and then leave for the rendezvous with St. Mike at the planned time.

"Thanks for telling me," I said to the ranger. "I'll hurry on down to Davenport Gap Shelter."

"You're welcome," he said, smiling with his dazzling white teeth. I couldn't take my eyes off them. My oldest daughter, who had loved men in uniform ever since seeing the movie *Top Gun*, would love this guy. "One more thing," he added. "Have you seen a hiker named Waffles?"

I thought back to the hikers I had met at shelters over the last few nights. No, I hadn't met anyone named Waffles. I told him so and asked, "What's he done? Is he in trouble?"

Ranger Dudley laughed (more teeth!) and said, "No, not really. But if you see him, could you call a ranger station?"

I assured him that I would, being the good hiker citizen that I am, and hiked on. I was glad to have the advance notice of the bad weather coming in so I wouldn't be caught out in it, and glad that I would be out of that weather tonight. But I was dismayed at the thought of the need for speed as I struggled down the long steep descent ahead of me. It was going to be a long, dull afternoon at the shelter.

It was, for once, pleasant enough to eat lunch on the trail, but I was afraid to take the time, and decided to wait until I got to the shelter to eat. I came upon the shelter at about one-thirty after completing the gauntlet of the long descent from the mountains. It was a particularly lovely shelter, situated in a scenic little cove. Prettiest of all, to me, was that all of the foliage was green! After spending some time in the winter atop the mountains, I had hiked back down into springtime once again. I was very relieved to be there—only one mile and four hours from Mike. As I walked closer to the shelter though, I saw that the open side was covered by chain link fencing. All the shelters in the Smokies used to have this bear-proof fencing, but it had been taken down some years ago, replaced by better policies to manage the interactions between bears and hikers. So why did this shelter still have it, I wondered. I opened the gate and stepped inside. A large sign on the wall instructed hikers not to cook or even open food packages at this shelter, because food odors attract bears. I decided that there must be a troublesome bear in this area, necessitating the sign and fencing.

I wasn't afraid of bears, in general. I had done my research, and I understood that black bears are timid, afraid of humans, and that they don't look upon us as prey. They do want our food, and are big enough to take it away from us, but they don't initiate confrontations, preferring instead to sneak it away from us in the night if we've been foolish enough to leave it within their reach. I actually hadn't seen a bear yet on my hike, although a hiker walking some distance behind me had told me at a shelter a few nights previous that he had seen one in a tree just over my head as I walked down the trail, oblivious. Other hikers had seen them, usually just their back ends as they ran away. I knew what to do if I saw a bear: stand still, don't turn my back on it and don't run. Make myself appear bigger by standing up, spreading my jacket to the sides, waving my arms. Make noise. The bear will turn and run. It's a little different if it's a mama bear with cubs. She will do what she needs to do to protect them if she detects a threat. I understand and sympathize with that motherly instinct and planned on never getting between mama and baby.

The ATC and the park officials have done a great job with educating hikers, and we all know what we need to do to prevent interaction with bears. Namely, *don't feed the bears,* even inadvertently. If bears don't see humans as a source of food, they will heed their natural reticence. So we hang our food at night. Most shelter have bear cables, so it's easy to clip the food bag on a carabiner and hoist it up into the air, out of reach of even the tallest bears. When camping away from a shelter we throw a rope over a tree branch, at least 20 feet high and 10 feet from the trunk of the tree and tie the food bag to it. We take our food garbage and food packaging with us and don't burn garbage at campsites. (In reality, though, there is no food garbage. Hungry hikers never have food scraps left over. We lick up every last crumb, every drip. But if there were to be any food garbage, we would put it back in our food bags.) With all these steps being followed so closely, bears and hikers co-exist peacefully on the trail, and bears don't look upon hikers as walking vending machines.

That doesn't mean that there isn't an occasional "problem bear," one who has become habituated to humans and lost its natural fear of us, one who has indeed come to see us as a food source. This is nearly always the fault of the humans, and sadly, usually ends in the bear having to be put down. There was one in the vicinity of Neel Gap while I was hiking through there, although I was slackpacking at the time and not camping. Hikers were cautioned to not camp overnight in the area unless they had a bearproof canister for their food.

Now I found myself all alone for a long afternoon in an area that I thought might have one such nuisance bear. I scoured the hillside around the shelter for firewood, carried it into the shelter, and pulled the chain link gate behind me, closing myself into my bearproof cage. I started a fire in the fireplace, more to have something to do than for warmth or light. This would be another day without lunch, as I was afraid to get my food out. If I attracted the bear I would be safe enough in my cage, but I was going to have to leave the cage at 5:30 to hike the remaining mile to the road, and I didn't want him following me. I hung my jacket and the Green Monster on a nail in the wall, got out my pad to lay on, my journal and pen, and my Sudoku book, and settled in for the afternoon.

Time passed pleasantly enough. There were no bears, and I even napped a while. Two other hikers showed up late in the afternoon, and I was glad for the company. They were two young males, section hikers, both medical students. We had a good conversation. They were less impressed by the bear fencing and signage than I had been, and I drew courage from their bravado. Finally it was time, so I left the shelter and hiked the last mile blithely, making it to the road crossing just as the rain started. It was only a few minutes until I saw the Jeep coming down the road, a welcome sight indeed.

I threw my pack into the back seat and fairly leaped into the front. I gave St. Mike a huge hug, and we caught each other up on the events of the last few days. The herb market was going well, although it had rained and was cooler than he had expected. I looked forward to working in our booth the next day, relieving him so that he could have a day off. Finally, the basics covered, I announced

"Let's eat!" It was great to be in a warm car, driving down the road headed for a clean motel room, and in the company of my dear husband, but what I really wanted was food—lots of it, and soon.

Mike paused. "Um, don't you really want to go to the motel and clean up first?" he asked.

"Oh, no," I said. "I'm starving. Let's stop somewhere along the way. I'm not picky, help me keep an eye out for a pizza place or a cheeseburger stop."

"Um, well, I could take you to the motel and drop you off, and then I could go get your supper and bring it back to the room," he countered.

Oh. It must be bad. He had seen me a couple of times since I had been hiking, and he hadn't been ashamed to take me out in public before. How many days had it been since I had a shower? It didn't seem like it had been that long. "Oh, well, ok," I said. "Just bring me a couple of cheeseburgers, large fries, a Mello Yello with ice, and something chocolate. Maybe two chocolate somethings. That should hold me until morning. Or maybe there's a vending machine at the motel and I can get some more food later."

He dropped me off at the little nondescript motel and went for my supper while I had a long, hot shower. He was back with the food when I emerged, and expressed surprise that I was able to eat all that he brought. I didn't tell him that I wasn't really full and could easily have gone out for pizza after eating all that food. The hiker appetite is a thing of beauty.

Asheville, North Carolina
May 5, 2013

The day dawned, not warm and sunny as I had hoped for my stay in town, but cold and drizzly. It was Sunday, so I dressed in the town clothes Mike had brought me, and we attended mass at St. Barnabus in Asheville, and then went on to the sprawling farmer's market where the herb festival was being held. It was a huge outdoor complex, with all the individual vendors' wares set up under one of several large roofs, offering protection from the rain coming from the sky, but not from sprinkles carried in sideways by the wind. Mike had done a good job of setting up our display in the long narrow space we were allotted, and he had had reasonable sales and feedback during the previous two days in spite of the weather. This was my business, these were my products, and yet I felt oddly removed from the process.

Mike had been running it nearly single-handedly for the last month during our usually busy spring season. I felt detached, simultaneously grateful that he was willing to take on this project to allow me to hike and guilty for the burden it placed on him. There was also a tinge of jealousy for the fact that he was doing so well without me, and I was apparently somewhat superfluous. I somehow felt that life at home would freeze in place while I was on the trail, and I would come back and resume my life as it had been, with no changes. It was uncomfortable to think that life went on without me, things happened and changed and I had no input in the process. Here was St. Mike, set up at a show I had never been to, with a new and novel approach to displaying our products, doing well. It felt foreign to me.

I had wanted to work in our booth to give him the day off, since he had been there for the last two days, but the weather was so cold and nasty that he had little desire to leave the market grounds to ride his bike or take any pictures, the two activities he enjoys most. So we both sat in the booth through most of the day, selling soap, greeting customers, and getting to know our neighboring vendors (who Mike was already quite friendly with, another reason I felt more like a visitor than the business owner.) There actually were plenty of customers despite the nasty weather, and by the day's end we deemed the show a success and looked forward to coming back the next year, hopefully in better weather. We took down and packed up the remaining product, the tables and shelves and signs, and I was glad I was there to help him.

After dinner I sewed up the rip in the seat of my hiking pants, again, and then we found a laundry and I washed all my dirty hiking clothes in preparation for my return to the trail the next day. Checking my guidebook, I saw that my next town stop would be Hot Springs, NC, only 30 miles further down the trail. That would be about three days, at my usual pace, and I looked forward to getting there. Hot Springs is an iconic trail town, a must-see stop for hikers. The Appalachian Trail goes right through the middle of the small town, with the white blazes embedded in the sidewalk. It's a tiny little town, but has several hostels, an outfitter, and other businesses that cater to the many hikers that pass through. I had heard and read about it for so long, and I couldn't believe that I was nearly there.

I was sitting on the motel bed poring over my guidebook when my phone rang. I picked it up and glanced at the screen. "It's Songbird!" I said in amazement. I punched the button and blurted "Hello!" into the mouthpiece.

"Hey, Tortoise, how you doing?" asked Songbird. "You

still hiking?"

"Yeah, I'm in Asheville for the weekend with Mike, but I'm going back to the trail tomorrow."

"Where will you be getting back on at?"

"Davenport Gap, where I got off yesterday. I'm finally through with the Smokies, you don't even want to hear about how horrible that was. How was your job interview? Did you get the job?"

"Oh, I don't know, I don't think I'll get it, though. I want to hike some more. If I actually do get the job I can leave the trail then. I can be at the hostel near Davenport Gap tomorrow, want to hike with me some more?"

And just like that, I had a hiking partner again. We made plans to meet the next day and hung up. I hadn't minded hiking alone, but it would be nice to see Songbird again, and it was fun to have company at the shelters and campsites in the evenings. The other hikers were always friendly and interesting, but Songbird was so much more outgoing than I was, and besides, she was funny. I looked forward to getting back on the trail. It almost felt more like home to me than civilization did. By this point, the real world was starting to seem almost like an intrusion, an obstacle preventing me from moving forward towards my goal. All except for St. Mike, cheeseburgers and hot showers.

Davenport Gap to Groundhog Creek Shelter
May 6, 2013

Mike and I had a huge breakfast at IHOP and then a quick stop for a resupply at a grocery store. I didn't need much, just enough for the estimated three days it would take me to reach Hot Springs. He then drove me back to Davenport Gap and we had our sad goodbyes. It would be two weeks until our next planned reunion at the hiker festival called Trail Days in Damascus, Virginia. We would be there as vendors, just to have an excuse to get together, and hoped that we might sell enough products to pay for Mike's trip there. My usual products, soap, lotions, herbal salves, and ointments, weren't really hiker related, so before starting my hike in April I had made up a line of hiker-friendly products to justify our presence at a hiker festival. I had made my usual herbal insect repellent in tiny, two ounce sizes, along with an herbal waterless hand cleaner, jewelweed soap (for poison ivy), and biodegradable liquid soap, all sized small for weight conscious backpackers. I wouldn't be able to walk the 200 plus miles to Damascus in the next two weeks, but I was going to walk as far as I could, and Mike would pick me up from wherever I was and take me to Damascus for Trail Days, then return me to my stopping point after the festival.

I liked having a plan, an itinerary of sorts, and this one felt comfortable. In three days I'd be in Hot Springs, and after a zero there I would head north, trying to get as close to Damascus as I could in the remaining time before Trail Days. I returned to Davenport Gap in much different conditions than I had left it. What a difference 24 hours could make! The day before I had been freezing in the rain in Asheville, but it was warm and sunny on my return to the trail. I hiked in shorts and a tee shirt, soaking up the warm sunshine. My pack felt light on my back with only three days worth of food and no rain-saturated items to weigh me down. From Davenport Gap the trail goes down a road and across a bridge over the Pigeon River, then under the interstate before it re-enters the forest. Tacked to a tree near the turnoff to get to the hostel was a paper sign with "BLUE TORTOISE" written on it in large letters.

"Trail mail!" I thought, delighted. It was from Songbird, saying she was restless to start hiking and would meet me at the next shelter, another seven miles further. I hiked on, starting the five mile ascent of Snowbird

Mountain. I took my time, enjoying the beautiful weather, sunny skies, and lovely scenery, and feeling, as usual, a bit bloated after a town stop. Coming out on the top of Snowbird Mountain, the view was so gorgeous it took my breath away. It was a true bald, with 360 degree views. I was the only person to be seen in all directions, and it was so quiet and peaceful, warm and sunny, with a brilliant blue sky, that I decided heaven wasn't Davenport Gap after all, it was Snowbird Mountain. If a choir of angels had appeared and started singing I wouldn't have been surprised. But there, on the top, was an odd structure. According to my guidebook it was just an FAA tower, but it was so wildly out of place that I wondered if the government was hiding aliens in there. It had an Area 51 feel to me, brushing aside my first impression of heaven.

Laughing at myself and my imagination I walked on, now starting my descent from the lovely mountain. A short two miles later I came upon tiny Groundhog Creek Shelter, a stone shelter with a capacity for just six hikers. I shrugged the Green Monster off my shoulders and heard the call, "Blue Tortoise!" There was Songbird, walking down the trail back to the shelter from the privy.

"Hey there, Songbird!" I called, and we greeted each other with a warm hug. I set up my pad in the shelter next to hers, deciding to forego the comforts of the hammock for the night so that we could spend the night together, talking and giggling and catching each other up on all that had transpired since we had seen each other last. A hiker slumber party, if you will. There were already two sleeping bags on the wooden floor, and Songbird explained that they belonged to two young men, David and Roadkill, who had gone out foraging in the woods. Eventually they returned, and David had some wild ramps which he added to their ramen noodles cooking over the fire. Their company made for a pleasant evening, as they were not typical hikers. They were not exactly hiking the Appalachian Trail as much as they were vagabonds, walking and hitchhiking and living off the land, who just happened to be on the AT at this time. David was quiet and had a shy smile, but Roadkill was friendly and talkative. Songbird and I—both middle aged women with real jobs and families and responsibilities in the real world—struggled to understand the life choices of these two young men. Songbird was much more pointed than I was in her questioning of them, but they didn't take offense, answering her questions in the same spirit in which they were asked, that of genuine curiosity, not criticism. As we lay on our pads on the shelter floor later that night, I thanked God for the variety of people I was being introduced to. I was reminded again of Chris and Mary in Bryson City and the lessons God was teaching me about acceptance and loving and holding off on the judging. David and Roadkill lived with a joy and appreciation of their surroundings that many office-bound people can't understand, and I struggled to understand as well. But with all that I had learned thus far, I did not have to struggle to love them and their infectious happiness. I thought of the other people who had shared my campfires over the preceding month, many of whom I would never have had occasion to interact with in my real life: people with piercings in various and sundry places and more tattoos than bare skin. Before hiking alongside them I might have avoided them, even made assumptions about their lives and morals. That is to say, I would have judged them. Instead, by sitting around campfires and conversing with them, I found that they had lives more like mine than different from it. They had homes, parents who loved them, siblings they worried about, and jobs they hated or loved, and questions about God and the universe and their purpose in it. In short, they were like me. They also were the apples of God's eye, and I pictured Him singing over all of us who were sleeping in shelters along the 2,000 miles of the trail.

The Lord your God is with you,

He is mighty to save.

He will take great delight in you,

He will quiet you with His love,

He will rejoice over you with singing.

Zephaniah 3:17

Groundhog Creek Shelter to Lemon Gap
May 7, 2013

Songbird and I packed our backpacks and started off in the morning after saying goodbye and good luck to Roadkill. David was out looking for mushrooms, but Roadkill promised to convey our good wishes, and we hiked away. Our usual hiking pattern had been that we didn't walk together most of the time but came together at rest breaks throughout the day and of course at our campsite for the evening. But on this day we walked together most of the day. We fell back into our familiar and comfortable routine of jokes, stories, and songs. We sang *"The Night They Drove Old Dixie Down"* through the morning. Songbird knew the Joan Baez version, and I liked the Band's version, and between the two of us we managed to remember all of the lyrics. The weather remained fine, with the cold, wet, windy days in the Smokies a distant, unpleasant memory. Nearly seven miles into the day we came to Max Patch, another iconic location on the trail that I had been excited to see. It was a huge bald, the biggest one yet, so big that it made Snowbird Mountain seem small by comparison. There were other people there, non-hikers sitting in small groups having picnic lunches and taking photographs. I wondered how they had gotten there until I looked down the hill and saw a dirt road and a small parking lot. I had to laugh, I had walked 254 miles to get there, and here were people who had driven to the parking lot and walked up the hill, enjoying the same views I had!

It was a breathtaking vista, though, however one got there. We lingered, taking pictures, trying to capture the grandeur with a cell phone camera. The AT was marked across the expanse of the treeless bald by metal posts driven into the ground bearing the white blazes I had been following for over a month. Finally we decided to walk on, leaving Max Patch to the day hikers. Songbird whispered to me, "I really, really have to pee." As there were no trees around, we decided it was time to resume our hike and followed the white blazes back down the bald and toward the trees. We reached the tree line and dropped our packs.

We were going to stop here in the shade and have our lunch. I was unpacking my food bag while Songbird was scouting a location for her business, when a sweet looking elderly couple emerged from the forest, holding hands.

"Well, hello there," said the lady. "Are you hikers?"

"Why, yes, we are," answered Songbird, the more talkative of the two of us. "We just came down from Max Patch. It's beautiful. Are you going up there?"

"Oh, honey, we've already been up there," she said, and then proceeded to regale us at great length with stories of her family, her children and grandchildren, hikes she had taken with her husband, and all about her home in Florida. Her husband stood at her side, smiling sweetly and nodding proudly. I was spreading peanut butter on crackers and murmuring polite answers, yes ma'am, and oh really?, and isn't that nice? when they seemed called for. I could barely keep from smiling when I glanced at Songbird, who was also apparently involved in the one-sided conversation, all while squirming uncomfortably, tears beginning to gather in the corners of her eyes. She was just about to begin the quickstep we used to call "the peepee dance" when my girls were small when the husband spoke up.

"Well, Sweetie, I think we probably should get on our way and let these young ladies get on theirs, don't you think?"

"Oh, do you have to go?" I asked, earning a glare from Songbird.

But they did leave, picking their way slowly up the hill toward Max Patch, while Songbird made her way, not quite so slowly, into a rhododendron thicket. In fact, she dashed over to it, unzipping as she ran.

After eating lunch we resumed our hike, and in a few short miles came upon another shelter. But it was still early in the afternoon, and we uncharacteristically weren't ready to stop yet, just over eight miles from last night's stop, so we hiked on another three and a half miles until we came to a cute little campsite called Lemon Gap and decided to stay there for the night. We were the only hikers there. We started a fire and had supper. Just before dark it started to rain, and we hurried to put up our hammocks. Songbird had gotten a hammock instead of a tent, and this would be her first night to sleep in it. We hurried to get both hammocks hung in the sprinkling rain. I got mine up and then helped her with hers, and we managed to get our gear stowed under the tarps and crawled into the hammocks just before the rain began in earnest. I said my rosary in the darkness of my little nest while I listened to the rain dancing on my tarp. I was warm, dry, and comfortable, and fell asleep easily.

Lemon Gap to Hot Springs
May 8, 2013

It was still raining when I awoke in the morning, although it was just a damp, drizzly kind of rain that seemed almost to be coming up from the ground as much as down from the sky. We were in the middle of a thick cloud of fog that covered our whole little gap in the mountains. It was so dreary that I wondered how it had earned the name Lemon Gap. I reluctantly emerged from my cozy cocoon, only to find Songbird rustling around with her hammock suspension, the look on her face a match for the gloomy weather.

"Are you dry?" she asked. When I said that I was, she spat out, "Well, I'm not. This damn thing leaked rain all night. Everything inside it is soaked, and I'm wet to the skin. I didn't sleep all night."

"Why didn't you say something?" I asked, incredulous. "I would have gotten out to help you arrange your tarp. We could have fixed it!" I didn't mention that I had heard her snoring in the middle of the night when I had awakened to empty my bladder.

I had never seen the usually ebullient Songbird so down. "At first I just thought it was a little leak. I thought I could live with it until morning. But it was leaking in underneath me and I didn't realize it at first. By the time I did, it was too late. My sleeping bag was already wet, and it was too late to do anything about it."

"At least it's not cold," I said, which earned me another glower. "Do you have some dry clothes to put on? Let's see what we can do with your stuff."

She wasn't interested in me helping her with her gear, which she continued packing into her backpack. "This pack is twice as heavy now," she said, Eeyore-esque.

I was sympathetic, my ordeal in the Smokies still fresh in my mind. She was wet, tired, and frustrated. We had a 14 mile day in front of us, including two mountains to climb, Walnut Mountain and Bluff Mountain, and then a long, four mile descent into the town of Hot Springs. Fourteen miles was just about our upper limit on daily mileage even under the best of circumstances, and I knew Songbird was not going to walk 14 miles that day. I consulted my guidebook for options.

"Hey Songbird, there's a road crossing coming up in two tenths of a mile. How about if we catch a ride into town from there, get a bed at a hostel, and let your stuff dry? Then we can shuttle back here tomorrow morning and finish the hike into town."

She readily agreed with that plan and we finished our packing and walked the short distance to the road crossing. I was anticipating a scenario like the day I hitchhiked into Robbinsville—a busy road, trucks and cars zooming past, and a vehicle stopping the moment we stuck out our thumbs. I assumed we'd be in Hot Springs in an hour's time, so I skipped my usual protein bar breakfast. I should have wondered why, if there was a busy road with zooming cars and trucks just two tenths of a mile away, all I could hear was the pitter patter of raindrops falling from the trees to the forest floor. When we reached the road I was dismayed that it was a narrow, rutted, dirt road, with no sign that there had ever been a car or truck zooming along it.

Plan B was always to call for a shuttle so we both checked our phones. "No bars," we said simultaneously. I wasn't sure what to do next, and Songbird wasn't much help, her usual cheery optimism and take-charge attitude drowned along with her sleeping bag. She was, literally as well as figuratively, under a dark cloud.

"Ok, I said," suddenly the plan-maker. "Plan C. Let's

just start walking down the road. At some point we will either get cell coverage, come to a house, or meet a car. It's really our only option at this point, if we can't walk on the trail and we can't just stand around here. Which way do you think we should go?"

That was a good question. We didn't carry maps of the areas surrounding the trail, just a guidebook to the trail itself, which was, under normal circumstances, more than enough information. I had a compass on my phone, but I didn't know which direction Hot Springs was from us. The trail itself, although it went in an overall north-south direction, also wiggled around through the mountains, so at any given moment while walking northbound on the trail you could be walking north, east, west, or even south. With no real idea which direction we wanted to walk, we looked at the road itself. It was on a slight grade, going downhill to our right and uphill to our left. We could see nothing in either direction except trees, as the road curved out of side both ways. "How about if you walk that way and I walk this way, for about five minutes or so, then come back here. Maybe we will have seen something to tell us which way to go—a house or a better traveled road or a view of town down below us."

So we split up, I took the high road and Songbird took

the low road. I saw nothing in my five minutes of walking, except more of the same. I turned around and walked back to Lemon Gap where she was already waiting, with the same story for her direction. I was stumped. A wrong decision here could be a disaster.

"I say we go downhill," Songbird said, reasonably. "Most little mountain roads like this go up the mountain when they turn off a main road. The big road is probably at the bottom of the hill." That made sense, and I was glad to see a glimpse of the old Songbird. So we started walking down the hill. It wasn't raining anymore, but drops fell from the trees with a plop-plop sound, incidentally the only sound we could hear. It was still foggy and eerie looking, and I took a picture of Songbird walking ahead of me, forlornly disappearing into the mist. The road wound its way down the mountain, curving right and curving left, so that at no point could we ever see very far into the distance. This led to our hopes being continually dashed—surely around the next bend......no. Well the next curve then? No. We walked on and on. The fog finally lifted but the day remained cool and damp as we trudged on. Road walking is harder on the feet than trail walking, I realized. Eventually we came to a crossroads, but the road that branched off was no bigger than the one we were on, and the signpost reading "Rattlesnake Branch" didn't sound appealing, so we stayed our course.

I prayed as I walked, my divine mercy chaplet and then my prayers offering up my sore feet and discouragement for my cause of the day. I had planned to make the day's prayers for an increase in vocations to the priesthood and religious life, but changed my mind after a few miles of endless walking. I had somehow been thinking of war refugees and decided to make them the focus of the day's prayers. My youngest daughter taught English as a second language and often worked with refugees. She had told me stories of the lost boys of Sudan. I had recently finished reading "*Left to Tell*" by Immaculee Ilibagiza, and I was moved beyond words by the trials some people have to suffer, and the grace and patience they show. I even thought of the Cherokee on the Trail of Tears which passed very near my own home. I found myself wearily trudging down this road from hell, this road that would never end, with my hopes for an end to the trek continually being dashed as I rounded each bend in the road, only to find more of the same, and another bend coming up. When I pondered the vast difference between refugees and my own hike down a peaceful country road, I was ashamed for having felt sorry for myself. I was out here by my own choice and had a nice home waiting for me at the end of my hike. Even at the end of the day's hike, however long it might turn out to be, there would be a bed in a hostel, a shower,and a hot meal, that I could pay for with a piece of plastic. The end of my day's hike might not be waiting around the next bend, but neither was there any danger. I asked God's protection on those who faced real dangers and His forgiveness on me for pettiness and ingratitude.

With my perspective thus restored, I realized I was hungry, so I dug the forgotten protein bar from my pack and ate it as we walked along. Rounding another of the interminable bends in the road I saw a rustic sign in the distance. It was a campground! Oh hallelujah, praise God, where there was a campground there were people with cars and a phone and a camp store! We rushed ahead and turned into the campground. There were no sounds, no sign of activity. No cars, no people. Songbird carried an emergency whistle, which she blew repeatedly, hoping to rouse some hiding campers, but there was no answer. It was entirely deserted. There were modern stone block bathroom facilities, of which we both made use. There was a big signboard, of the type you see in state parks, with identification pictures of the local flora and fauna, and instructions not to feed bears, but of more interest to us, there was also a map of the area. I was able to place our campground on the map, but oh, dear God, where was Hot Springs? Surely not the other direction? We seemed to be heading toward Del Rio, a town I'd never heard of, which was so small it barely registered as a blip on the map. I was in favor of turning around and going the other way, but Songbird wasn't convinced. We debated it for a while. She strongly believed in the reasoning behind going downhill from the mountain to find a major road. I did too, but my compass plus the map seemed to indicate that Hot Springs lay behind us. I wasn't sure though, and just because the town itself might lie in that direction didn't mean that we would find a major road any easier going that way. I didn't trust my map-reading skills, and to tell the truth, I didn't want to be wrong. If I insisted on going back up the way we had come and it turned out to be a mistake, which it very well could....well, I'd rather not be to blame. We had already come quite some distance from Lemon Gap and the idea of backtracking was not attractive, so we put our packs back on and walked back to the road and continued down.

After another couple of hours we heard an engine whining as it came up the mountain toward us. We excitedly called, "Car, car!" to each other as we raced around the next bend, waving our arms. An ancient pickup truck rolled to a stop, two men inside. The driver was an old man, tobacco chaw in his cheek, wearing worn overalls. His passenger was a young man, maybe in his late teens, with matching overalls and tobacco chaw. His grandson, I wondered?

"Hi there! Are we ever glad to see you!" Songbird said with a big smile, turning on the charm. I was glad to see the old Songbird back. "We were hiking on the Appalachian Trail and got off on this road, hoping to get to Hot Springs. We're so tired of walking. I wonder if you could give us a ride?"

The old man spit a stream of tobacco juice out the open truck window and smiled. "Well look at you all! You sure did walk a long way didn't you? I hate to tell you, but we're going up the mountain, not down. And Hot Springs is a pretty far piece yet. But you all can walk on down this road and when you get to the bottom, turn on the paved road and there's a store just a few more miles."

"Oh, we will pay you for your gas and your time!" Songbird pleaded.

"We can ride in the back of the truck," I chimed in. "We don't mind."

The young fellow joined the conversation to say that

the store was only eight or ten miles from where we stood. This seemed to make our point more than theirs, I thought. By truck we could be there in 15 minutes, and we would gladly pay them for their time. By foot it would take us several more hours at the tender-footed pace we were hiking. Songbird didn't give up easily, and chatted with them for several more minutes, telling them that we were both nurses, that she was from North Carolina and I was from Tennessee. (The AT straddles the state line so we were never sure which state we were in. Hot Springs was in North Carolina, Del Rio was in Tennessee. She was covering our bases, hoping that they might be swayed if one of us was from their home state.) But it was all to no avail. The old man finally said that they were on their way up the mountain to their cattle herd, that they had some fencing down and they had to repair it before the cows wandered too far afield. He gestured to the bed of the pickup, at the large bundles covered by tarps, evidently his new fencing and tools. We saw that he wasn't going to budge and backed off. The truck took off up the hill and we resumed our weary trek downhill. Songbird said they must be Tennesseans, because no good North Carolina gentlemen would leave two women in distress. I didn't bother to stand up for my statesmen. I had no way to disprove her hypothesis.

We trudged on for another ten minutes while I ran the scenario through my head, then I said, "Songbird. There are no cattle on this mountain. This is all federal land. It's a national forest. What do you suppose they were really up to? They sure weren't letting us anywhere near the back of the truck. Have you ever heard of a farmer wrapping up his tools in tarps? And you're right, any men I know of from either state would have given us a lift down to the store and then gone back to whatever they were doing. Something was fishy there." We decided that somewhere buried in the folds of the mountain these two men probably had a marijuana patch or maybe a meth lab. Maybe even a still, but certainly not cattle.

As the day wore on we finally began to see signs of civilization. Through a break in the trees we caught a glimpse of a church steeple off in the distance. We came upon a lumber mill. There was no one there, but we were very encouraged by the sight. There was a log cabin, evidently abandoned. The road became paved. I was walking some distance ahead of Songbird when I burst out of the forest and into farmland. There was a house! And a real road, just a few hundred feet further on. We had made it. I didn't know where we were or where we were to go from here, but we had made it. The sun was shining now, and I laid down in a patch of mowed grass, my head resting on my backpack, to wait for Songbird. I had nearly dozed off when I heard her worried voice, " Blue? Blue? Are you dead?"

I opened my eyes and we both laughed. I stretched and sat up, and just at that moment a car pulled out onto the road from a driveway a hundred feet away. Songbird ran to it. She wasn't going to let this one get away. When I reached the car she was leaning over to talk to the driver, another older man, and chattering eagerly. She identified us, again, as two nurses, from North Carolina and Tennessee, and gave other details about our real, civilized lives, evidently not wanting to scare this sweet elderly couple away. She wanted to make sure that they realized that we were responsible, productive, citizens, and not homeless or hobos or criminals, despite our appearances. I'm sure they weren't used to being accosted by two shaggy looking women with big packs. Yes, the AT ran along the top of a mountain less than 15 miles from their home, but most trail traffic was on the other side of the mountain, in Hot Springs. Del Rio probably didn't see many hikers.

Songbird was using every ounce of her considerable charm on Butch, the driver, and his wife, Betsy. She pleaded for a ride to anywhere, knowing we could call a real shuttle if we could just get to a main road. I hung back to let her work her magic. Butch and Betsy offered us a ride to Newport, another town I had never heard of. They were going to a doctor's appointment. They would be happy to take us to Newport if it would help. We were overjoyed and put our packs into their trunk when Butch got out to open it for us. We climbed into the back seat.

We made conversation on the way to Newport, telling them about our lives and adventures on the trail and our decision to get off the trail this morning when Songbird's gear got wet in last night's rain. At that moment I took my rain jacket off, and Betsy turned around to say, "Maybe when you get to Hot Springs you can go to a laundry," in her sweet voice. I wasn't sure if she was referring to Songbird's wet gear or my evident need of soap and water on removing my jacket. Songbird must have had the same thought, because we grinned at each other, both still giddy with the joy of being off our feet and in a moving vehicle.

Butch went out of his way to drop us off on a highway closer to Hot Springs, and he pointed down the road. "It's that way," he said, "About ten miles." Like all my previous trail angels they refused any money and wished us luck on getting to Hot Springs. We could have called a shuttle at that point, but I had had good luck with hitchhiking on previous occasions and thought we should try that first. Songbird was a bit reluctant, but I stuck out my thumb and within minutes an SUV pulled over for us. The driver was a neatly-dressed man in his fifties, with a nice big dog curled into the back seat. He evidently had experience with hikers.

"Hey there," he said. "Going to Hot Springs?"

"Sure are," Songbird said.

"Can you take us there?" I asked.

"No problem, I'm going there myself. Hop in."

The ten mile drive to Hot Springs went quickly. Our latest trail angel was polite and interested in our hike. When he pulled into the little town of Hot Springs the first thing I saw was the Smoky Mountain Diner. I had seen photos of the sign in so many trail journals that I recognized it instantly, and, like Pavlov's dog, my mouth started to water. "Oh, can you let us out here at the diner? My stomach is telling me it's past suppertime."

He pulled to a stop, we thanked him profusely and made the routine offer, routinely refused, to pay him for his kindness. Then we eagerly jumped out of his SUV and soon found ourselves seated in the diner with plates of cheeseburgers and fries in front of us. It was wonderful, and the diner more than lived up to my expectations. Finally, satiated, we asked the waitress where Elmer's was, and she pointed to the big white house that was just across the street. "Just go around to the back door," she added.

Elmer's Sunnybank Inn was another landmark hostel on the trail. I had read about it in many trail journals over the previous year and was excited to be this close. We walked across the street. The hostel was a huge white house, set on a small hill, with a yard sloping down to the sidewalk. It was an old historic house that had in previous incarnations served as a girls' school, among other things. We walked up the sidewalk around to the back of the house. The back porch was lined with hiking boots and trekking poles, a heart-warming sight. Our people were here. Unsure what to do we knocked on the back door, and a young man came around the corner of the house at the same time and greeted us warmly. He asked us to leave our boots and poles with the others, but said that we could take our packs up to our rooms with us. (Some places ask hikers to leave their packs outside.) Then he held open the screen door, and we stepped into a crowded and fascinating kitchen. It was small, but evidently well-used and well-loved. There were cooking implements everywhere, on the kitchen counters and on the huge butcher block center island. Bottles of oils with fresh herbs floating in them lined the windowsill, and there were plants, books, and colorful crockery everywhere I looked. I loved the look and feel of this kitchen. There was a white board on the refrigerator with room numbers and hiker names written on it. The young man said "Room three is empty. I'll put you all in there. What are your names?"

"Songbird and Blue Tortoise," I said, punching Songbird as I noticed the name Maple by one of the numbers. I had told her about my encounter with Maple in the Smokies and his persistence in berating me for having accidently picked up his food bag instead of my own. She gave me a typical, mischievous Songbird grin, her good humor quite restored by now. We were led through the house, which, like the Smoky Mountain Diner, lived up to my expectations. It was a gorgeous house dating from 1840 when the town was bustling with tourists coming to soak in the famous mineral hot springs that give it its name. The house was huge, with room after room furnished in an odd mixture of beautiful antiques, hiker memorabilia, whimsical touches, and hippie chic. There was a music room filled with musical instruments, a television room, and there seemed to be more than one dining room. The rooms opened one off of another like a rabbit warren, with reading nooks tucked here and there furnished with cozy chairs, lamps, and shelves full of fascinating books. I could have lingered to give it all a better look, but after being shown the downstairs rooms we were taken upstairs and shown our room, which was lovely and very old world. It was a big corner room, with windows on two sides. There was a double bed in the middle of the room, covered with what looked to be an antique lace coverlet. Not the typical hiker hostel bunkbed for sure.

"This is my bed," Songbird said, indicating with a wave of her hand that I could have the daybed in an alcove in front of the window. I didn't care. After having slept on dirty wooden shelter floors and on the hard ground in cold rain, the sweet little daybed looked wonderful, and after her bad night in a wet hammock, I felt she deserved the queenly bed. The rest of the room appeared to be furnished with antiques, the desk and dresser made from dark wood, intricately carved. Our room opened off from a breezy landing with a screen door onto an upstairs balcony furnished with wicker furniture. We carried our wet tarps and hammocks and Songbird's soggy sleeping bag onto the balcony and spread them out to dry in the warm spring breeze, draped over the furniture.

Back in our room we reconnoitered, making our plans

for the next couple of days. The next day would have to be our zero, as Songbird's gear wouldn't be dry by morning. Songbird was in favor of hiking north out of Hot Springs on the day after that, but I was concerned about the 14 mile unhiked stretch behind us, from Lemon Gap to town. I couldn't, in good conscience, hike off and leave that section. I wanted to shuttle back to Lemon Gap and hike into town from the point at which we had left the trail.

"But we hiked the same amount of miles, maybe more," Songbird countered. "We just hiked them on a gravel road instead of on the trail. You know we walked at least 14 miles before we got to Butch and Betsy's. What's the difference? That should count."

It was a difference in hiking philosophy. Songbird didn't mind taking shortcuts or even leaving off sections of the trail she thought might be too hard. She liked the blue-blazed alternate routes and had bypassed Blood Mountain in the first week of the hike on one such trail. She had wanted to bypass Albert Mountain for the same reason and had skipped the Smokies entirely. If we skipped this section of the trail it would be considered yellow-blazing (going by road, with yellow dotted lines), not blue-blazing (hiking an alternate, usually shorter, blue-blazed trail). I didn't consider myself a blue-blazer, let alone a yellow-blazer. I wanted to finish the whole trail, and when I did, I wanted to know that I had walked every inch of it.

Hikers often use the acronym "HYOH" which stands for "Hike your own hike." In other words: hike your hike your own way. Don't preach to others that your way is the only right way, and also don't judge them if their way is different. Here was a philosophical difference between Songbird and myself about what it means to be an AT thru-hiker. It was okay for us to have different approaches to hiking the trail, but if we were going to hike together this one would have to be resolved.

I went downstairs to talk to the young man who seemed to be our host. Elmer was out, he said, and he was just helping out to make money to resume his own hike. He checked shuttle prices and told me that a shuttle to Lemon Gap would cost 55 dollars. Our room here at the hostel was only 20 dollars, but we already knew there was going to be a second night. Figure in several restaurant meals and the total for this town stop was creeping up, higher than I could afford. I was in a moral quandary, but faced with Songbird's refusal to hike the missing section and my own reluctance to part with that much money, I made the difficult decision to skip that section for now and come back to hike it when my hike was over. I was conflicted and knew that I couldn't keep skipping sections. But this was just one section, I told myself. I would hike it at the end.

Finally, foot–sore and tired and with an uneasy although resigned spirit, I went to bed and slept like a baby.

Summer 2016

I did go back and hike that missing section the next summer with St. Mike. I enjoyed showing him the town of Hot Springs, which I was to come to love. We hired the shuttle to drive us to Lemon Gap and then we slackpacked the 14 mile trek back to town, and we thought we would die doing it. We hobbled the last mile in the near dark, and when we reached town I could have lain down on the ground and kissed the dirt. We were not in the same good hiking shape as I had been the year before, and my beloved boots were too small, the result of my feet having grown by a full size during my hike, as is common. It was brutal, harder than it would have been for Songbird and me the year before. We would have probably gotten to town earlier by trail than we did by making the long trek down the dirt road followed by two hitched rides. Of course, we had no way of knowing that at the time, and we made the best decisions we could, given the information that we had available. The biggest irony, though, was that if we had turned left instead of right at Lemon Gap and walked uphill, it was only a couple of miles to the Max Patch parking lot, where there would surely have been dayhikers and shuttle drivers coming in from the opposite direction from Hot Springs.

Hot Springs
May 9, 2013

I had many occasions while hiking the trail to remark on how much difference 24 hours can make, and this was one of those occasions. The day after trudging wearily for miles in a damp drizzle, sore and hungry, we found ourselves on a warm sunny day in a charming small town, well-fed and well rested, strolling down the sidewalks, greeting other hikers, ice cream cones in hand. Hot Springs was tiny, much smaller than I had imagined, but it was lovely, a hiker's paradise. Songbird and I went into the outfitter, and I could have swooned. Outfitters had become my third favorite places in the world, right behind hostels and restaurants. I still love being in an outfitter. The clerks and the other customers seem like my people, part of my tribe, they speak my language. I love every item on every shelf, I want every gadget (although I don't want to have to carry them, so I don't buy much.) I wander through the aisles, touching the fleece, stroking the wool, caressing the nylon. I am not, in my real life, a shopper, unlike most women I know. Shopping malls make me alternately bored or anxious. I find myself just wanting to get what I came in for and get out, quickly. But at an outfitter I become a browser. The outfitter in Hot Springs also sold food, not just the dehydrated meals available at most such places, but also fresh food in small, hiker-friendly quantities. The AT ran right through town, right down the sidewalk in front of the store, with the white blazes embedded in the sidewalk.

Songbird and I went into the library, which had computers available for hikers. I ordered flowers for my mother. Her 90th birthday was coming up in just two days, as well as Mother's Day. She didn't really like fresh cut flowers, but she did like hanging baskets of blooming flowers which she could hang outside on her little porch. I called her, knowing that I would likely be on the trail without phone service on her actual birthday. She was never really in favor of my hike. She was, I guess, like most people, in that she couldn't believe that this was something anyone would actually choose to do. She saw it as a series of hardships, not something enjoyable.

Like many of her generation, she had had a hard life, born in 1923 to a large family in the poverty of Eastern Kentucky. She had lived through the Great Depression and World War Two. She had borne six children. She had always worked hard, and had been blessed to enjoy a few years of leisure and comfort with my dad after retirement. Then he became ill, first with a stroke and then with an aortic aneurysm that left him an invalid for the last few years of his life, and she became his sole hard-working caregiver. During that time she lived with fear and anxiety that the aneurysm would rupture and she would be faced with his "sudden" death. Eventually, of course, that's exactly what happened, and she had grieved him mightily and found herself faced with a life she didn't know how to live after six years of having done virtually nothing except care for him. I was grateful that my three sisters still lived close to her, since I had moved 500 miles away to Tennessee nearly 30 years earlier. They took her to church, to lunch and shopping, even to a senior exercise class, and gradually she found herself again. She still missed my dad and bemoaned the signs of aging as they showed up, but she was still vibrant, active, and funny.

We had a lot of "momisms," her funny and innocent commentary on life, as the world around her changed.

From her point of view, my hike didn't make much sense. She had known real hardship in her life, such as I never had, and why would I choose to voluntarily undergo hardship? Why would I want to carry a heavy pack on my back and walk for miles every day, foregoing warmth and comfort and shelter? Why would anyone sleep outside in the cold and rain, when there were motels in every town? She didn't get it, but on this day, as I stood on the sunny sidewalk and described some of my adventures (always careful to leave off the most harrowing details) she said my hike was "interesting." It was the most positive comment she had ever made about my hike, and I considered it as acceptance and praise. I knew she worried about me and wanted the best for me, that at 54 years of age I was still her baby.

Songbird and I visited the mineral hot springs and enjoyed a long, hot soak, letting the heat seep into our sore muscles. We browsed local art in the ice cream store/craft shop. We ate lunch in a small restaurant and ran into Maple, who was friendly, though wary, towards me. I still wasn't sure if he was crazy or just different, so I treated him in a friendly but cool manner. I wondered how our confrontation in the Smokies would have gone if Songbird had been with me. She was outspoken and blunt, although warm and insightful. Might she have been able to get to the bottom of that strange encounter and defused it early? Maple was with a couple of other hikers, and we made arrangements to meet back for supper at the same restaurant, which was having live music that night.

We went back to the hostel. Our plan was to hike north out of town in the morning of course. I was trying to decide between taking a nap and watching a movie when Songbird approached me, guidebook in hand. She had a plan. We could get a shuttle, she said, and take it to Allen Gap, 15 miles north of town, and then walk those miles south, back into town, and have another night at the hostel. We could slackpack, leaving the heavy gear back in our room. Then, the morning after that, we could shuttle back to Allen Gap and continue on north from there.

Of course. Songbird, queen of the hostel and the slackpack, was back. I was enjoying my time in Hot Springs, but this sounded like a very expensive proposition to me, involving not one but two shuttles, another night in a hostel, and more restaurant meals. I couldn't afford this.

But she had already figured this out. Shuttles prices are figured by the mile, and divided by the number of passengers. The more people on your shuttle with you, the less each one pays. She had recruited a few other hikers staying at Elmer's to go with us, so our shuttle costs really were negligible. There was another hostel in town, Laughing Heart, which was cheaper than Elmer's. I knew I shouldn't go for it, but I found myself back in the role of lily-livered accomplice and agreed. It really is difficult to turn down a night in town, and Songbird was very persuasive.

We moved over to Laughing Heart, owned by Chuck Norris. (No, not the movie star Chuck Norris. The hiker Chuck Norris.) He was friendly and cheerful, and our room was a bunk room, lined with metal bunk beds. A far cry from the opulence of Elmer's, but it had a warm and happy vibe. We had met Elmer and found him to be cool and standoffish. He had made a cutting remark pointed at me about "real hikers," evidently making the point that I was somehow not a real hiker. He had refused to let Songbird and me keep our room another night after she came up with her shuttle and slackpack plan, even though he had several empty rooms. That was all right because it prompted her to move us over to Laughing Heart, which saved money, but I didn't understand. Was the "real hiker" comment because we were slackpacking after taking a zero or something else? Either way I found Chuck Norris' warmth and friendliness very welcome.

We went to dinner as planned. We had a big table with Maple and his friends: Hard Drive, who we had met at Aquone Hostel; Treasure Hunter and Catskill, a brother and sister who were going with us on the slackpack the next day; Dogfight and Leo, two hilarious middle aged men who were army buddies from years past and had multiple funny stories to tell, keeping us in stitches all evening; and a couple of other hikers who were new to me. The food, music, and company were all great, and we retired to our bunks at Laughing Heart Hostel well past hiker midnight, which is generally around nine o'clock.

Allen Gap to Hot Springs
May 10, 2013

We boarded our shuttle to Allen Gap early in the morning, Songbird, myself, Treasure Hunter and Catskill, and one other hiker we didn't know. Chuck Norris drove us to Allen Gap, and when we disembarked the single hiker took off north, and the other four of us headed south, back toward Hot Springs. Treasure Hunter (who I mistakenly called Gold Digger! He was a gentleman about it, though, and I quickly corrected myself) was living his dream of hiking the Appalachian Trail, and his sister Catskill was along for the ride. They were extremely nice and, like most people, stronger hikers than Songbird and me, and they quickly left us behind.

The first two miles of the 15 mile hike were uphill. It became my first real taste of hiking in hot weather, as it warmed up considerably as the day wore on. I felt that I had no right to complain about the heat since I had done so much complaining about the cold, so I didn't. Much. Along with the heat came the bugs, swarms of tiny little insects that I called North Carolina Bugs, because I didn't know what they actually were. They were a maddening combination of flies, mosquitoes, and gnats, with the worst traits of all three: biting, buzzing, and an unpleasant predilection to fly into my nose and mouth. They seemed to love hikers and stayed in neat little swarms around us, so that we looked much like Pigpen in the Peanuts comics, except that our swarms were made of bugs instead of dirt. Each hiker had his own individual, personal swarm.

Now that I was north of Hot Springs my concern turned to the norovirus I had been hearing so much about at shelters and hostels. There was a dreaded hiker virus that caused virulent GI symptoms rampant on the trail from Hot Springs to Erwin, Tennessee. The ATC had had crews out bleaching the shelters and privies, and the health department had been checking the hostels. I had been keeping my eye on it for a month or so, hoping that it would be over with by the time I reached this part of the trail. It was better, seemed to have reached its peak and was receding, but it wasn't over yet. I resolved to wash my hands scrupulously and stay out of shelters and privies until I was past Erwin.

The middle part of the day's hike was more pleasant than the beginning had been. The weather cooled down. There was a light off and on rain, which actually felt good and drove the North Carolina Bugs away. The trail was varied, with terrain that was new and different, which was always interesting. We walked down a quiet country road, past pastures, and around a scenic pond which had a bench to sit on. It was all very lovely and a nice change of pace.

The final third of the hike was challenging again. As we grew closer to Hot Springs and started the long descent, the trail suddenly became very steep and rocky. Songbird and I were hiking together by then, and we were both quite tired and worried about making it back to town in time to go to the laundry and wash our dirty clothes. We walked by the romantically named Lover's Leap, a steep cliff. From our vantage points as we climbed down the rocks we could see the rollicking French Broad River churning down below us. Finally we made it down to river level and walked along beside it for awhile until it led us to the road. We climbed wearily up to the bridge over the scenic river and walked the rest of the short distance into town. We were wet with sweat and rain, hungry, and absolutely exhausted. Just another day on the trail! We did manage to get our laundry done and went to Dollar General for our resupply. The next day we would start a 53 mile trek to Erwin, Tennessee, our next town stop. I bought enough food for the four or five days I estimated it would take us. Much as I loved Hot Springs, I found myself looking forward to getting back on the trail. I ate a cheeseburger and went to bed, more than willing to trade them for some Ramen and a hammock in the woods.

Allen Gap to Little Laurel Shelter
May 11, 2013

Chuck Norris drove us back to Allen Gap in the morning as we left Hot Springs for good. We had spent three nights there, and I loved the little town, but I was anxious to return to trail life. I wanted to hike the 53 miles to Erwin in five days, which was a very reasonable goal. St. Mike was picking up the two of us, Songbird and myself, in Erwin, and then we were all planning to go to Damascus, Virginia, for Trail Days. The craft show which was part of the festivities lasted for three days, and I planned to work at our booth all three days to give Mike some well-deserved time off. Songbird was excited, because her husband Joe was coming to Trail Days, also. So we started this leg of our journey with high spirits in spite of the weather report Chuck Norris shared with us on the drive to Allen Gap.

"There's some rain moving in," he told us. "It's going to rain all afternoon and evening, and the temperature's going to drop, too. Going to be 38 degrees tonight!"

That took a little of the wind out of our sails. It's not good to get wet on the trail, because in such a damp climate things have a hard time drying out. That explains why hikers never wear cotton and certainly not denim. Once those fabrics get wet, it seems like they will never dry. Basically all of a hiker's clothing and gear is made from synthetic material or wool. I like natural fibers, so I preferred wool and wore wool shirts and socks. My wool shirts were so thin and soft they felt like tee shirt jersey, they were light and stretchy and comfortable, and they breathed better than synthetics. The fact that wool does not hold odors as much as synthetic was definitely a plus, as well.

I was weary of hiking in the wet and the cold, but that definitely fell under the category of "things I could not change," so there was no use worrying about it. Instead I expended my energy hiking. The Green Monster felt terribly heavy on my back after a zero, a slackpack, and the addition of five days of food. The hike out of the gap was all uphill, as usual, and the day proved to be quite warm and humid. I was sweating heavily as I made the four mile ascent up the mountain. There was a shelter less than five miles from Allen Gap, and although we arrived there in the early afternoon we decided to stay for the night and wait out the coming rain. It was almost seven miles to the next shelter, and we weren't sure we could get there before the rain started. Besides, we had five full days to hike 53 miles, which meant we had time to take a short day.

The rain started shortly after we arrived at the shelter, and we were glad to be there early and find spots out of the rain. It was a small shelter, capacity only five according to the guidebook. There was a tent already set up near the shelter, and its occupant emerged to greet us. He was young, with a round, friendly face and full beard. His name was No Rush, and his demeanor matched his trail name perfectly. We were at the tail end of the northbound thru-hikers heading to Mt. Katahdin. Most of them were past us now, and we were starting to see more section hikers who emerge after the "bubble" of thru-hikers has passed through an area. But No Rush, like Songbird and me, was a thru-hiker. At least, technically he was.

"I'm hiking for the fun of it," he told us. "If I get to Katahdin in time, that's great, but I'm not going to break my neck to do it. I'm enjoying the hike." He went on to explain that, unlike most hikers, he slept in most mornings, emerging from his tent to pack up and hike only when he felt like it. If he liked a place he stayed in it a little longer. Most thru-hikers are fairly easy-going, it is true, but they all do have a strong drive to hike north, to keep going, to make miles. Katahdin is a beacon, calling to them, and they are focused on getting there. No Rush was the first hiker I'd met who said he really didn't care if he made it to Maine or not.

"What do you do, No Rush, in your real life?" I asked. He smiled and stated that he was a bartender. I thought that was a good fit for him. He was easy to talk to and inherently likeable. As the afternoon wore on I found out that he actually trained the bartenders for a popular chain of restaurants and travelled the country (and outside the country, as well), training the bar staff when new restaurants were opened. His job was one of more responsibility than he let on, and I respected his innate humility. We tried to make a fire, but all the wood we were able to find was just too wet to burn.

A group of six men of varying ages arrived at the shelter. They spread their gear out on the floor, and it seemed that there was plenty of room for all of us, in spite of the listed capacity of five. They were section hikers, friends and Boy Scout leaders. They were smart and funny, and we spent an enjoyable afternoon and evening in their company. An older gentleman arrived and set up his homemade tent behind the shelter, then came into the shelter to fix and eat his supper with us. His name was Ringmaster, he was a magician, and he entertained us all with magic tricks! I tried hard to keep my eyes on the tricky parts and not get distracted by his sleight of hand, but I couldn't see how he did any of the tricks. He was very good. He was the first true "ultralight" hiker I had seen. All of his gear including food and water weighed about twelve pounds, he said. (My packed weighed twenty four pounds, fully packed with water and four days worth of food.) He had made it all: tent, backpack, sleeping bag, and stove.

We sat under the roof of the shelter watching the raindrops fall, and I bemoaned the lack of a fire on this chilly night. George, one of the Boy Scout leaders, said he could make a fire, and immediately pulled out a huge knife, which no thru-hiker would carry, and started whittling down the wet wood that No Rush and I had gathered earlier. It took some time, but eventually he had a roaring fire going. I gave him the trail name of Fireman and enjoyed the warmth of his blaze immensely for the rest of the night. All of the men in his group were friendly, and their jovial banter made them pleasant shelter-mates for a damp afternoon and evening. I enjoyed their company, and I was glad that men of this character donated their time to the boys of their community. They were great role models, and I told Fireman to be sure and teach his fire making skills to his boys. Eventually it got dark, which means bedtime to hikers, and we all straightened our pads out, bid each other good night, and drifted off to sleep. My realization of the night was that Boy Scout leaders are great snorers.

Little Laurel Shelter to Flint Mountain Shelter
May 12, 2013

I woke up early after spending the night sleeping fitfully on the chilly, hard shelter floor, surrounded by the snoring hikers. I picked up the Zip loc bag containing my bathroom articles, put on my Crocs, and walked down the muddy path to the smelly privy. After attending to business, I washed my hands with water from my water bottle and a drop of liquid soap and then brushed my teeth with baking soda. I started to walk back up the muddy slope to the shelter, but stopped halfway up to look around. The woods were a marvelous shade of green in the very weak, early morning light, and were coming alive with birdsong. The view of the horizon was breathtaking—layer upon layer of mountains in varying shades of blue, indigo, and purple, with the sun coming up behind them all in a brilliant display of pink and orange. No artist's pigments could match those colors, I thought. There were no roads or cars to be seen, no electric lights, no power lines. No people, except for the congenial group of hikers just beginning to stir up at the shelter. And I knew that in that moment I was the luckiest girl in the world.

That's thru-hiking. It's not always (or even usually) comfortable or pleasant. But it is magnificent. I thought about how many people that I knew were rushing through a hurried morning routine so that they wouldn't be late to a job they despise. But I was surrounded by God's glory, and at peace.

Two sections of Holy Scripture came into my mind, both pieces from the Liturgy of the Hours that I had inadvertently memorized:

When I see the heavens, the work of Your hands,
the moon and the stars which you arranged,
what is man that You should keep him in mind,
mortal man that You care for him?
Psalms 8:3-4

In the tender compassion of our God
the dawn from on high shall break upon us,
to shine on those who dwell in darkness and the shadow of

death,

and to guide our feet into the way of peace.
Luke 1:78-79

Songbird and I walked twelve miles, over terrain that was varied enough to be interesting. There was a true rock scramble that required some climbing. When even my guidebook, which doesn't usually comment on the difficulty of a section of trail, warned that it would be "rocky and strenuous," we knew we were in for a challenge!

About halfway through the day's hike I passed another milestone, my 300 mile mark! I was excited about it, but had to downplay my emotion when Songbird seemed diffident and dismissive of the accomplishment. I know she felt bad that we couldn't celebrate this milestone together as we had the first hundred mile mark. We had been hiking together for so long and had had so many adventures together, but this was my accomplishment and not hers, and it seemed to upset her. Oh no, I sensed gloomy Songbird making her reappearance. I did ask her to take a picture of me holding up three fingers to mark the occasion, and then I just let it go.

We walked through a lovely grassy bald called Bald

Ridge, then we came to a mountain charmingly named Big Butt Mountain. We joked that it was named after us, and I saw cheerful Songbird returning. The mountain reminded us of a side trail early in the hike, back in Georgia, called Chunky Gal Trail. We had taken our picture with the sign for that trail, and we now took one with Big Butt Mountain.

Songbird walked on ahead of me when I sat down on a rock to take a break. Reflexively I pulled my phone from my hip belt pocket to see if I had a signal. I didn't, but there was a long email from my sister Pat. She had sent it two days earlier, although with my lack of coverage I had just gotten it. In it she explained that our mother seemed to be having more pain now, and she wasn't sure if this constituted a change in her condition. Pat knew that I wanted to be kept abreast of any possible changes, because when and if Mom began to decline I was going to leave the trail to care for her. I was still unconvinced that she actually had pancreatic cancer. Her condition just didn't match that diagnosis. As a hospice nurse I had taken care of patients with pancreatic cancer, and they all had many more symptoms and were much sicker than she was. In fact, her only symptom was pain, and she was frustratingly vague in her descriptions of that pain. I had been with her many times when her own hospice nurse asked her the usual nursing question: "On a scale of zero to ten, with zero being no pain at all and ten being the worst pain you can imagine, how would you rate your pain right now?" Mom unfailingly gave the same answer every time. Ten. Even if she was chatting and joking with the nurse and drinking a cup of coffee, she always claimed her pain level was a ten. If pressed on the point, she might downgrade it to a nine.

I had been taught in nursing school that the definition of pain was "whatever the patient says it is," but that definition only counted on exams. In real life, while pain is indeed subjective, it is often easy to see that the patient really does not know what pain is, or for some reason willfully assigns their pain a number they know to be inaccurate. Some stoic types might give a lower number than the pain they are actually experiencing, but more often they inflate the number. This might be done for a variety of reasons: to get more narcotics, or sympathy, or attention, or maybe just because they have a low tolerance for pain. Nurses learn to consider the pain score that the patient gives us, but also to look for other cues to help understand the patient's pain level. I didn't know exactly why my mom inflated her pain score, but I had a couple of theories. I believed that she had a low threshold for pain. She was a tough woman and had endured many hardships in her life without complaining, but tolerating acute pain was not one of her strengths. I think she also wanted to be sure that her doctor and nurses took her complaints seriously, and she believed that high pain scores were one way to get their attention. I think she believed that a low pain score might make them inclined to take her other complaints less seriously. I also think she had difficulty with the idea of levels of pain. To her mind, she was either in pain, or she wasn't. Pain equals ten. I do not believe that she wanted more pain medicine and inflated her scores in order to receive it. As a hospice patient she had liberal access to narcotics. I had no doubt that she had pain, I just questioned that the cause of her pain was cancer in the complete absence of any other symptoms.

She was also frustratingly vague about the location of her pain. She could never pinpoint it, and when asked to try she would usually just say, "It hurts all over." One problem with rating all pain as a ten, of course, is that it leaves you with nowhere to go from there. She had been rating her pain as a ten since last November, now she was saying it was worse. According to Pat, she still couldn't pinpoint a location for the pain, just saying she felt bad all over. Pat also wrote that nothing else had really changed as far as her mobility, independence, or her cognition or mental state. She might be a little more willing to nap in the afternoons, but otherwise she remained independent and mobile. Pat wrote that she knew this wasn't the kind of change that would require me to leave the trail and come to her bedside, but she wasn't sure if this was a prelude to that final change. She knew that I wanted, needed, to be kept informed and updated as to Mom's condition. "I don't know if this is a significant change or not," she wrote, "but I knew you would want to know."

I did want to know and was grateful to be kept in the loop. I knew this whole situation was extremely difficult for my sisters, who lived close to Mom, saw her every day, and were so grieved at the thought of losing her. I felt guilty for not being with them, but I knew that even if I wasn't hiking I couldn't just go to their home and stay, waiting for the end. Mom was still caring for herself and wouldn't want all four daughters hovering over her. My home was in Tennessee, and if I wasn't on the trail I would be there, not at Mom's bedside in Indiana. As I came out on a high ridge just before the trail started a steep descent into Flint Gap I unexpectedly got a few bars of service on my phone. "Thank you, God," I whispered, and called Mom. She sounded the same, just tired and maybe a little depressed. After we spoke for a few minutes I asked to speak to Pat, who took the phone into another room to be able to talk. I told her that I didn't know if this change in pain level had a deeper meaning, a progression of her disease. I reiterated that I would come as soon as I was needed, but that I didn't think that time was yet. Pat agreed with me that it probably wasn't yet, but she was worried. I told her to contact me through Mike if she felt like she needed to get a message to me, because I sometimes went days without either internet access or phone service, but that Mike always knew pretty specifically where I was and would be able to reach me. He knew Songbird's number, and her cell provider had greater coverage in the mountains than mine did. He also knew approximately when and where I would be in a town or hostel, and if all else failed he could drive over to where I was on the trail and find me. After we hung up I said a brief but heartfelt prayer for Mom and Pat and my other two sisters, shrugged the Green Monster back on my back, and resumed my hike.

After a sharp descent I came to a little shelter nestled among the trees and knew that it was our home for the night. I caught up with Songbird on the blue-blazed trail into the shelter. It somehow felt more isolated to me than other shelters we had seen, but there was no logical reason for me to have that impression. It sat back off the trail but was really no further from civilization than anywhere else on the trail. There was a small group of young section hikers there when we arrived, and they had a few obvious differences from the thru-hikers we were accustomed to camping with, and even from other section hikers. They had a flag flying outside of their tent, and a few travel games (Battleship, Connect Four, etc). They had a CD player with which they played their music loud enough for all to hear, and had a dog, but not a trained trail dog, just a pet tied to a tree near the tent. Thru-hikers generally don't carry such luxuries as games and flags and never play their music out loud. Every trail dog I had seen had been solidly trained, even Mika who took my cheese at the Fontana Hilton. These section hikers were all very nice, but they were a different breed than thru-hikers, and I was acutely aware of the differences. They had come for a weekend party in the woods with their friends and were just on a different wavelength than thru-hikers. I separated myself from the group to walk to the privy and stopped on the way back to the shelter to sit on a log. I turned my phone on and was surprised to see that I had some cell service. When it finally found its satellite, the first line of every text message I had received during the day flashed across the top of the screen, one at a time. Over and over, it read, "Happy Mother's Day," one from each of my three daughters. It made me cry, to be so far away, in such a sometimes brutal environment, and get messages of love from those who mean the most to me. My needs on the trail were simple, basic, and vital--food, water, shelter. Those messages seemed to come to me from a whole different world. To know that someone in that faraway world loved me and was thinking about me seemed almost too much to bear. I felt lonely and removed, separated from my family at home by the miles, from the other hikers at the shelter by hiking strategy and goals, and even from Songbird as I was coming to realize that we had fundamental differences in our hiking philosophies. I thought about mothers and daughters. It was the first time I cried on the trail. It wouldn't be the last.

Flint Mountain Shelter to Hogback Ridge Shelter
May 13, 2013

It had been a bitterly cold night, the coldest night I had spent on the trail outside of the Smokies. One of the section hikers had a thermometer, and he told us that it was 33 degrees when we woke up. I slept poorly because of the cold. Once I got up and started moving I warmed up quickly, as usual. A great deal of energy is expended while hiking, and I was almost never cold during the day, unless it was also wet. It was only at night that the cold bothered me. Depending on which source you read, the type of backpacking you do on the Appalachian Trail burns anywhere from 4,000 to 6,000 calories a day. It is just not possible to eat that much food, you can't carry that much in a backpack, so long distance hikers are always in a calorie deficit. This explains why when we get to town, we consume huge quantities of food and yet never really feel full. It's interesting to watch hikers in a grocery store doing their resupply. They frequently read the nutrition information on the packages, but they are looking for much different criteria than might be expected. They want high calories. They want the most calories for the weight of the item itself, calorie-dense food. They also may be looking for protein, as I did, or have other personal requirements, but the number one best attribute of a hiker food is high-calorie.

The appearance of thru-hikers changes over the course of a long trail in interesting ways. Men generally become very gaunt as they lose weight. Their hair and beards grow, of course, and hikers are known for their hirsute status, as few hikers shave. But the men also become thin, sometimes nearly skeletal by the end of the hike. Women, by contrast, seem to become better looking as their hikes progress. Early on they lose whatever extra weight they may have carried, and then start adding on muscle. Our female metabolism seems to prevent us from becoming as gaunt as the men do. After a few months of losing fat, adding muscle, becoming tan and healthy from all the outdoor living, the women look like they've been to a health spa, while the men resemble refugees.

I warmed up as I walked on, and the melancholy of the evening before lifted. We hiked less than nine miles for the day, and the terrain was pleasant, interesting, and varied. We crossed a stile over a fence and through a pasture. There were quite a few charming little streams and one glorious waterfall along the trail. We arrived at Hogback Ridge Shelter and decided to stay for the night. Only one other hiker showed up to spend the night with us. His name was Stretch, earned because he was six and a half feet tall! Stretch was an ultramarathoner, and with his long legs he easily hiked 30 mile days. He planned to arrive in Erwin the next day, while Songbird and I had budgeted another three days to get there! It was just over 25 miles to Erwin. I wished Stretch could put me on his back and carry me. I couldn't imagine being able to hike 25 miles in a day.

It was cold, and we gathered wood and had a nice big campfire. I was hoping for a warmer night than the previous night had been.

Hogback Ridge Shelter to Bald Mountain Shelter
May 14, 2013

This day was so full of beautiful sights and wonderful people, it was easily one of my favorite days of the entire hike. It was also my last day of unrestrained joy, the last day without fear or sorrow, regret or confusion. The last day of pure, innocent enjoyment of the Appalachian Trail, although of course I didn't know it at the time. God is good and made this last day before the bottom fell out a spectacular one.

Songbird and I woke up early after a good night. Stretch was already gone when we got up, and we joked that he would be in Erwin eating a pizza at about the same time that we cruised into the next shelter, ten miles farther up the trail. We heaved our packs onto our backs and started walking. The weather was perfect for hiking: clear, sunny, and cool, with a slight breeze. Our shelter had been near the top of a mountain, so for once our day started with an easy downhill. The mountains were not as steep as they had been earlier on the trail. After two and a half miles of walking we came to Sams Gap, with a big road crossing. There was both a state highway and an interstate highway in the gap. According to my guidebook, there was a café and a market about three miles down the state highway. "How about a little midmorning snack?" I asked Songbird. "The next car that comes along, let's see if we can hitch a ride to the café. It's only seven or eight miles to the next shelter, and we've got all day. Wouldn't a cheeseburger taste good right about now?"

She agreed and I went to stand by the road, ready to put up my thumb at any vehicle that came our way, while she sat in the grass repacking her pack. After ten minutes with no cars in sight, we gave up and headed back into the woods. There was a set of stairs leading up to the trail, but I had a surprise for Songbird. The gap marked a milestone for her, two hundred miles walked. I opened my food bag and brought out the chocolate chip cookies I had bought in

Hot Springs and saved for this event. She thanked me and we enjoyed our cookies, but I could sense the return of her blue mood. She seemed to have two distinct faces that she presented to the world. There was her cheerful, talkative, fun side, and then there was the sullen, withdrawn face that I was seeing more and more. I had first seen her gloomy side on the long trek from hell down the road from Lemon Gap, and now it came and went. It wasn't always possible to identify a cause for either its coming or going. I generally just left her alone when she seemed to want to withdraw, which was easy since we didn't actually hike together most of the time anyway. I didn't pressure her or try to get her to tell me what was wrong. I just let her be, figuring that if she wanted to talk to me about it, she would. I was always close by.

I could feel her pulling away from me now as she sat on the steps eating her cookies, so I walked on. It was a fairly easy, short uphill walk from Sams Gap to the top of a little unnamed mountain. At the top, my guidebook told me, I would find "meadow." Two miles later, when I reached the top, I wasn't expecting much from such a generically named landmark. No name was given for the mountain, which was only 4,414 feet tall. No bald was listed at the top, and the meadow didn't even seem to have a name. Just "meadow." But when I emerged from the woods and followed the white blazes out into the sunshine, I was absolutely enchanted with the gorgeous meadow and promptly re-named it "Blue Tortoise Meadow." It needed a real name because it was magnificent. It stretched out into the sunshine around me on all sides, green and dotted with yellow flowers, under a bright blue sky with puffy white clouds. It looked like a picture a child would draw, filled with clear primary colors. A line from the Psalms came to me, a scrap memorized from the Liturgy of the Hours: *"The hills are girded with joy."* If ever there was a hill girded with joy, this was it. Songbird followed me into the knee high grass, her mood lifted by the utter loveliness around us. It was so spectacularly beautiful, and Songbird and I were the only people there to see it. It seemed that, in that moment, it was there being beautiful, just for us. It seemed to exist for our eyes and hearts only. Grinning wildly, we walked deeper into the meadow, becoming drunk and giddy with joy. Almost at the same instant we raised our arms, trekking poles and all, and started twirling around. It seemed to be the only logical response to the situation. Songbird lived up to her name and broke into song. "The hills are alive, with the sound of music....." I tried to join her, but quickly remembered that I am no Julie

Andrews, and neither of us knew many of the lyrics anyway. Twirling is very difficult to do with a heavy pack on your back, so we subsided, with much laughter, and reluctantly started down the trail away from Blue Tortoise Meadow. "I will be back," I whispered.

Songbird took the lead as we walked on down the slope, and I quickly lost sight of her. At the bottom was a gravel road crossing which looked like it hadn't seen a car in many years. I walked on and stopped at a spring for a drink two miles further. Songbird was there, and we filled our water bottles and filtered our water together. "Have you seen anybody since the meadow?" she asked me.

"No, I haven't seen anybody but you all day."

"I saw some people back at the road crossing," she said. "They weren't really hikers. They were wearing nice clothes, button up shirts tucked into their pants. Like salesmen or Mormons or something."

"Did you talk to them?" I asked just to be polite. There was no one Songbird didn't talk to. She genuinely liked everyone and was naturally outgoing and friendly. If she had gotten close enough to talk to them, she would have known their entire life stories, and we wouldn't be having this conversation.

"No, they were quite a way ahead of me," she said,

confirming my suspicion. "I just wondered what they were doing out here, without a vehicle, dressed like that." "Were they headed up the trail?" I asked. When she confirmed that they were I said, "Well, I suppose we'll catch up with them sometime."

I walked on, leaving her at the spring as I continued up the trail. We were making an ascent now, climbing a mountain called Big Bald, which was indeed big at 5,516 feet of elevation. I hadn't gone far when I came upon the people Songbird had seen earlier. They were a group of four young brothers, the oldest being about eighteen years old. They were well-dressed, as Songbird had noted, and well-spoken, too. They stopped to talk to me and I was quite impressed with their articulate good manners. They were polite and friendly and made good eye contact while they spoke, and their speech was not peppered with the words "dude," "like," and "you know" that so many young people seem to be unable to form a sentence without using. All four were loaded down with bags and boxes of camping gear. They were on their way up to the top of Big Bald to set up a tent and spend the night. It turned out that they lived nearby and had camped up there before. They were in high spirits, happy to be together and looking forward to their night of adventure. I discovered in our conversation that they were home-schooled, and I mentally congratulated their parents on raising such well-mannered young men. We said our goodbyes and they hurried off, eager to reach the summit. The oldest brother solicitously took the youngest brother's load and added it to his own burden. Their camping gear that I could see was not the efficient, lightweight stuff that hikers carry, but older, WalMart style sleeping bags and such.

I toiled on up the trail and soon came out on the windy summit of Big Bald. It was much like Max Patch, a huge, domed expanse, with 360 degree views of the surrounding mountains. The wind was so fierce that I was worried about the young brothers, but when I reached their spot their tent was already set up, with all their gear (and maybe a brother or two) inside to keep it from blowing away. They greeted me cheerfully, and I walked down the trail, trying to get to the tree line to get out of the wind. I hoped that the sky would be clear that night so they could see the dome of stars over their heads, and I envied them their exuberance and innocent appreciation of life.

Just over a mile down from the summit I came to Bald Mountain Shelter, our home for the night. It was only a tenth of a mile off the trail, but somehow it felt isolated and a little creepy to me. Songbird and I were clearly out of the bubble of thru-hikers now, everyone we had started with being much further north on the trail than we were. When you're in the bubble you can be sure that there will be other thru-hikers at every shelter you stop at for the night to offer their company and their stories around the campfire. Now that we were out of the bubble, there were no guarantees that anyone would show up to share our fire. If anyone did come, they would be section hikers with no plans to walk to Katahdin and therefore a different set of priorities. There was a sense of security and camaraderie in being with the rest of the pack, everyone with the same goal, to make it to Mt. Katahdin, the end of the trail. There was a reason to try to make good time, Katahdin closes for the season on October 15, and even earlier if the weather warrants it. A thru-hike takes an average of six months if the hiker averages 15 miles a day. I had started my hike on April first, giving me just a couple of weeks over that six month schedule—if I hiked 15 miles a day. I hadn't to this point hiked a single 15 mile day, and had taken entirely too many zero days. I never said I was hiking to Maine when asked, it sounded absurd, like saying I was hiking to Mars, but it was still my plan. I always said I was hiking "as far as my knees would carry me," but my knees, which I considered my weak point, were doing surprisingly well. I babied them by keeping my pack light, my speed slow, and my distance short, and by wearing knee braces and taking daily ibuprofen. So far, so good, as far as my knees were concerned. There was just the problem of my distance and speed and getting to Maine in time.

I actually wasn't really worried about that, either. I knew that my daily mileage would increase with a few changes that were right on the horizon: the days would be getting longer and the weather better, the terrain would be getting easier as we left the largest mountains behind, and my legs would be getting stronger. All of this was already happening. And I had a backup plan, to ensure that I would finish my thru-hike this year: the flip-flop hike. Whenever I got to the point that I was sure I would not be able to reach Katahdin before October 15, I would get off the trail and travel to Maine by some other method, climb Katahdin, and then continue hiking south from there, back to the same point I had gotten off the trail. A flip-flop hike is a valid hike, and many people do planned flip-flops to take advantage of the best weather at each end of the trail. Often the midpoint of the trail, at Harper's Ferry, West Virginia, is used as the jumpoff to leave the trail, and thus the place to end the flip-flop hike. Harper's Ferry is also the home of the Appalachian Trail Conservancy, the headquarters of the trail, so it makes a fitting place to end a hike. With the idea of the flip-flop in my back pocket I still planned on finishing my hike, even though I was behind the pack, and I still assumed that at some point I would be called upon to leave the trail to care for my mom, if and when her health required it. She had sounded strong and upbeat when I called her from Hot Springs, still in her usual state of health and mind, and only slightly tired when I had last spoken to her.

Bald Mountain shelter felt lonely and somehow discarded. It was dirty, and there was trash in the "yard," which infuriated me. Hikers are supposed to adhere to "leave no trace" principles, not only because it's the right thing to do, but for safety's sake. Food trash attracts bears. Songbird showed up and really wanted a bath, after several nights on the trail and sweating on these warm days and strenuous climbs. She went behind the shelter to do what she could, with me on guard in front to keep any hikers who might show up from walking around the building. I found a broom and swept out the shelter, which was filthy, and even some garbage bags which I used to pick up the trash in the yard. Songbird came back around the corner, looking and feeling much better, so we changed places. I took my two liters of water, a little liquid soap, and a bandana around to the back of the shelter and gave myself some semblance of a bath in the great outdoors. I then gathered wood for a fire, but the area had been picked pretty clean and I didn't end up with much. It wasn't cold enough to justify a fire anyway, it was just a reflex on my part and a habit—that's what you did at night, build a fire. The only place on the trail where we hadn't had a fire every night was the place we needed it the most, in the Smokies. Everyone had just always been too exhausted (or wet, or cold) to have any interest in starting a fire, although that doesn't sound logical, when every night was so cold.

My pitiful fire going, I gathered and filtered more water to replace what I had used in my "bath" and made my supper. The night's meal was macaroni and cheese with tuna and a Payday bar for dessert. While Songbird and I were eating and chatting, three more hikers showed up. I hadn't quite lost my sense of unease over the campsite, so I was glad to see them. They were indeed section hikers, a father named Brian, and two of his nine children, teenage boys with the trail names of Mayonnaise and Moccasin Man. Brian was friendly and joined us on the edge of the shelter, wearily dropping his pack and pulling out his food bag. While Songbird, Brian, and I got to know one another the two boys, "M & M," got to work on my struggling fire.

They scattered out into the surrounding woods and came back with piles of burnable firewood that had somehow hidden from me on my foraging foray. They squinted at my fire, and decided that there were just too many ashes and set to work on it. While the fire was still burning they somehow dismantled the ring of rocks that surrounded it and scooped out the thick pile of ash. Under all the ash they found a second ring of rocks that they unearthed and added to the first ring. By the time they finished, a blazing fire burned brightly in the center of a fire ring that looked like it had been laid up by a pair of stonemasons, not by two teenage boys. M & M, unlike the four brothers I had met on Big Bald, didn't talk much, but they were also very polite and, coincidentally, home-schooled. Brian, Songbird, and I sat on the edge of the shelter watching the refurbishment of the fire pit with interest. I complimented Brian on his fine sons. He seemed quite proud of them, and rightfully so, and when he left to visit the privy Songbird said, "That's the kind of family that *ought* to have nine children. The world could use more people like this." I agreed wholeheartedly.

When the boys finished the firepit I innocently remarked that it was a shame the shelter was so high, it was actually difficult to climb up into it. Without a word they wandered off and came back with a plank they had found somewhere and a few flat rocks scavenged from the firepit construction, and we soon had a step that made it easier to get into and out of the shelter. Later, as we readied ourselves for bed Songbird noted that the wind was supposed to get pretty strong that night, and, oh, wasn't that a tarp over in the corner? Before we knew it the tarp was stretched across the open side of the shelter, blocking the wind. "Can we take these boys hiking with us from now on?" she asked Brian, who laughed along with us.

I lay in the shelter that night in wonderment at the warmth. It was my first night since beginning my hike a month and a half earlier that I slept without wearing my down jacket, gloves, and hat. The wind howled outside of the shelter and I was grateful for the tarp and for the young men who had hung it. Some days on the trail it was the scenery that was beautiful and inspiring, some days it was the people I met, and some days, like this one, it was both.

Bald Mountain Shelter to Spivey Gap
May 15, 2013

We had sixteen miles to hike to get to Erwin, which fit into our schedule perfectly. Our plan for this day was to hike ten miles to the next shelter, leaving six miles for the following day, putting us in Erwin about noon. Mike would be there to pick us up at about that time, and we would all go to Damascus for Trail Days together.

I was a bit concerned about going to Trail Days in my current disheveled state. We would be camping in Damascus, as the small town would be packed with both current and past hikers and other trail aficionados. Every motel room in the area had been booked for months. In addition, I would be manning our booth, attempting to sell soap, lotion, bath salts, and other "smell good" products. My so-called bath the day before notwithstanding, I was still dirty, and my hair and clothing were worse. I didn't worry about these kinds of things on the trail, but this was to be a town stop. And unlike most town stops, there wouldn't be an opportunity to clean up while there since we would be camping and not staying in a hostel or motel. Looking at my guidebook, I made what turned out to be an ill-conceived suggestion to Songbird.

"We could walk ten miles to the next shelter. Or we could walk five and a half miles to Spivey Gap. There's a US Highway that crosses the trail there. We could hitch a ride into Erwin and get a motel room, take showers, do laundry, and be all cleaned up when Mike picks us up tomorrow. He's bringing us back to where we got off the trail after Trail Days, he could just as easily bring us back to Spivey Gap as to Erwin. What do you think?" As I had suspected, Songbird was not hard to convince, and we hiked down the trail, excited about getting to town by noon. Town food, hot showers, and real beds awaited us.

We reached Spivey Gap, took up our position on the side of the road, and waited for a car to come along. And we waited, and waited, and waited. I couldn't figure out why there was no traffic at all on this road. It wasn't like the gravel forest service road at Lemon Gap, this was a wide, paved road. There were no cars at all, going in either direction. Soon it was past lunchtime, and I had gone light on breakfast, in anticipation of the big cheeseburger waiting for me in Erwin. Eventually we decided to call for a shuttle, although we much preferred the free hitchhiking to a paid shuttle. I was distressed to find that we had no cell service. We finally decided that our only choice was to start walking. It was about 15 miles by road to Erwin, but we felt that a car would come along eventually or that we would get cell service as we got closer to town. So we walked, and walked and walked, down the side of the road. It reminded me of our trek at Lemon Gap, and I fervently hoped that this one would be shorter, because as the day wore on it was becoming uncomfortably hot. This was a new experience for me on the trail. It had been warm a few times—very few—but never what I could consider hot. We were out of the shelter of the trees, and with the blazing sun reflecting heat from the blacktop road I was soon sweating. The Green Monster felt unbearably heavy, and I was thirsty. I hadn't filled my water bottles, looking forward to an ice cold Mello Yello in town. We trudged along, and I wondered how many people had faced both hypothermia and heat exhaustion within a few weeks of each other. Songbird seemed to be taking the heat in stride better than I was. After about a mile we came upon a house, and I didn't hesitate to walk right up to the door and knock. A sweet little older lady answered the door and, upon hearing my request, she very willingly let this strange, dirty, smelly hiker with a huge pack on her back come into her neat little house and use her phone. I arranged for a shuttle to come pick us up and retreated back onto the porch to wait for it.

The shuttle driver delivered us to the motel in Erwin

after a stop at a convenience store to stock up on cold drinks and snacks. We immediately called in a pizza order when we realized that, although it was a trail town, Erwin was not laid out in a fashion that was friendly to hikers. Instead of being compact it was all spread out, so that walking from establishment to establishment was not easy. The last thing I wanted to do was walk anywhere. The laundry was a good mile away so I decided to wash my clothes in the motel room bathtub. I filled the tub with warm water and some trail soap, dumped all my dirty clothes in it, and swirled them around. The water turned brown so I squeezed the water out of each garment, drained the water, cleaned out the dirty tub, and filled it up again with cool water. I added the clothes again and swirled them around. The water turned only slightly brown this time, so I repeated the process with cold water. This time, the water stayed clear, so I decided I was done and wrung each item out one last time, and hung them up on towel bars and hangers all over the room, grateful that I didn't have many clothes. Songbird was not impressed with the process and decided that she would walk to the laundry in the morning while we waited for St. Mike to arrive. I wasn't at all sure my clothes would dry in 24 hours but I didn't really care. I had four town days in a row, the excitement of my first Trail Days, and a weekend with St. Mike. Wet clothes were inconsequential. Besides, Mike was bringing the overnight bag he brought to our every meeting, that I had packed before I ever started my hike, so I would have town clothes. Jeans and sandals to wear! Unlimited cheeseburgers! And Mike! It was a wonderful prospect. I ate more pizza and switched on the television, sighing deeply as I lay on the bed, Songbird already snoozing on her own bed.

Damascus, Virginia
May 16-May 19, 2013

Mike arrived to pick us up at the motel in Erwin right on schedule, just after noon on Thursday, May 16. Songbird had done her laundry, and I had packed my (admittedly still damp) clothing into my clothes bag, and we were waiting in the lobby when he arrived. We all crammed into the van which was already quite full with all of our products and the display equipment for the craft show in Damascus. It was, as usual, great to see him. It was always a feeling of great relief to be around him, knowing that I could let my guard down, that he had my back. I didn't realize until I was with him how tiring it was to be without him, knowing that I had to be constantly on my toes on the trail, watching out for myself every minute, because no one else would. I am not a helpless, pampered woman, but he is a gentleman, and I could relax better when he was around than when I was alone.

We were in high spirits at the thought of Trail Days and hopefully seeing all the hikers we had met over the preceding month, but I could feel Songbird's mood slipping even as we rode along. She was withdrawing again. When we got to Damascus her husband Joe was there waiting for her, and she was palpably relieved to see him, much as I had been when I saw St. Mike, I supposed. We introduced Mike and Joe to each other, and then Songbird and Joe took off while Mike and I set up our booth for the Trail Days craft show. I assumed we would get together with Songbird and Joe for supper later that afternoon. We hadn't been sure where we were going to be able to stay, the motels and rental houses having long since been booked solid. I was reluctant to stay at Tent City with most of the other hikers, because it was pretty much party central. We were fortunate to meet two former hikers named Fidget and Dotcom who lived in Damascus. They had a house with a nice flat yard right across the street from the little park where the craft show was to be held, and they offered to let us set up our tent in their yard. Mike had brought a little two-person tent to sleep in. There were no bathroom facilities, but that prospect was not daunting after spending six weeks in the woods. I was glad that Songbird and I had spent the night in Erwin, having a shower and doing our laundry, though, as it appeared we might not get another chance to do so in Damascus. Joe and Songbird also set up their own tent in Fidget and Dotcom's yard, but we didn't see them again that evening, so we went to dinner on our own, assuming that they had also wanted some privacy.

Damascus was a cute little hiking town, filling up with hikers as the day went on. There was a festive atmosphere, as everyone looked forward to all the activities coming up the next few days. The tent was cozy, and we had a one-person air mattress to sleep on, but Mike was by my side, so what was there to complain about?

The next day was Friday, the first day of Trail Days. I stayed in our booth at the craft fair most of the day, while Mike went off on his bike to ride the Virginia Creeper Trail, a bike trail that conveniently passes right through Damascus. Sales were slow, but the people-watching was fabulous. I saw many of the people I had met along the trail, and it was fun to reconnect and see how much farther

ahead of me they had gotten. Little Janie came by and I
was glad to see that she was still on the trail and only a day
or two farther along the trail than I was. I was pleased to
be able to give Mike a much-needed day off, as I knew that
he was working hard to keep our home, his job, and the
business all going without me. It was a pleasant day. I
didn't see Songbird and Joe all day, but I could see their
tent in the yard next door. I wondered where they were, but
I also knew they had a lot of catching up to do and again
still assumed that we would see them at dinnertime.

After the craft fair closed for the day Mike and I went to
Tent City where we had found that free showers were being
offered for hikers. I started to protest that I had taken a
shower only two days before and couldn't possibly need
another one yet, until I remembered that normal people do
take showers more than once a week. After showers and
dinner (alone, still no sign of Songbird and Joe) we went to
one of the activities of Trail Days, a lecture and slideshow
given by one of the gurus of hiking and the Appalachian
Trail. It had been a great day, and I looked forward to the
next day, Saturday. The craft show would be open again,
and in the middle of the day was the highlight of Trail
Days, the hiker parade down the main street of Damascus.
I was looking forward to walking in the parade, having

earned my place with the class of 2013. We retired happily back to our little tent after the lecture, walking down the dark street with the stars glittering over our heads, peaceful.

STRIKE ONE

I poked my head out of the tent on Saturday morning, and the first thing I noticed was that Songbird and Joe's tent had disappeared overnight. "Mike," I whispered back into the tent. "Songbird's tent is gone. Where do you suppose they went?"

"I don't know," he said, logically. "Maybe they were able to find a motel room somewhere."

"Wouldn't you think she would have come by to tell me?" I asked.

"Well she doesn't have to report to you," he said, again, logically. "You'll probably see her later at the hiker parade."

We opened our booth for the craft fair, and soon it was time for me to report to the other end of town to line up for the hiker parade. It was going to proceed down the main street of town and end up back near the town park where the craft fair was set up. Then there would be a hiker talent show to be held in the park, with marvelous prizes for the winners. The prizes were being donated by the vendors of hiking gear who were located in their own area of the park. There were manufacturers of all the best known hiking gear and clothing and gadgets, who were selling as well as servicing and repairing the hikers' equipment. Trail Days really is a hiker heaven.

I walked to the beginning of the parade route and found my place in the class of 2013. There were hikers from many previous years marching as well. Some years had their own banners to walk under, and they went in chronological order, with the biggest group, the current year, at the back of the parade. Spirits were high in the staging area. I saw many hikers I had known previously, including No Rush, the bartender trainer, and Fresh Step, from the Smokies, who invited me to a BYOB (bring your own bowl) hiker feed to be held at Tent City that night. A tradition of the Trail Days hiker parade is that the locals who line the parade route arm themselves with squirt guns, even water cannons, and spray the hikers as we pass by. I'm not sure how this tradition started, but I wouldn't be surprised if it was an allusion to the fact that most hikers do need to take a shower. Hikers often dress in funny costumes for the parade, and I saw a man in scuba mask and flippers, men in dresses with large bosoms and red lips, some Mardi Gras style masks and beads, and several raincoats and umbrellas. "Where did they get all this stuff?" I wondered.

Eventually we got the go-ahead to start walking, and we flooded onto the street. I tried to stay in the middle of the pack to avoid the water being sprayed at us by the spectators. Some of the hikers had squirt guns also, I saw, and sprayed back at the little boys who were aiming at us. It was all great fun, and I took many pictures of the colorful characters walking around me.

I heard screaming behind me. At first it sounded like the shrieking of someone who had been a target of a water cannon. Then it didn't. It got louder, more shrill, with a sound of terror instead of surprise. I turned to look behind me and just as I did, a car drove past me, just inches to my right, and I stumbled and fell to the blacktop. My mind couldn't process events as quickly as they unfolded around me, but as I got back to my feet I realized that I had been tripped by a pair of legs protruding out from under the car as it continued moving. There were shouts around me now, of outrage and pain and warning. The car had people, hikers, swarming all over it. Some were holding onto it, evidently trying to drag it to a stop. Some were crawling onto it, trying to get into the windows to reach the brakes or the ignition or the gear shift, anything to stop it. And some were being dragged along under it, like the legs that had tripped me. There was a young woman hanging from the front hood, who seemed to be being run over by the front wheels. I looked back down the street behind the car and saw a wide swath cut through the hiker parade, with people lying on the ground here and there.

Turning back to the car I realized that it had finally been brought to a stop. Male hikers were actually lifting the car off the ground, and others were helping people who had been under the car to get out. I was in some kind of shock, but my nursing instinct kicked in, and I rushed over to assist a woman who had just gotten to her feet. She looked dazed but was standing, and I took her gently by the arm and led her over to the curb where she could sit down and I could assess her injuries. She had a large wound on her lower leg, but once I realized that it wasn't actively bleeding I turned my attention to her breathing, which was shallow and labored. "Hi, I'm Blue Tortoise," I said, my voice sounding strange to my own ears, calm and normal, no match for my internal emotions. "I'm an RN. How do you feel?"

She was about my own age, I saw, and she looked pretty calm herself. "I think I might have broken some ribs," she said. "I heard them crack when the car ran over me, and it hurts to take a deep breath. And my leg hurts."

"Ok, can you just take nice slow breaths with me?" I asked. Her color was good and she didn't seem to be in imminent danger. I just wanted to keep her calm and her breathing slow and shallow until help arrived. I couldn't tell how many other people were hurt, or how badly, or where this woman would rank on the triage priority list. I assured her that I would stay with her until the paramedics got to her. I asked her to sit up straight and not panic or move around too much. She was a wonderful and cooperative patient, and we sat calmly on the curb together and waited in the middle of chaos. Time was moving strangely, and it seemed we sat there for hours although I suppose it was really only a few minutes. All of the small town's resources had been out for the parade, so there were police officers on site within minutes and ambulances shortly afterward. I stayed with my lady, talking trail talk, while I tried to attract the attention of the medical personnel arriving on the scene, trying to get someone to come over to us, NOW, without alarming her with my sense of urgency. An EMT responded to my furtive gestures and approached us.

"Are you injured?" he asked me, looking at my knees, scraped from my fall to the pavement.

"Not me, her," I said. "Possible broken ribs."

He knelt beside her, and I gave way, moving over and standing up, stopping as I did so to kiss her forehead. I couldn't say why I did that. I felt somewhere in between nurse and friend in my relationship with this stranger, oddly protective of her, and proud of her stoicism. My kiss was my blessing, I supposed. They had a stretcher which she compliantly sat on while they put the required cervical collar around her neck and looked at her leg. "Compound fracture," I heard one of them say, and I was shocked. It had just looked like a gash to me, but admittedly I hadn't looked at it closely, just enough to make sure it wasn't bleeding profusely, then I had shifted my attention to her possible rib fractures. They asked her to lie back on the stretcher and, again cooperatively, she tried, but the pain in her chest prevented her from being able to do so, and they immediately changed the plan to allow her to sit upright on the edge of the stretcher instead.

A police officer came along and asked all of us bystanders to please clear the street to allow emergency vehicles to have access to the injured. "Oh, I'm a bystander now. Thank God," I thought, moving over to the sidewalk. Suddenly remembering the camera in my pocket, I pulled it out and took pictures of the scene all around me, the ambulances up and down the street with hikers in each one. I turned to look at the car that had caused the whole scene, still parked in the middle of the street. The driver, an elderly gentleman, was sitting sideways in the driver's seat, his feet on the pavement, his head in his hands. I took a picture of him. He was all alone, as all the attention was on the injured. I started to walk down the sidewalk as I heard the drone of helicopters overhead. Mike! I thought. He was probably worried, not knowing if I was injured or not. I dialed his number and was surprised that he knew nothing of the events on the parade route. How could he not know? Hadn't this made the news? Wasn't everyone talking about it? Couldn't he hear the sirens and the helicopters? I realized, shocked, that all of the drama had probably taken place in less than 15 minutes, and the news hadn't had time to filter even down the street yet. I told him, roughly, what had happened, then hung up and started toward him. Suddenly, I wanted nothing more than to get to him, to get in his arms, to be held. I walked quickly down the sidewalk. Two blocks from the accident site people were still lining the parade route, squirt guns in hand, laughing and chattering. It seemed unreal, obscene, but I realized that word of what had happened hadn't even trickled this far yet. I walked faster, nearly running into the park, the craft show, our booth, and Mike's arms, where I finally lost it and started sobbing.

Summer 2016

Now, three years later, as I look back on the hiker parade, I find that I don't really remember it in the same way that I remember the other parts of my hike. I remember the parts that I told people about, what I wrote in my journal that night, and the things I took pictures of. My memories of the events themselves are static in my mind, like a series of still photos. Sometimes I think that I am actually remembering only the things I photographed, but I do have images in my mind that don't match any of the pictures I took.

It could have been worse. I suppose the fact that the car was going so slowly minimized the injuries. The final tally was that three people were airlifted out by helicopter, and another twelve went by ambulance to local hospitals. They estimated 30 to 40 people treated on the scene, although that seems a little high to me, and I suppose most of them were people who had scraped themselves up leaping out of the path of the car. No one died, and within just a few days all were out of the hospital. I have never heard a good reason given for the driver driving down the parade route or why he was unable to stop the car on his own. It was stopped by a hiker crawling into the open window and pulling the keys from the ignition. "Medical emergency" was blamed in the newspaper accounts I read later. The driver hadn't looked to be having an emergency to me, but he did look completely befuddled and confounded. My own theory is that he mistakenly pulled into the parade route, hit his gas instead of the brake, and in shock didn't react quickly enough. I could be wrong.

My own response to the incident is what befuddles and confounds me. It seems out of proportion to what happened. I wasn't injured, no one died, and everyone did recover. Still, later that day sitting back in my booth at the craft fair, a car drove slowly through the craft fair grounds, and I panicked. I froze in place, heart pounding, unable to catch my breath. I wanted to scream to everyone to get out of the way, and I wanted to run away, but I could neither speak nor move in terror, even after I realized that it was just another vendor pulling up to his booth to restock his wares. It even happened after my return home after my hike. Much later, in a parking lot my first week home when a car drove slowly past me towards a parking spot, I again seized up, my heart racing and pounding in my own ears, my body frozen between fight and flight. And then again at an Atlanta Braves baseball game, walking toward Turner Field, in the middle of a crowd of fans, suddenly I was unable to catch my breath. My pulse was pounding and racing, but I was able to move this time and jumped out of the crowd of people to the safety of a lamp post which I grabbed and held onto. As my breathing slowed I realized that it was much like the parade had been, a crowd of happy people all walking in the same direction at the same time, festivity in the air.

It was all people on the trail talked about for a day or two, but very soon, with the news that all the injured were going to be okay, it seemed to be over. I have felt guilty over my response to it, which was mild depression and panic attacks, because I felt I had no right to those emotions. I had not been injured. I was okay, and so was everyone else, so why did it continue to haunt me for so long afterward? Even now, three years later, my hands shook as I wrote this description of the parade and its aftermath. Surely it wasn't a serious enough event to warrant my reaction.

It shook me up, badly. It was strike one.

After the parade, Trail Days continued. The talent show went on as planned. There was a difference, a low humming energy, and every conversation started with "Did you hear....." but the scheduled events went on. I felt like I had been kicked in the stomach and like life had gone from color to black and white, but I was already feeling like I had no right to be so upset about it if no one else was, so I tried to continue as usual, too. My hiker appetite was gone, and town food held no appeal, but Mike and I went to the contra dance that we had been looking forward to that evening. Once we got there, I couldn't dance, though. My body felt too heavy and I couldn't imagine skipping and twirling across the floor. Mike was wonderfully supportive and understanding, as is usual for him, although I'm sure he also wondered why I was dealing with it so poorly.

On Sunday morning we drove to nearby Abingdon, Virginia to go to mass. Kneeling in the pew before mass started, I thanked God that I hadn't been injured. Then I felt guilty for being grateful. If I was grateful for the path the car took, missing me by so little, didn't that mean that I was glad it ran over other people instead of me? Why shouldn't it have hit me? How could I reconcile being grateful that I wasn't injured when it meant that someone a couple feet away from me was injured instead? It all seemed so arbitrary.

After mass we went back to Trail Days for the last day of the craft show. The weather alternated between sunny skies and thundering rain. Attendance was sparse, so we decided to take down our booth a little early. I had hiking errands to do to get ready for the next leg of my hike and an empty food bag to fill. There was still no sign of Songbird, but their car was gone, so we could only assume they had left. I didn't know why she didn't tell me she was leaving, but with my churning emotions over the accident, I didn't take time to ponder it as I might have otherwise. We drove back to Erwin, to the same motel that we had left three days earlier, and checked in, Mike and me this time, instead of Songbird and me. I would be hiking alone again.

Spivey Gap to Erwin, Tennessee
May 20, 2013

Mike had an idea for me to be able to slackpack my
first day back on the trail, which was a good one and I was
grateful that he thought of it. After we checked out of our
motel in the morning and had a hot breakfast, he drove me
to the hostel in Erwin called Uncle Johnny's. It sat right on
the trail itself, where it crossed a road. We reserved my
bunk for the night and left most of my pack's contents
there, while I carried just the few things I needed for a
dayhike on my back. We then drove to Spivey Gap where I
had gotten off the trail to walk into town, and I said
goodbye to Mike and headed north on the trail, toward
Erwin. It was about ten miles to the hostel, a good day's
hike with the late start. It wasn't hard to decide what to
pray about for the day. I offered the day's hike for
everyone who was injured during the parade, for the driver,
and for my own peace of mind.

I didn't feel much like hiking when I started. It felt
wrong, my stride felt off, I was stiff and awkward and had
trouble finding a rhythm as I walked. This wasn't really
unusual after nearly four days off the trail. But the trail
itself was lovely. The air was cool and the scenery was

sweetly beautiful—lots of the rhododendrons that I loved, now covered with buds. A sparkling little stream followed the trail, keeping me company as I walked along, occasionally breaking out into little waterfalls. Even the trail itself was soft, the ground covered with a thick layer of leaves. It was like walking on gym mats. It seemed like all of nature was trying to make it easy for me to get back into the rhythm of hiking. The trail gently and tenderly welcomed me back.

With only ten miles to go, such little weight on my back, and such gentle terrain to hike, I slowed my already slow pace down to a crawl. I literally strolled, stopping to look at everything that caught my interest. It was so quiet. I didn't see any other thru-hikers all day and only a pair of sobo section hikers. I had the whole day with just my own thoughts, and I needed it. Every time I thought about the parade I was overcome with fatigue. My feet suddenly felt like they weighed 30 pounds each, too heavy to lift.

But I walked on in the quiet and peace and beauty of nature. Eventually the trail seemed to decide it had babied me long enough and once again became hard, rocky, rooty, and steep. It was time to pay attention to my footing again and get walking. I had found my rhythm and headed down the trail toward Erwin.

I reached the hostel, took a shower, and put my hiking clothes in the washer. It had been terribly humid during the day and I had sweated profusely. Humidity was a new aspect to hiking. The nights were definitely warmer, which was a great improvement over all the many nights I had shivered and yearned for morning, but evidently I was to pay for comfortable nights with hot sweaty days.

The hostel also had a different atmosphere than I was used to. Normally at a hostel all the customers were hikers, meaning that they were all my friends, and we all immediately had something very personal and important in common. It was different at Uncle Johnny's. The thru-hikers had long since passed through, of course, but I had been enjoying the company of all the section hikers I had camped with also. However this hostel also served bicyclists and even people traveling by canoe, located as it was on the Nolichucky River. There were a few section hikers there, but a large group of bikers, who evidently didn't believe they had to be friendly to hikers. I carried my supper to the picnic tables and sat down at a table of people, prepared for the friendly greeting and questions with which hikers started every conversation. No one at the table looked at me or acknowledged my presence in any way, continuing their own conversations with each other instead.

"Hi," I said. "How you doing? I'm hiking, trail name Blue Tortoise." If my feelings hadn't been hurt by it, it would have been comical, as they looked at me for just the barest fraction of an instant and then quickly away, as if they hadn't seen me, and continued their conversations. I felt invisible and wondered if anyone would say anything if I jumped up on the table and started dancing the Highland Fling. "Anybody have change for the drink machine?" Again no response. Maybe I really was invisible. Maybe I had died in Damascus and no one could see me and that's why everything had seemed so strange for the last three days.

I gave up and strolled over to another part of the compound and sat down on a bench in tears. A section hiker named Canada Dry came over and we had, finally, a regular hiking conversation. Based solely on that, the fact that he could see me and hear me, made me decide that life was going on, and I still had a trail to hike. He had change for the drink machine. I drank a Mello Yello and went to bed, determined to pull myself together on the next day's hike.

Erwin, Tennessee to Beauty Spot Gap
May 21, 2013

STRIKE TWO

I woke in the morning refreshed after a night in the bunk, convinced that my negative feelings of the night before had been an illusion, a hangover from the trauma of the hiker parade at Trail Days. I am a natural optimist, and I felt ready to resume my life on the trail with hope and joy. It was a new day and a beautiful one. I felt that a new chapter of my hike was about to begin, and I resolved to welcome it with open mind, heart, and arms.

I left Uncle Johnny's and walked down the road and across the bridge over the Nolichucky River, marked with the white blazes that I had been following for almost two months. Once across the bridge, the trail re-entered the woods, where I felt comfortable, safe, and at home. I came into a clearing and walked across a set of railroad tracks, which reminded me of Mike, a train fan. I was blessed to have him in my corner, supporting me and my hike. I gave God thanks for him like I did every day, as I walked back into the cool shade of the forest. I reflected how the trees were always my friends, always on my side whatever the weather. In the Smokies they had protected me from the worst of the howling wind, and I had missed them when I came out on the trail above the tree line and had to deal with the force of the wind. Now in the warmth of early summer I hastened into their coolness and shade for protection from the sun. I thanked God for the trees and realized I had an incredible amount of things to be grateful for. I resolved to spend this day's hike in gratitude, not supplication. As I walked I thought of all the blessings I had enjoyed my whole life and gave Him praise and glory and love for them as I tried to list them all. It made for a nice day as pleasant memories were replayed over and over in my mind.

The terrain was not strenuous, although it was a gentle uphill grade all day. My plan for the day was to hike twelve miles to a campsite called Beauty Spot Gap. I might have preferred to stop for the night at a shelter, where I would be more likely to find other hikers, but there were no shelters conveniently located for a stop that night. The first one was only five miles from Erwin, and the next one was 18 miles. Beauty Spot Gap, at twelve miles, was just the right distance for me to hike, and situated right before Unaka Mountain, which at 5,180 feet I wasn't eager to climb at the end of a long day. Better to face it in the morning when I was fresh.

It grew warm as the day wore on, and then hot, with the humidity a constant, oppressive presence. The gentle uphill grade began to seem less gentle. My pack was full with five days worth of food, and I hadn't had a fully packed weight on my back since before Trail Days. I felt sluggish and began to struggle, and it became harder to find things to be grateful for, but I did keep trying. I only met a couple of other hikers along the way, sobo section hikers who barely spared a glance at me as we passed on the trail. It was so different from the beginning of my hike when I was with thru-hikers who were all so excited to be there and so helpful and friendly with each other.

I was sweating so heavily I began to wonder if I was drinking enough water to stay hydrated as my head began to hurt and my mouth became dry. I chugged what was left in my water bottle and walked on. I have never been able to handle heat well and had actually passed out from becoming overheated a couple of times in my teenage years. It hadn't happened in years, mainly (I supposed) because I was old enough to take better care of myself and not allow myself to become overheated. I wondered what would happen if I fainted on the trail. The thing I remembered most about having passed out from heat was the overpowering headache I had felt just before I blacked out. My head hurt, but not like that, so I powered on.

I met a pair of hikers coming down from the peak of Beauty Spot as I was walking up at the end of the day. "There's trail magic at the top!" they informed me. "Some locals have set up a camp for the night, and they've got hot dogs and cold drinks for hikers coming through."

"Just what I need! Thank you!" I told them as I quickened my pace a little, buoyed by the possibility of a drink that wasn't body temperature. I pushed on along the uphill trail and finally came out on Beauty Spot, which was a pretty little bald, a clearing in the forest. At first I didn't see any sign of trail magic as I walked across the bald. Finally, there ahead, was a tent set up, with a table and a couple of chairs. There were a few hikers lounging in the chairs and on the ground. I wasn't sure though, if it was trail magic or a private picnic among friends. It just didn't have the look of trail magic, somehow, it seemed private. I wasn't sure what I should say when I reached the little encampment. If I asked if it was trail magic, and it wasn't, was that rude, to be horning in on a family outing? There's a word for it in hiker lingo. It's called yogi-ing, which means to somehow wheedle food out of non-hikers, to coerce them into giving you some of their picnic supplies.

It's named after Yogi Bear, famous for appropriating picnic baskets in Jellystone Park. If you can get a non-hiker to give you food or other supplies without actually asking for them, that's a successful yogi. If the people on Beauty Spot were not offering trail magic and I assumed they were, then I was inviting myself to their picnic, which was a type of yogi. Surely if they were trail angels offering magic they would tell me so as I passed through. So I greeted them all in a friendly manner when I reached their encampment, but I didn't make a move toward the food table. As I looked at it, I realized that it was empty anyway, just a few loose buns still in a bag with no sign of either hot dogs or cold drinks. I stood around for a few minutes, feeling increasingly uncomfortable as I tried to make conversation. Maybe it *was* a private party, I thought, because if I had come too late to the trail magic, wouldn't one of the trail angels have said so? "Oh, I'm sorry, you just missed the trail magic! We just ran out of hot dogs," I would have expected to hear, but no one spoke up, so after a few awkward moments I took my leave, wishing them a good evening as I walked down the hillside toward the campsite at the bottom of the bald.

There was a gravel forest service road, allowing locals access to the bald for picnics and outings. I found the campsite in the trees at the side of the road, identifiable by a fire ring with a log pulled up beside it. I sat on the log, exhausted, fatigued, aching all over, with a pounding headache, covered in sweat. Immediately the North Carolina bugs found me and swarmed my face and skin, biting, buzzing, and flying up into my nostrils. There were no other hikers at the campsite, and I began to hope someone would come along to share this isolated spot with me.

I went to the water source, which was a little streambed. I filled my water bottle and dumped the entire liter straight over my head. It was cold and made me feel slightly human. "Who needs ice?" I said to myself. I filled the bottle again, filtered it, and drank it straight down. Better yet. I filled both bottles with filtered water and went back to the fire ring. What I needed was a smoky fire, not a hot one, to keep the bugs from devouring me, so I gathered a little firewood and a lot of green pine needles. Once the fire was burning I laid the pine needles on the top and positioned myself directly in the path of the smoke, turning my back to keep it out of my face. Voila, no more bugs. Sitting on the log in the smoke, I fixed and ate my supper and drank another liter of water. My mood now greatly improved and my headache gone, I cleaned my Jetboil stove and found a tree to hang my food bag, high out of the reach of bears. I brushed my teeth and wiped my face and hands with a wet bandana and was just about to sit back down on the log in the smoke when I heard the low distant rumble of thunder. "Of course it's going to rain," I thought. "Why *wouldn't* it rain?" Remembering my theme for the day of gratitude and looking for blessings I mumbled to myself, "Well at least the rain will cool things down. And get rid of the bugs."

I pulled the tarp and hammock from the Green Monster and quickly selected two trees the correct distance apart, measured by standing between them extending a hiking pole in each hand. The right trees would be just beyond the tip of each pole, or about twelve feet apart. I hung the tarp first, then the hammock under it. I had just finished securing the pack itself and its contents when the first few fat drops of rain plopped onto the tarp. I crawled into the hammock and zipped the bug net up behind me, then nearly jumped out of my skin as the world lit up at the exact moment a bolt of thunder crashed with a sound like cymbals. "Wow, that was close," I thought, a bit uneasy. Normally I like storms, even thunder storms. Streaks of lightning against a dark sky, booming thunder, pounding rain, and wind are exciting, exotic, carrying a hint of danger while at the same time being *almost* completely safe. It is the *almost* that makes them exciting, I think, the knowledge that they are wild and unpredictable, as well as beautiful and powerful. I laughed at myself for having jumped at the sound and settled back into the hammock. It was just getting dark but it didn't matter because I couldn't see anything from inside despite the transparent bug net, because of the tarp, which I had pitched low to the ground and close to the hammock to keep out the rain.

I had just relaxed when it happened again. A flash of light bright enough to hurt my eyes, simultaneous with a clap of thunder too loud and sharp to call rumbling, which I suddenly decided was my favorite kind of thunder. I didn't like this cracking kind of thunder at all. Before I had a chance to reflect on this, all hell broke loose in the woods around me. The flashes of lightning and cracks of thunder became continuous, a kind of storm I had never seen before. Instead of being just an occasional burst of lightning, this was a single bolt of lightning that only rarely blinked off, and instead of a periodic clap of thunder, there was a single, continuous crashing coming from somewhere above me. God wasn't bowling, as I had been told as a child, He was demolishing entire cities. In the rare moments of silence between the crashes from Heaven I could hear the wind, screaming, moaning, whistling, as if all the demons had been unleashed at once and were running screaming laps around Beauty Spot Gap. The sound was so eerie and unnerving I was actually glad when the crashing of the thunder sounded again, to drown out the sound of the wind. In the continual lightning I could see clearly when my tarp pulled loose from the ground where I had staked it, and went whipping and swirling over my head. Without the tarp to cover me, I could see the treetops high above me in a bizarre and macabre dance, bending this way and that, seemingly writhing in pain. The driving rain was able to come into my hammock without the tarp, but I was worried less about staying dry than about blocking the sight of those poor tortured trees from my vision, as I got out of the hammock to snatch at the tarp, darting and taunting me from the branches of the tree. I grabbed it and reattached it as best I could, then darted back into the meager shelter of a nylon hammock. I ended up having to keep one hand out of the hammock to hold onto one corner of the tarp that I had been unable to reattach in the whipping wind.

"Pray.....pray," my heart told my mind. My body was paralyzed by fear and tension, but my heart and my mind did their best to reconnect with the only One who could rescue me from this maelstrom. I asked Him for protection, for courage, and for the faith to trust Him in the storm. I ran through as many of the Psalms as I could recall, all of the parts referencing God as my shelter, my stronghold, my ever-present help in times of danger. I prayed the Our Father, the Glory Be, the Hail Mary. I thanked Him for all the times in my life when He had protected me when I didn't even know I was in danger. I asked, pleaded, begged, for comfort. As the storm raged on my prayers lost their focus, devolved, and became simply, "Oh please, oh please, pleasepleasepleasepleaseplease."

I wasn't used to panic, or terror. As a naturally calm person, as a mother of four, and as a nurse who had been involved in many stressful, emergency situations, I had always been able to handle calamity with equanimity. Even the moment of "panic" in Damascus, when a car drove through the craft fair after the parade, had been a biological event, a surge of adrenaline through my body in response to a stimulus. This was uncharted ground for me—pure, unadulterated, blind terror.

I tried to regroup. I tried to remind myself that my chances of actually dying were slim. What were the odds that I would actually be struck by lightning or that a tree would fall on me or that the wind would whisk me up into the air and set me down on a distant mountain peak? What if I died in my hammock, maybe of a heart attack, which seemed a definite possibility? How long would it be before my body was found? Would it be when a hiker passed through and noticed the smell? Would it ruin the hammock? Would a bear find my remains before a hiker did? Bears had been known to eat human carcasses.

That line of thought wasn't helping. I returned to prayer. I had no concept of time, but the storm seemed to have been raging forever and showed no signs of abating. "God help me!" I begged. "Help me! I'm scared! I know You could stop this storm! Why aren't You helping me? *I'm scared!*" Anger was beginning to creep into the already crowded swirl of emotion in my brain. What could I do to help myself? I pulled my phone out of my pocket. Unbelievably, I had cell service. I was on a forest service gravel road. That meant that vehicles could get here. I could get out! Maybe God wanted me to help myself, I reasoned.

I wouldn't be able to talk on the phone because the sound of the storm was too loud, but I could text. I sent a text to St. Mike, my hands shaking so violently from fear that it was difficult to type even short messages. He responded immediately. It gave me a thin, white-knuckled grip on reality to be able to communicate with someone who communicated back. He reassured me that he could see the storm on radar, exactly over where I was, and that it would pass in another hour or so. *"An HOUR??"* I typed, my nerves frayed. "I can't stay out here another hour!" I checked my guidebook and got the phone number for the nearest hostel. "Call it," I typed. "Ask them if they will drive out to Beauty Spot Gap and pick me up. Please."

Within minutes he was back. The hostel owner wouldn't venture out in the storm to get me. They were 45 minutes away by car, it was dark and stormy, it was late, and the storm would be nearly over by the time they got here. I was devastated. I couldn't blame them, but I was devastated. We continued texting back and forth. I loved him, I missed him, I wished he was here beside me. My body ached from the tension of being held rigid by fear. My hand, still holding the corner of the tarp, was numb. I reluctantly let Mike go, knowing he was worried about me, but knowing at the same time that he had no real idea of how frightening it was here in the eye of the storm.

I'm embarrassed to admit it now, but after I said goodbye to Mike, I dialed 911. I don't know what I expected. I was just so scared. The emergency operator was calm but firm, at least as much as I could hear between the cracks of thunder and howls of wind. No, they had no personnel to send to Beauty Spot Gap. They were spread thin, dealing with flooding in town. The best thing for me to do was hunker down and wait out the storm. I was not injured, not in need of rescue. She had to get off the line because there were actual emergency calls coming in.

The storm raged on for awhile, probably about the hour that Mike had predicted, but eventually it did begin to lessen. I was exhausted: physically, emotionally, mentally, and spiritually spent. I got out of the hammock to tie down the corner of tarp I had been holding for the last few hours. "What the hell just happened?" I asked myself. I was angry. Angry at God for not helping me and angry at myself that I had turned from God to a phone for help. Where was my faith? That line of thought ushered shame into my emotional stew. It was all too much to deal with, and as my body relaxed after hours of tension and rigidity, my mind gave up trying to puzzle it all out, and I fell into a deep, dreamless sleep.

Beauty Spot Gap to Iron Mountain Gap
May 22, 2013

My eyes flickered open, shut, and then stayed open. It was daylight, the soft morning light filtered through my green tarp. I could see the tarp clearly through the bug net, and it was still. All was quiet, except for the twittering of little morning birds somewhere in the tree over my head. I was safe.

I stretched, my hammock moving gently with the extension of my arms and legs. I unzipped the bug net and stepped out from under the tarp onto the damp ground. I half expected to see a post-apocalyptic world, a lunar landscape, after the night's drama. Instead I found the world much as I had left it when I had entered the hammock some ten hours earlier, save for a few tree branches scattered around the gap. I felt sluggish, slow, both mentally and physically. I broke camp. My food bag was miraculously still hanging from the tree where I had tied it. My pack and boots were muddy and my tarp was wet, but this was nothing I hadn't dealt with many times, and I mechanically wiped things down with the chamois cloth as I reloaded the Green Monster.

I still felt numb as I started the climb up Unaka Mountain. I tried to mentally process my ordeal and assign some meaning to the events, but they seemed slippery and hard to grasp. Maybe it had just been a storm, and I had just been frightened, and I should just leave it there and continue with my hike. Maybe it had been a spiritual epiphany that I needed to dissect. But if that was it, the lesson seemed to be that God would not answer me when I called out to Him. Did He not hear me, or did He not care? This was an uncomfortable line of thinking, so I moved on. Maybe the whole event had been a test of my faith. If that was the case, I had failed. I couldn't cope with any of these scenarios, so I dismissed them all and hiked on. I found it hard to pray as I usually did when starting a day's hike, so I murmured a simple, "God help me. God forgive me. God show me," and walked on.

It was a reasonably strenuous hike up the mountain, and for once I was grateful for it, because it gave me something to focus on besides my swirling thoughts and emotions. When I reached the top I was rewarded with a dense spruce forest, a new type of terrain. It was charming, the ground underneath soft with a thick mat of pine needles, the air fresh with their scent. I had to pay close attention to the white blazes painted on the trees as the trail was not obvious through the maze of trees. It was warming up considerably as I left the evergreen forest and started down the mountain. The humidity returned with a vengeance and so did the infuriating little bugs. I found it hard to hike with any rhythm as I had to try to swat the bugs away from my face continually. With a hiking pole in each hand, it was awkward and ineffective. Sweat was dripping from my chin when I reached the bottom of the mountain.

I heard again the low rumble of thunder as raindrops began to lightly land on my face. "Oh, swell," I thought as I walked on. The rain was light and cool and felt good, and I didn't bother to pull my rain jacket out of my pack. The bugs disappeared as suddenly as they had appeared. About five and a half miles into the day's hike I came across a little shelter, Cherry Gap Shelter, and decided to duck into it to wait out the rain. It was lunch time anyway, and I was out of water. There were two hikers already in the shelter, both young men. One was lying on his sleeping bag, perhaps asleep, and the other was sitting hunched over in a corner, reading a book. "Hey there," I said. "Listen to that thunder! Do you think we're in for another storm like we had last night?"

Neither one looked at me, but the one with the book grunted something unintelligible. Suddenly I felt utterly bereft. Where was the famous hiking community? Why wouldn't these people look at me or talk to me? I had people at home who loved me and missed me, who cared for me. No one out here knew or cared if I was alone in the storm or if I was afraid. What was I doing out here, where my children could only reach me via text message, and my grandchildren grew older without me? I went to the stream behind the shelter and gathered and filtered two liters of water, then went back to the shelter with my sullen shelter-mates to eat my cheese and crackers and plan my escape. I wanted out, more than I had ever wanted anything. I wanted to get away from storms and mud and dirt and bugs and rain. I wanted to go someplace where people knew me and cared about me, someplace where if I were to die in a hammock my body wouldn't be left to be eaten by bears. I checked my phone and, amazingly, still had service. I called the closest hostel, the one St. Mike had called for me the previous night, the Greasy Creek Friendly, to see if there was any chance of a shuttle anywhere. Connie, the owner, told me that there was a free shuttle leaving Iron Mountain Gap in an hour, going to town for dinner, if I was interested. Without hesitation I told her I would be there, and hung up. I was three miles from Iron Mountain Gap according to my guidebook, and I had never walked three

miles in an hour. My top speed so far on the trail had been
two miles an hour. I didn't care, I was going to be on that
shuttle, so I packed up and took off at a near run. The three
miles of trail were perfect for trail running, mostly level
and wide with few loose rocks. I skimmed over the ground
with a light heart, pack bouncing on my back and poles
gripped in my hands. I came out at the road crossing at
Iron Mountain Gap in one hour and ten minutes, and there
was an ancient Bronco waiting. A cute, bubbly blonde
came out from behind the wheel. "Are you Blue Tortoise?
I'm Connie. Let's get to town before the sky falls in on
us!"

I glanced at the sky, roiling with black clouds, which I
hadn't even noticed in my single-minded determination to
get to the gap. I took the pack off my back and Connie
tossed it into the back seat and we both climbed in. She
turned the key and the engine roared to life. With a
grinding of the gears she pulled out on the road, and we
were on our way to town, which, I found out, was Johnson
City, Tennessee. "I hope you don't mind," she said, "But
I've got several stops to make. I need to go to Walmart and
get some groceries and….."

She continued her list, enumerating the errands she
needed to do, and finished with, "And I was going to stop

for dinner. How do you like Zaxby's? They have really good chicken, and the salads are pretty good, and they're not too expensive…" Connie was a talker, with a cute, girlish voice and a blonde ponytail. Now that I was close to her, I could see that she was older than she first appeared, probably close to my own age, but with an energy and a giggle that made her seem years younger. By the time we reached the edge of Johnson City I knew all about her, and her ex-husband and the hostel that she called "Greasy Creek Friendly" because, she said, "We're friendly, not hostile!" This was followed by the giggle that told me how much she enjoyed the play on words.

Before we reached Johnson City the sky did indeed fall as she had predicted. The rain fell so hard that visibility was reduced to mere feet, and she pulled the Bronco off the road under an overpass which meant that we could hear one another again without the pounding of rain on the hood of the car. This in turn meant that she could talk again. She turned to face me and saw the Miraculous Medal around my neck. "Oh, I see you're Catholic," she started with. "I'm a Messianic Jew, and…." Then she went off on a history of her religious affiliations, which included all the grievances she had with the Catholic Church, all told in a matter-of-fact way, as though they were indeed facts and not opinions and misrepresentations. "But I like everybody," she concluded with, "and I know that everybody is on their own spiritual journey and has to find their own way to God and sometimes those ways are different than mine and...." she continued, obviously not concluding yet. I had never had a non-Catholic be quite so honest with me about their objections to the Catholic Church, and found that I quite liked her lack of guile. With Connie, what you see is what you get, and she is so likeable and honest that it's impossible to be offended by what she says. Besides, she meant it when she said that she liked and respected everyone. I was fascinated by the conversation. She made no attempt to convert me or convince me of the error of my ways, she just stated her beliefs and went on. It was all so refreshing and light-hearted and ...different, than any other conversation I had ever been part of.

The rain eventually let up a little, and we drove into Johnson City and did her errands. We went to dinner, and by the time we were on the ride back to Greasy Creek I knew all about her difficult next-door neighbor who continually sabotaged her hostel, because he didn't like the steady stream of hikers ensconced there, and others in her community who whispered that "every time you see Connie she's with a different man! And they're all younger than her and have long hair and beards besides!" We laughed and I found that I liked Connie more and more all the time.

The conversation eventually got around to me and my hiking experience. I told her about the incident at Trail Days and the frightening storm the night before. I told her that I was lonely and having a crisis of confidence, and that I was considering leaving the trail, quitting, and going home. She was sympathetic, but practical. "I thought you would try to talk me into staying on the trail," I told her. "I would have thought that since the trail is such a big part of your life you would think getting off is always a mistake."

"I don't know if it would be a mistake for you to leave the trail or not," she said quite logically. "Maybe you've learned what you needed to learn already. Maybe you're done. But maybe you're not, and I don't think you know yet either. One thing I do know is that you should never quit the trail on a bad day. Don't make a permanent decision based on a frame of mind that might turn out to be temporary. Take a day or two first. Take a zero tomorrow, I think it's going to rain, anyway. Hang out with the hikers at the house. Maybe after some time has passed you'll feel differently." That made a lot of sense. I could see the logic in it, even in my confused state. I would sit on my decision for 24 hours.

We left the interstate to go back to her hostel. We rode on a highway for quite a while then turned onto a country road. I thought we had to be close then, but we kept going and eventually turned onto a gravel road and started up a steep incline. *Now,* I thought, we must be almost there, this little road can't go much further. But it did, and so did we. The houses thinned out, and eventually, at the very end of the dirt road, she pulled to a stop in front of a little house that looked like a strong wind might blow it down. And yet there was something homey and friendly about it, the front porch filled with chairs, a clothesline hung with hikers' tarps stretched between the porch rails. It looked great to me.

Connie instructed me to go around to the back door and take off my boots in the mud room and leave my pack and poles there, then go immediately to the bathroom and wash my hands. I was to see this ritual repeated with every new hiker that arrived. The norovirus was still around, and Connie was doing her best to keep her hikers healthy. Gear stowed and hands washed, I went into the living room/dining room/ kitchen that constituted the bulk of the little house. This was Connie's home as well as her hostel. Unlike most hostels which have an area for hikers which is separate from the owner's living quarters, Connie lived here, with the hikers. We actually came into her home for our brief respite from the trail.

The inside of the house looked much like the outside: a little worn, humble and in need of repair, but welcoming and comfortable. And the house was like its owner: simple, honest, unadorned, without pretense, and utterly charming. There were a few other hikers already there and two that I recognized. One was Sunshine, whom I had met the first week of my hike while I was slackpacking out of the Hiker Hostel. She still had her little dog, Flycatcher, and now had her boyfriend Sam with her, too. He wasn't hiking, but was riding his motorcycle as near to the trail as he could, meeting her at road crossings, taking her to hostels to spend the night, and driving her back to the trail in the mornings. She was truly enjoying her extended slackpack while Sam was on a two week vacation from his job. The other was a photographer, Artgirl, a young woman who photographed the trail and made beautiful prints that she sold at craft fairs. Mike and I had met her the year before at a craft show in Abingdon, Virginia, when she was set up next to us. There was also a young man sick with the norovirus who kept his distance from the rest of us, looking up wretchedly when I said hello. They were a jovial group, besides the sick hiker, warm and friendly, and a balm to my wounded soul.

Connie showed me my bed in the back bedroom, a small room entirely taken up by three twin beds. There was a shed in the back yard that Connie had decked out as a bunkhouse, and even a daybed on the front porch that had a young couple staying on it. I showered, and Connie did my laundry, and then we joined the group around the table, swapping trail stories. Connie was very entertaining. When one of the hikers mispronounced the word "Unaka," she recited a poem she had written to help people remember the correct pronunciation. It started out: "You naked on Unaka? Nay, nay, nay!" Several verses later we were all convulsed with laughter. It was like the old days on the trail, with a dining table in place of a campfire, but the gentle and welcoming hiker spirit was present.

I went to sleep in the twin bed that night easier in mind and heart, but I knew I had a decision to make. I didn't know what I was going to do, and I was glad I didn't have to decide yet.

Greasy Creek Friendly
May 23-24, 2013

STRIKE THREE

The rain seemed to be moving out, and most of the hikers left in the morning, eager to be back on the trail. Sunshine and Sam stayed on, as well as Artgirl and me. The morning passed gently. Connie made us breakfast, and we enjoyed the stories about her crazy, hiker-hating neighbor (she showed us signs he had put up in her yard over the years, saying things like "Hostel closed due to bedbugs.") Around midmorning I retired to my bedroom, planning on doing some reading or maybe taking a nap, when my phone rang. It was my sister, Pat.

"I'm so glad I got you," she said, her voice thin and tight. "Mom died this morning."

"What? What? How, I mean what happened?"

"She made her breakfast and coffee as usual and sat down at the table with the newspaper. I turned to walk into the living room, and a minute later I heard her coffee cup hit the floor. I went back to help her clean it up, and she was...gone. As quick as that."

My throat was tight. I was shocked, and didn't know what to say. What do you say when your mother dies? "I'll….come," I told Pat. "I can be there tomorrow, probably. I'm so sorry. Are you okay?" A foolish question. How was she supposed to be? She attempted to answer me, but her voice choked off. "I'll call Mike. I'll be there tomorrow. I love you." I heard a gargle from the other end of the phone, and the line went dead. I called Mike, who said he would arrive in the morning, and we could drive straight from East Tennessee or North Carolina, wherever we were, to northern Indiana, and be there that night. I clicked "end call" and sat down on the bed. A pain new to me seemed to well up from somewhere under my ribcage and convulse my whole body. How can you live to be 54 years old and then find an entirely new type of pain you never knew existed? I put my head in my hands and sobbed like a baby who has lost its mother, which is what I was. At that precise moment Connie came through the door. In a heartbeat she was beside me on the bed, arms around me. I laid my head on her shoulder, and she stroked my hair. I could barely get the words out, but I managed to tell her that my mother had died. She patted and murmured and rocked, while I gave myself over to grief. I would never get to see my mother again. I wouldn't get to go take care of her. I was glad, for her sake, that she never became the invalid she feared to be and had died suddenly in her own home, in her right mind, caring for herself. But I realized how much I was counting on having that final time to learn how to say goodbye and to somehow prove my love for her. That time was for my benefit, not hers, I realized, and seemed selfish. I felt cheated of my final time with her, but that was my time, not hers, and I wouldn't wish it upon her.

I sat up, wiping my eyes and nose, and thanked Connie for her concern. She squeezed my shoulder and walked back into the kitchen. Within minutes Sunshine and Artgirl were in the room, hugging and crying along with me. I welcomed their expressions of love. It didn't seem odd then that I known them for such a short time. They felt like family. They left me alone then, and I lay on my bed and poured my heart out to God. I could almost *feel* Him listening. I could almost sense Him saying to me, "Do you see now? It was all for you. I didn't want you to be alone when you found out. I wanted you to be in a warm and friendly place, and I wanted you to be able to go to her."

I realized that if it hadn't been for my experiences of the previous few days, I wouldn't have been at Greasy Creek.. More than that, I would have been out on the trail without cell service. Pat wouldn't have been able to reach me by phone. I might not have known until it was too late to attend the funeral. There were a lot of ifs, but the confusing pieces of the puzzle started to drop into place, and I could sense God's presence in my life, where it had always been, even when I doubted.

I don't remember much of what happened the rest of that day. Mike came and picked me up the next day. I thanked Connie, and we got in the Jeep and drove to Indiana. Mike drove 900 miles that day. We got to Indiana after dark, and the funeral was the very next day. All four of my adult children were there, even on such short notice, and from such distances. I was numb and in pain at the same time, and it didn't seem real. I saw cousins I hadn't seen in years and managed to smile and make conversation and eat the pot luck meal her church provided. Back at Mom's house later, it just felt wrong. She couldn't be gone, she was such a big presence. There was a hole-- in the house, in the family, in my heart-- and I didn't know how any of it could ever be filled.

Then, just like that, it was over, and I was on my way back to the trail. St. Mike drove me back, and in my numbed state I never considered getting off the trail and going home. What would I do at home? What does one do the week after one's mother dies, in a house they haven't seen in nearly two months? The trail was my home, my job, the place for me to go back to. Logically, I thought the trail would be a great place to grieve. I would have quiet and space and peace. I could walk and think about Mom and begin to heal, maybe, or at least make peace with the pain.

Iron Mountain Gap to Greasy Creek Gap
May 27, 2013

Mike drove me back to Iron Mountain Gap, where Connie had picked me up less than a week before, a lifetime ago. It was a gorgeous day, and the countryside was the prettiest I had ever seen. I hugged him and kissed him and thanked him, then put the Green Monster back on my back and turned to walk up the hill. Near the top I turned to look back down on the road from my high vantage point and watched the Jeep pull away, to go back down the long country road, back to the highway, then to the interstate, to begin the long drive home, without me. I wanted to run down the mountain, waving my arms and shouting for him to come back. But I didn't. Then I realized that I still had my phone, and I could call him even after he was out of sight, and he would come back. But I didn't. I wondered why in the world I was letting the best man in the world drive away from me, and what I was doing standing on a lonely mountainside by myself. But I turned around and trudged on up the steep trail.

It was about one PM when I started hiking, so I had set a modest goal for the day, just over six miles to the Clyde Smith Shelter. That was an easy distance for me, and I planned to walk slowly and think. But as I walked, nothing seemed easy. And more than that, nothing seemed interesting or adventurous or magical like the trail had always felt. I didn't feel like I was "hiking the Appalachian Trail," with all its mystique. I felt like I was dragging myself up a path. A path to what? I couldn't have answered that question, or what I was doing there, or where I was going, or where I wanted to go.

At just over four miles, with two more to get to the shelter, I came to the turnoff which led to Greasy Creek Friendly, half a mile down an unmarked side trail. I didn't even hesitate at the turnoff. I didn't make a decision to go back to the hostel. There was no decision. My feet just turned off the AT and onto the side trail, almost of their own free will. I walked the half mile without doubts.

When I reached the hostel I opened the back door and walked in. Connie was standing in the kitchen as usual, and she didn't seem surprised to see me. After washing my hands I sat down at the table, and Connie got the Mello Yello I had left in the refrigerator and handed it to me. She greeted me warmly and without question and said, "Your bed is still available." I knew I had some thinking to do.

Greasy Creek Gap to Johnson City, Tennessee
May 28, 2013

I was the walking definition of "turmoil." I didn't want to keep hiking, and I didn't want to quit. The word quit made me recoil in horror and the word hike made me cry. I couldn't pick a direction to go; north on the trail by foot and west by car both sounded equally repulsive. I didn't have a third option, so I knew I had to decide between them, and all I really wanted to do was go to bed and sleep. Maybe when I woke up it would all be different. I was too tired to make such a big decision.

The four miles I had walked the day before had been painful, physically as well as emotionally. It was more than just the normal aches that happened while hiking after taking a few days off the trail. It had only taken me a couple of hours to hike the four miles, but it had seemed interminable, every step a struggle. The trail had lost its beauty and was now just hard. I had no heart left for the trail. I had a lump in my throat that had been there so long it felt permanent, like the stinging behind my eyes. I couldn't imagine doing that all day again, putting myself through that pain, trying to hike 15 miles a day. Why would I do that to myself? Shouldn't you only hike while it is fun to hike? Why do it if I hate it, if it makes me miserable? What was I trying to prove? Days on the trail were now going to be long and hot and lonely, and I could see no good reason why I should keep doing it.

But then again, maybe I was rushing this important decision. It had only been five days since Mom died. Maybe I just needed more time. Maybe I hadn't given the trail enough of a chance. Four miles! That was nothing. I needed to get back out there and hike some more, give myself a chance to heal. Walking alone in the beauty of nature, of God's very footprint, I would find peace. I loved the AT. I had watered the trail with my sweat, lots and lots of it, with my tears, quite a few of those, especially that last few miles, and even with my literal blood, although fortunately not much of that (just from scratching my multitude of bug bites.)

At the same time, I was quite disappointed in myself for even entertaining the idea of quitting. I'm not a quitter by nature and have a strong drive to complete the tasks I set out for myself. This was a very big task, and few that start it actually do finish it. I wanted to be one of those. Approximately 2,000 people set out to hike the Appalachian Trail in any given year, and somewhere from ten to 20 per cent finish it. I hated to think that I was part of that 80 to 90 per cent who quits. Before I started hiking I had read in many trail journals and books that most people don't quit for physical reasons, but for emotional reasons. I had found that hard to believe because it seemed such a daunting physical task to walk over 2,000 miles. I had been sure that I was up to the challenge mentally and emotionally, and that if I didn't complete the trail it would be because my body just wasn't strong enough and my knees gave up. But here I was, physically strong and seriously considering quitting. I had no doubts by this time that my body, knees and all, could carry me all the way to Katahdin. But my will, my mind, and my heart…that was another story.

I went back and forth between these thoughts, but it all boiled down to the fact that I just didn't want to walk anymore. For whatever reason, I had checked out. I couldn't stand the thought of putting the Green Monster on my back and walking out of Greasy Creek. I didn't want to quit, but more than that I didn't want to hike.

I didn't call Mike. I didn't want to give him the chance to talk me out of it. And I didn't want to ask him to get back in the Jeep and make that long drive again, so I decided to take the Greyhound bus home. Connie drove me to Johnson City where I got a motel room, made bus reservations for the next day, and then called Mike to tell him I was coming home. He was surprised, and probably a little dismayed, and of course he offered to come get me. I told him that I looked forward to an afternoon and an evening in a motel room alone and a long bus trip alone, and that he could pick me up at the bus station in Chattanooga the next day.

I spent the rest of the afternoon, the evening, and the next morning lying on the motel room bed, watching television, dozing, and not thinking. I was going home. I prayed for peace with my decision.

Home
May 29-June 15, 2013

It was good to be home. When I walked into my house for the first time in nearly two months the first words out of my mouth were, "This is a really nice house!" which made Mike laugh. My small ranch style house is nobody's idea of upscale lodging, but I had stayed in so many places that were so much worse, my own home looked luxurious by contrast.

I tried to get back in the swing of life off the trail. I did housework and went to mass on Sundays. I found myself avoiding most social occasions, though. I am a member of a secular Franciscan order and couldn't quite bring myself to attend the fraternity meeting for June, something I normally love and look forward to. "I just need more time," I told myself. "I don't want to answer any more questions about why I am off the trail," I told myself as I turned down another invitation. "I'm just too tired," was another one I used a lot. "I think I must need a lot of rest after two months of hiking."

I knew I needed to get a job. I couldn't bring myself to return to nursing. The hospice unit I had worked at had closed, and I didn't want another nursing job. Now I believe that I didn't want to take a job taking care of sick people when I hadn't taken care of my own mom, but that's a much deeper realization than I was capable of making at that time. I thought of taking a job in another field, but I had no skills or experience in any other area, and in a small town jobs are not plentiful. I meant to go out and look for one, but "tomorrow" always seemed like a better time for that. "I haven't updated my resume/printed my resume/it's too hot/it's too late/it might rain/I don't feel good/no one will hire me anyway," take your pick, I had no shortage of excuses. I felt guilty that I wasn't working, guilty that I wasn't on the trail, and guilty that I hadn't been with my mom when she passed.

I knew I was depressed. I started taking a supplement called sam-E after hearing Dr. Oz talk about it. (I was watching quite a lot of television.) It was supposed to help both mood and joints, so I thought it could do double duty for me. I felt that I had several very good reasons to be depressed: the sorrow over losing my mother, the physical end of my hike, and my readjustment to life off the trail. When a person is incredibly physically active (like a long-distance hiker) and that activity comes to a sudden and complete stop, the body does not know what to do with all the endorphins that it's used to having on hand due to the activity. Evidently they decide to get together to just make the hiker feel bad. That's physiology, and there was nothing I could do about that. Except maybe be more active, but it's hard to do that when you don't even want to get off the couch. Readjusting to the non-hiking life was depressing, too. Life seemed so real and vital on the trail. Everything was important. The highs were higher and the lows were lower than life in a house. This life seemed pale and colorless in comparison, superficial and petty. As a Franciscan and a hiker I did not value material possessions, and I was shocked and disgusted by how much *stuff* there was in my house. I wanted to get rid of a lot of it, but I didn't have the energy to get started. I believed that my depression would improve with time, and so I was just waiting and letting time pass, all the while maintaining a pleasant façade and not letting people know just how bad I really felt.

I had only been home for a couple of days when Mike first told me he thought I should go back to the trail. I was quite surprised, shocked even, and assured him that I didn't know yet what I was going to do about getting a job, but one thing I was sure of, I did not want to go back to the trail. He left it alone for awhile, but a few days later he brought it up again. "Are you trying to get rid of me?" I asked, half in jest. "I thought you would be glad I was back!" He said that of course he was glad I was back, and he was not trying to get rid of me. He left the subject alone again. He is not prone to nagging. He also didn't nag at me to get a job or to take better care of the house or him or myself. He was just there for me, giving me the space and the time I needed to get hold of myself again, while planting the seeds that he knew I needed to have planted in my brain.

The seeds took root, and I began to consider the little fledgling plants. I had said so many times that I really did not want to get back on the trail that I had almost started to believe it myself. Almost. I was afraid to go back to the trail, but more than that I was disappointed in the way my hike had ended. I knew that no matter what I did, I wasn't going to be able to complete a thru-hike that year, but the hike I did want to make had ended badly, with a whimper. There was no desire to complete the entire trail, even though I knew I could still do it as a flip-flop hike. It wasn't about finishing the Appalachian Trail, it was about finishing *my* hike. It was about hiking until I decided I was done hiking. I hadn't made that decision for myself, I had let events make it for me. I had quit because I was overwhelmed by circumstances, not because I was ready to quit.

This is another example of the selflessness that makes St. Mike a saint. He was happy to have me home (and we needed a second income), but he knew that I was unhappy and confused and not making good decisions. He knew me better than I knew myself at that time. He realized that the trail was a great big piece of unfinished business for me and that if I didn't go back I would always regret it. I was trying to hide my unhappiness from him, and even from myself, and I was most emphatic that I didn't want to hike anymore, but he had the wisdom to see right through all of that, the gentleness to help me see through it too, and the unselfishness to want me to go back to finish my dream, even at the price of continued hardship for himself.

Eventually I came to see that he was right. I found some joy and some purpose. I wasn't going to go back out to finish the trail, I was going to go back to hike until I was finished, whenever that was. I got the Green Monster out of the basement. I had never really unpacked it, except for the dirty clothes and the food. It had been sitting there, waiting for me to come back. I got my guidebook out to see what came next. I had hiked 360 miles. I wanted to make it to at least 400. If I walked to Damascus, Virginia, the site of Trail Days and the infamous hiker parade, that would make 466 miles, only another hundred. That seemed like a fitting place to stop and a good distance to shoot for. I was ready. I bought my resupply, filled up my food bag, and St. Mike drove me back to Greasy Creek Gap.

Greasy Creek Gap to Clyde Smith Shelter
June 16, 2013

It was a Sunday morning when we made the 300 mile drive back to Greasy Creek. Mike joked that the Jeep knew the way by itself now. We stopped along the way to attend mass, and it was early afternoon when we pulled up to Greasy Creek Friendly. It was good to see Connie again and catch up on trail news. She said the norovirus was still not eradicated and she had had three hikers throwing up in just the past week. Mike did some work on her Bronco, and finally I bid goodbye to them both and started hiking the trail behind her house, the half mile trail that connects to the AT. I felt good and wondered what adventures awaited me this time around.

The weather was lovely, in the mid seventies, but still quite humid. Remembering how badly I had fared in the

heat I had rethought my hiking strategies. I was
determined now to get an earlier start each day, and try to
get most of my hiking done in the cool of the morning. If
the afternoon got hot I resolved to stop in the middle of the
day for a break, taking a couple of hours to rest in the shade
or by a stream if one was available. I could even hang my
hammock and take a nap. Then in the early evenings I
could hike a little longer, until dark, which was much later
than it had been when I started my hike on April first. I
also resolved to drink more water, and I appreciated the
fact that my backpack was lighter without the winter
weight gear I had left at home.

The first shelter was only two and a half miles from
Connie's house, but I stopped there for the night anyway.
The next shelter was another seven and a half miles, and I
was resolved not to push myself after I had gotten such a
late start for the day. It was still afternoon when I cruised
into the shelter area and looked around. I was the only
hiker there, but it was early. I knew that the thru-hikers
would all be gone by now, but I was hoping for the
company of some section-hikers. The silent woods and
empty shelter seemed eerie to me after having spent a few
weeks at home. I wasn't yet used to being back in the
woods, and my overactive imagination kicked into gear. I

started imagining rabid bears and serial killers. I'm not usually prone to such fears, but I became edgy and nervous. I decided to talk to God about it.

"Lord God, I know I am actually safe. I know that I thank You for having protected me thus far, and I pray for Your continued protection. But could You please help me today, not just to be safe, but to *feel* safe. I hope it's not lack of faith in Your protection making me feel so scared, and if it is, forgive me. I know that I will adjust to life back out on the trail, but for tonight, I ask for the special grace of being able to feel safe. Thank You."

I decided I needed to stay busy. I walked around to the stream and gathered and filtered two liters of water. Back at the shelter I realized that there were no bear cables, so I hung my food bag high from a tree branch. I gathered wood for a campfire and laid it in the fire pit, but I didn't start it yet. I looked for the trees to hang my hammock and found myself leaning toward sleeping in the shelter. The hammock was much more comfortable, but I thought that with my skittishness I might feel better sleeping surrounded by a roof and walls. I still felt spooked, but I started working on a Sudoku puzzle, not yet ready for supper. I was just about reconciled to staying alone when I heard voices on the trail. Two older gentlemen came down the path and into the shelter area. David and Darrell were from North Carolina and were old friends who hiked a section of the AT together every year. They were amiable and pleasant, very good company. The eerie feeling dissipated immediately with their arrival, and I thanked God, who is so good to me and watches out for me. Being section hikers, they carry things that thru-hikers won't, and they had pudding in little cups and fresh apples. I didn't realize it at the time, but I was still thinking of myself as a thru-hiker, even though I was now officially a section hiker, albeit one with no definite endpoint. We got a blazing fire going, more for the cheeriness than for the warmth, as the evening was pleasantly warm. We had a lovely conversation and it felt like old times on the trail. Just before dark we were joined by Ross, a young law student. Soon enough it was nine o'clock, hiker midnight, and time for bed. I was the only one sleeping in the shelter, as all three of the men chose to put up their tents. When I was alone in the shelter in the dark, my imagination started back to work again, conjuring up mice in the shelter, and snakes to eat the mice, and bears, and maybe even Bigfoot in the woods. I slept with my headlamp on my head and snapped it on at every sound. I asked God again to have patience with me and to protect me from my own fears and imagination. The shelter floor was hard—I had forgotten how hard and uncomfortable it could be—so I dozed fitfully. Once when I woke to a familiar sound, I tried to get my bearings and figure out what I was hearing. Oh, of course, it was rain. How many nights had I lain awake listening to rain on a shelter roof? I was glad to be in the shelter at that point, because it meant I wouldn't have a wet tarp to deal with in the morning.

I woke to a dim light and looked over the edge of the sleeping platform. I saw Ross moving his wet tent into the shelter, and finding himself a spot to sleep on the lower platform (it was a double decker shelter.) I was glad that I had awakened to see him moving in, because later in the night he started snoring quite loudly. If I hadn't seen him moving into the shelter I might have thought there was a bear in the shelter with me. Somehow, a bit illogically, I felt safer just knowing he was down there, and I slept better. If Bigfoot did come in, he would find Ross first.

Clyde Smith Shelter to Hughes Gap
June 17, 2013

In spite of a rather poor night's sleep I woke up feeling optimistic about the day ahead, my first full day back on the trail. I was happy to be there, and I looked forward to the day's hike. My plan was to hike eight miles to the shelter on top of Roan Mountain, the highest shelter on the entire trail at an elevation of 6,194 feet. The four and a half mile ascent of the mountain was said to be long and steep, but the upcoming section was often called the most beautiful section of the entire trail, and I was looking forward to it. By passing through later than thru-hikers I would have the advantage of seeing the famed rhododendrons in full bloom. I had kept the day's mileage short to allow myself time to spend on top of the mountain where there were ruins of an old hotel as well as the rhododendrons, and also so that I wouldn't feel the need to push myself on the long climb to the summit. If by some chance I reached the shelter with energy to spare I could always walk a little further.

I waited in the current shelter later than usual because of the still-drizzling rain, but eventually I put my rain jacket and pack cover on and started hiking. It was a very light rain, and the walking was pleasant, the morning cool, and the woods serene and lovely, the mythical creatures that had inhabited it the night before having fled with the morning light and my growing confidence. Three miles into the hike I came to Hughes Gap, which had a wide road crossing. Just as I reached the gap the skies opened up and buckets of water began pouring right down onto my head. Within minutes I was soaked to the skin, my rain jacket plainly giving up in the face of such an assault. I took off my pack and pulled out my tarp, the one that I hang to cover my hammock, and draped it over my head. It kept off the rain, giving me time to decide what to do. I didn't want to walk three miles back to the shelter, I definitely didn't want to walk four and a half miles up the mountain in the pounding rain, and I didn't want to hunker down under the tarp and wait for the rain to stop, although that seemed like the best option of the three. While I was waiting a trail runner came lightly skipping down the mountain. "Hey, how's the weather up top?" I asked him.

"Oh, it's terrible. It's raining harder up there than it is down here, believe it or not. The trail coming down was a sea of mud and slippery too. I'd wait it out a bit, if I were you, before going up." With that he blithely continued running down the trail. I wished that my body was cooperative enough to consider running on the trail, but walking was giving me all I could handle and more. I found a rock to sit on and pulled the tarp more fully over me, so that I was entirely covered by green nylon, like a gigantic toadstool, and waited another five minutes. When the thunder started I decided to give up on options A, B, and C, and I went straight for option D: the phone. I had cell service, so I unhesitatingly dialed Connie's number, which by now was programmed into my phone. I was only five miles from Greasy Creek by trail, longer by road, but Connie told me to sit tight, she'd be there to pick me up in 20 minutes.

When the Bronco pulled up to the gap I tossed my wet pack and tarp into the back and joined Connie in the front seat. We both laughed, and I asked her if there was a huge magnet under her house, and if she had put metal filings in my pockets, because I just couldn't seem to get past her hostel. "No magnet," she laughed, "but I do hate to tell you that there is more rain forecast for tomorrow! There won't be a break in the clouds until Wednesday."

"Story of my life! Or at least, story of my hike," I replied. "Well, I'll pray for sun and we'll just have to take what comes along, won't we?" Connie felt like an old friend by this time, and we chattered happily on the way to the Friendly. I knew the routine well by this time and I walked around to the back door, leaving my poles outside and my wet pack and boots in the mud room. I then went straight to the bathroom and washed my hands before touching anything in the house. Finally, I changed out of my wet clothes and hung them and my wet tarp from the clothesline on the front porch. Then I went inside to meet the other hikers.

There was an interesting and affable group gathered there, resigned to spending the day waiting out the rain. Kiwi Don was a soft-spoken New Zealander about my age. Jane, a lovely young woman from Louisiana, was a schoolteacher hiking with her well-behaved dog, Lola. Kiwi Don and Jane would be sharing the back bedroom with the three twin beds with me, while in the shed turned bunkhouse in the back yard was a group of four women from Ohio, all friends who taught school together, all roughly my age. Deb was the leader of the group, or at least the organizer, and the story of how they came to be hiking together was fascinating. Deb and her husband came down to hike for a week or two every summer, with it being Deb's dream to complete the whole trail. She realized she could never get it done at that rate, so she proposed to her husband, who couldn't leave the family farm in the summer for longer than that, that she come down to the trail without him and hike for six weeks, to knock off some serious miles. He agreed, as long as she could get someone to go with her, as he didn't like the idea of her hiking alone. She had contacted her friends and co-workers and set up a schedule of revolving hiking partners, each coming down to hike a week or a weekend and then being replaced as the next "shift" arrived. A new hiker or two would drive down from Ohio, and the previous shift would drive back. I was quite impressed with her ingenuity in setting up this schedule, and that she had that many friends, most of them novice hikers, willing to come hike with her. I had invited friends and family and not gotten a single taker, not even for a weekend! Her group was at the hostel to trade shifts, and the three women who were currently with her were going back in the morning to be replaced by the next woman in the rotation. One of her group, with the trail name Princess, was sick with what we assumed was the norovirus, but the rest of them were a lively group with a great sense of humor, always laughing and teasing each other, sharing their trail stories, and generally making the mood at the Friendly light and fun.

The afternoon and evening thus wore on in a pleasant, friendly fashion, although the rain never let up. We all went to bed at the usual hiker time, nine PM, hoping the weatherman was wrong and the morning would bring us some sunny hiking weather.

Greasy Creek Friendly
June 18, 2013

Kiwi Don was gone when I woke up, evidently deciding that hiking in the rain was better than a day cooped up in a house full of women. We realized as we gathered around the table for breakfast that we were currently an all-female hostel. "Girl Power!" we toasted ourselves, before one of the Ohio contingent announced that Jane was the only person present who qualified as a girl. "Middle-aged Women Power!" we amended our toast.

After breakfast we gathered around the television to watch the radar, hoping for a break in the weather, as we were all eager to get back on the trail. "Love ya, Connie, but we're hikers," I said.

"And hikers gotta hike," added Jane.

According to the radar, it looked like there would be a break in the clouds in the early afternoon. The rain was supposed to stop for awhile, then resume in the early evening. That was the break we were looking for, and we all repacked our packs, ready to head out after lunch. I thought I would be able to walk up Roan Mountain and get to the shelter before the rain started again. We kept an eye on the weather report throughout the morning, and the same break in the clouds remained. The next hiker in Deb's rotation appeared: Lynn, accompanied by her husband Mark. Lynn was going to stay and hike with Deb, and Mark was going to drive the other three ladies back to Ohio. Princess was feeling a little better, and they all said their goodbyes, and Lynn settled in with the rest of us to watch for the chance to hike out. When it finally appeared to be close, Connie drove me, Lynn, and Deb back to Hughes Gap to resume our hike. Jane was going to hike out from the hostel. We pulled up to the gap in the driving rain and sat in the Bronco. None of us really wanted to get out and start up that mountain in the rain. I felt guilty asking Connie, who had other things to do, to sit and wait with us for the break in the weather we were expecting, so eventually we made the decision to go back to the hostel and try again the next day. The Bronco turned around, and we all returned to Greasy Creek, and I asked Connie again about that magnet. I just couldn't seem to get away.

Back at the hostel we found Jane still sitting on the

couch, and we laughed as we realized we had all come back. Connie had to leave to run some errands, so she asked Jane and me to watch the place while she was gone. We had both been there long enough to know the routine if any new hikers arrived. Sure enough, she hadn't been gone half an hour when we heard a rustle at the back door. We went to the mud room and opened the door to find two hikers who looked like nothing so much as drowned kittens. They were wet from head to toe and from the skin out. We ushered them into the mud room and helped them with the routine. The two hikers themselves had little or nothing to say in response, apparently completely exhausted, cold, and half-drowned. One of them took a towel and some loaner clothes from Connie's rack and went into the shower, while Jane and I tried to get their wet gear hung on the porch or in front of the wood stove. When the first hiker emerged from the shower the second one went in. The first hiker now sat at the table with the rest of us, drying her hair with a towel, her spirits much improved now that she was clean, warm, and dry. They were two women from Virginia, both nurses, which tied us with Jane, Lynn, and Deb: nurses and teachers, three each. The second nurse came out of the shower, and we were all getting to know each other better when the phone rang.

Jane answered it. "Greasy Creek Friendly," she said in an official sounding voice. It was Connie, getting our orders for supper, which she would bring back from town with her.

"Can she get us a bottle of wine?" the nurses asked.

Jane relayed the request to Connie. "Red or white?" she asked. "I've got red there at the house."

That was fine with the nurses, whose names were Donna and Susan. When Connie returned with the food she gave them a bottle of wine, with the request that she be able to pray the blessing of the wine first. They assented, and we watched, fascinated, as she proceeded to recite a long prayer in a language I could only assume was Hebrew, delivered with a southern accent. Trail life is never boring.

The evening passed pleasantly. Although I really enjoyed the slumber party atmosphere, I was heartened that the next day's forecast was for clear skies with mild temperatures and low humidity. In other words, perfect hiking weather.

Hughes Gap to Overmountain Shelter
June 19, 2013

The weatherman redeemed himself for the previous day's broken promise of a break in the rain by bringing us a beautiful, clear, sunny day. The fears and sensation of vulnerability that had plagued me on my first day back on the trail were gone. I felt strong, confident, and ready to hike. Connie drove me back again to Hughes Gap, and I knew that this time I was leaving Greasy Creek for real. I gave Connie a sincere hug. She had been such a special trail angel to me. I was hiking alone, as all the women from the hostel were starting from different points. I started up Roan Mountain, and found the walk to be less difficult than I had imagined. My stride was strong, and the woods were beautiful. The steep mountainside was covered in jewelweed, acres and acres of it, and on each plant the dew had beaded up, turning the water droplets into the crystal jewels that give the plant its name. Little orange newts were out en masse on the forest floor, their bright color in sharp contrast to the muted browns of the leaf mold. I took pictures of the newts for my grandson.

Four and a half miles up the trail I came out of the forest onto the summit of Roan Mountain. It was a beautiful high meadow and a popular picnicking spot for locals, as there was a road that drove straight to a small parking area. There were a lot of people there enjoying the first sunny day after the rain. There were picnic tables and real bathrooms. I wandered around the area, taking in the sights. A resort hotel had once stood there in the late 1800s, when it was popular to come up to "take the mountain air." The state line between Tennessee and North Carolina had gone right through the building, so that at one time alcohol had been legal on one side of the dining room but not the other. The hotel is gone now, except for part of the foundation, but there was a large placard giving details on the era. The views from the mountain were amazing, and the rhododendrons, as suspected, were out in full, showy bloom. A group of artists had assembled to take advantage of the gorgeous scenery, standing behind their easels in a rough circle. I thought that if I could paint, I would paint the artists themselves, their presence on the mountaintop such a charming scene.

After eating my lunch I walked back to the trail to resume my hike north. I came to the sign for Roan Mountain Shelter, but it was too early in the day to stop for the night. I wanted to go see it and take a picture because of its status as the highest shelter on the trail, but the blue blazed trail to the shelter did not look inviting, and I still had a good distance to walk, so I contented myself by taking a picture of the sign and continued on down the mountain. The trail became very rocky and steep, my least favorite kind of trail. It hurt my feet, knees, ankles, and toes. My right pinky toe, in particular began to hurt very badly. I limped and picked my way down Roan Mountain to Carvers Gap.

I had frequently heard hikers talk about Carvers Gap, but I knew little about it. A road ran through the gap, which is why hikers often get on and off the trail there, and I expected a typical road crossing with the woods coming right to the edge of the road, with a little break in the trees and a white blaze to mark the Appalachian Trail. Instead it was a huge open meadow, filled with blooming rhododendrons and flame azaleas, as well as with day hikers, sight-seers, and photographers. Several people, seeing my backpack, stopped me to inquire about my hike, and as was usual they all expressed concern that I was walking alone. I had faced these questions many times since starting my hike. The most common questions were: aren't you afraid, walking all alone? What does your husband think? And then, sotto voce, they all assumed that I had a gun, but asked just to verify the fact. Surely no woman would venture out into the wilderness alone without a gun. I usually gave them a wink and a nod that I was well-protected and let them interpret that however they wanted to.

One gentleman in Carvers Gap asked me a question I had never been asked before, though. After we talked in generalities for a few minutes he asked, "What is the most important thing you've learned on your hike?" I was surprised at the question and equally surprised at how quickly the answer formed itself in my mind and came out of my lips. Without thinking about it, I found myself saying, "The most important thing I've learned is to value all people. I was more judgmental before my hike. I've met so many hikers that I would never have had opportunity to get to know before my hike, and they are all just people, just like me. We all walk the same trail, the same way."

He looked thoughtful and maybe impressed. This clearly wasn't the answer he expected, nor was it the answer I would have given if I had taken time to formulate a response. But as we said our goodbyes and I hiked on, I realized it was true, and I was grateful he had asked me the question. It was only much later, after my hike ended, that I came to understand that this lesson, as important as it is, was only the first part of what I was ultimately to learn. It was the introduction, the foundation, for the true lesson of my hike.

I walked on, over Round Bald, and Jane Bald, and Grassy Ridge Bald. Beautiful places, all. The sun grew warm. I hadn't been out of the shelter and shade of the woods for this long in quite a while. I found a couple of trees whose branches hung low, making a little hideaway, and stepped inside the canopy. The grass was long and soft, and the shade was cool. I lay on the grass and sipped water. From my hiding place I could see the trail and an occasional hiker walking on it, but I was hidden from sight. I enjoyed feeling like a kid in a secret fort, but eventually I got back on the trail and walked on. The day hikers and sight-seers thinned out this far from the road, and I was alone again.

A little further on I came to Stan Murray Shelter, and although it was a bit early I considered stopping for the night. As I approached the shelter I saw that there was someone lying down inside. Odd, it was early to be down for the night. As I got closer, I saw that the hiker looked familiar. It was Kiwi Don, whom I had met at Connie's. He was curled on his side and didn't look at all well. "Kiwi Don, are you all right?" I asked.

"Oh, I'll do," he said in his musical New Zealand accent. "I've been sick, though. Right after I left the hostel yesterday morning I started throwing up, and I haven't kept anything down yet. Probably caught it from that woman at the hostel. Don't get too close, now."

"Oh dear, you poor thing! What can I do to help? Do you need water?" The water source was down a steep trail from the shelter, and I offered to go down the trail to collect his water, but he had just been, he said, and his bottles were both full. "Can I call someone for you? Do you want me to call Connie? Maybe she can come up and bring you something, or help you back to Carvers Gap and take you back to her place."

He refused though, saying he was feeling better, hadn't thrown up since morning, and just wanted to rest out the day and try to hike again the next day. I changed my mind about staying in the small shelter and gave him some Gatorade powder to add to his water, telling him he needed to replace some electrolytes and to sip at the Gatorade and not try to eat anything else until he was able to keep the Gatorade down. I felt rather helpless as I walked away from him, wishing I could do more, but Kiwi Don was a stoic sort and obviously uncomfortable with my attention, so I gave him my phone number, and Connie's, and walked on.

The next shelter was one I had really wanted to see anyway. Overmountain Shelter is a converted barn, making it one of, if not the, largest shelters on the trail. It was a lovely red barn, very scenic, situated as it was in the green countryside, with striking views of a deep valley and distant mountains. There were a few hikers already congregating when I arrived, and I found a spot and spread out my pad up in the loft, then joined the group for conversation. I was eating my supper when Jane arrived, whom I had last seen that morning as she hiked out of Connie's. She told me that she had seen Kiwi Don at the previous shelter, and that he was sitting up and drinking Gatorade when she left him.

I had taken off my hiking boots on arrival at the shelter, as usual, concerned now about the pain on my right little toe. I had yet to have a blister, and I definitely didn't want to start now. Blisters can be disastrous for hikers. The toe was red and very sore, but the skin was smooth, with no sign of a blister. I resolved to pad it with a bandaid in the morning before hiking, after letting it air out all night. I made a wonderful dessert of instant chocolate pudding, powdered milk, and water, in a Ziploc bag. Then I added some chocolate mint cookie crumbs (carrying them in a backpack does a nice job of pre-crushing them.) It was very tasty. I shared it with Jane and finally made my way to my bed on the hard shelter floor, and to sleep.

Overmountain Shelter to Roan Mountain, Tennessee
June 20, 2013

I woke up tired and achy in the morning. Shelter floors were definitely harder than I remembered them being, and I hadn't slept well because of it. I resolved to never sleep on another shelter floor (and I didn't). The group of hikers downstairs had awakened at six o'clock and proceeded to greet the day with loud voices and booming laughter. The barn loft, where I was sleeping, was still dark and quiet, and I would have loved another hour of sleep, which was impossible with the festivities occurring down below. Reluctantly I got up and stretched and started my day.

According to my guidebook, the next shelter was 18 miles away, an impossible distance for me to hike in one day. Although I didn't plan on sleeping in the shelter itself, I still wanted to camp in a shelter area for the other amenities provided: roof and walls in case of rain, nearby water source, bear cables, privy, picnic tables, firepit, and especially the company of other people. Hikers were scarce by this time, with the thru-hikers all gone. There were some section hikers, but it was possible to go all day without seeing a single other person. I would have loved to have seen a shelter ten miles away providing me a place to hang my hammock for the night with the likelihood of company. Instead, about nine miles away was a major road crossing, a US highway. It is common knowledge among hikers that it is not a good idea to stop for the night too close to a road crossing because of the possibility of partying locals in the vicinity. Especially for a woman hiking alone, it's a better idea to stay away from road crossings. So this narrowed my choices for where to stop for the night. I would want to go a couple of miles past the road crossing. Unfortunately, there was another road, albeit a country road and not a highway, one mile further on. Might a country road actually be more dangerous than a major highway? And two miles further there was what was listed as a "jeep path." What was that? Could it be more of a draw for teenagers out for a night of drinking? I could always "stealth camp," go just far enough off the trail to not be seen and hang my hammock behind a screen of foliage and forego a campfire. In the entire time I'd been hiking I had only spent one night all alone, at Beauty Spot

Gap. I wasn't afraid of camping alone under normal conditions, at least I didn't think I was, but I remembered my first night back on the trail at Clyde Smith Shelter, and how I had imagined Bigfoot and rabid bears in the woods until David and Darrell showed up. I was definitely feeling more vulnerable on this second iteration of my hike, a bit more wobbly and less self-assured. I even missed the layers of down and wool and fleece that I had wrapped myself in on those cold nights. I didn't need them now for warmth, but I felt somehow more exposed at night without being encased in my cocoon of insulation.

I hiked out of Overmountain Shelter not entirely sure of where I would stop for the night, but I asked God for inspiration, safety, and faith as I walked, and I knew that it would all work out. It was an extraordinarily beautiful morning. The sun was shining and the trail was a vivid bright green, now in the full foliage of early summer. It was such a contrast to the brown winter forest I had started my hike in. I wasn't in forest at all for most of the day, as the trail took me over two really spectacular balds, Hump Mountain and Little Hump. Both mountains were well over 5,000 feet of elevation. From any given point on the trail you could look far ahead and see a tiny thin line disappearing around a bend or a hillock—the trail itself.

You could also look behind and see where you had walked the last hour or so, that same thin line in a sea of dazzling green. It was on Hump Mountain that I finally found the panorama feature on my camera and put it to good use trying to capture the grandeur of the 360 degree views, but the camera just couldn't do justice to the true beauty that surrounded me. I don't think that it's possible to capture in an image the feeling of being able to look at all the world spread out before you on all sides. I thanked God that I was able to see something so indescribably gorgeous, and I asked St. Francis if he didn't agree with me that this was one of God's most beautiful footprints.

I was in total awe of my surroundings, but I was also beginning to struggle physically again with the heat. There was no shade to be found on these treeless balds, and the sun was blazing down on me. My right small toe was hurting again, too, a tenderness that became an ache that became a constant pain that became excruciating. Every step became painful. I tried to lead with my left foot on the downhills, to take the pressure off, but discovered that I am extremely right-footed, and it felt too weird to lead with the left. Late in the afternoon I was sitting on a gigantic rock formation by a spring, having a snack and sweating in the heat and humidity, when Jane and her dog Lola came along. We chatted for a few minutes about how beautiful the trail and the weather were. "Where are you planning to stop for the night?" I asked her. I knew that she was capable of hiking much longer distances than I was, and that her Louisiana-trained body handled heat and humidity much better than my Tennessee-based body did, besides her young age, and I assumed that she was going the 18 miles to the next shelter. But she surprised me.

"There's a hostel at the road crossing. That's only eight miles for the day, but I think I'll stop there anyway. Why don't you come too?"

I hadn't thought about making another hostel stop. I thought my days of frequent hostel stays were gone with Songbird, queen of the hostels, but I found myself seriously considering Jane's offer as I walked the long steep downhill from Hump Mountain, my foot hurting more with every step. As I approached the road crossing I gave myself many reasons why I should just keep walking, looking out for a place to camp for the night. But when I reached the road, the lure of a shower and a cold drink won out again, and I turned onto the road and limped the three-tenths of a mile to the Mountain Harbour Hostel. I found Jane and Lola already there, along with Kiwi Don, now apparently recovered from his short-lived bout with the norovirus. They were setting up their tents beside a creek in the wooded side yard of the hostel, which was also a bed and breakfast. All the rooms were full with vacationers and sight-seers, but for a few dollars we could camp in the yard and use the shower, while the owner would drive us to town for supper and his wife did our laundry. This sounded like a slice of heaven to me, and I eagerly hung my hammock near Jane's and Kiwi Don's tents. I took a delightfully cool shower, washing away layers of sweat and grime. My dirtiest clothes went to be laundered while I looked at my toe. I expected to see a huge blister, but the skin was intact. It was swollen and red and exquisitely painful to the touch. I couldn't figure out what was wrong with it. It looked and felt like an injury, perhaps as if it were broken, but I knew it hadn't been injured. I padded it up with layers of moleskin and bandages just for cushioning and wore my Crocs to town.

The hostel owner drove the three of us to the tiny town of Roan Mountain, Tennessee. As if it were a beacon calling to us we descended without discussion on the local burger joint and placed our orders. Kiwi Don was apparently entirely recovered, as he ate a huge burger with bacon. He said it was the first food he had been able to keep down, and I watched him with the experienced eye of a nurse and mother who has been thrown up on a few too many times, but all was well. I also had a cheeseburger, with fries and a large, ice cold Mountain Dew, and afterward we all had double ice cream cones. There was a facetious sign in the diner about handguns being welcome on the premises and judicious marksmanship being appreciated. Kiwi Don remarked on it, because evidently in New Zealand handguns are not the norm. He assumed the sign had to be a joke, which it mostly was, but I explained to him that here in Tennessee, many people carried guns. Jane concurred that the same was true in Louisiana. I told him that if he looked around, a good many of the men in southern small towns would either have a gun in their pants or a rifle in the gun rack of their pickup truck. I told him about a patient of mine, an elderly man who was in the hospital parking lot when a young man came to the window of his new truck with a knife and said, "Here's what's going to happen, old man. You're going to get out of this truck and give me the keys. Then you're going to turn around and walk away and not look back. If you do all that, you probably won't get hurt."

My patient pointed the barrel of the gun he had pulled out from under the seat at the young man and said, "No, here's what's going to happen, sonny. You're going to drop that stupid knife and stand right there. And if you're lucky you won't get shot or run over while I drive off."

Kiwi Don laughed and said it sounded like living in the Wild West. Jane and I both agreed that it wasn't that bad, but that guns are an accepted part of southern culture: many people hunt, and everyone believes in protecting their own—lives, family, property. He told us about New Zealand culture, and it was an interesting hour learning about another part of the world. The trail never ceased to amaze at the opportunities it brought.

Back at our little campsite we made a fire and continued our conversation from the diner until we were all yawning and stretching. Then we said our good nights, and I hobbled over to my hammock and gratefully crawled in, and slept like a baby.

Roan Mountain to Upper Laurel Fork
June 21, 2013

Kiwi Don was gone before I even woke up. I didn't hear him leave, but all that remained of his campsite was the faint impression his tent had left on the ground. Jane and I got up at about the same time and walked down the road to the trailhead together, but she hikes much faster than I do, so she was soon out of sight too, and I walked on alone. It was June 21, the longest day of the year, the summer solstice. In the hiking world, it was also Hike Naked Day. I couldn't gauge how widely observed it was, since I didn't see a single other hiker the entire day. Among section hikers, I was sure it was ignored, and that few even knew the significance of the day. But farther north, among the thru-hikers, there were probably a few who participated. I still mistakenly thought of myself as a thru-hiker, but I did not celebrate the day.

The trail was, for the most part, fairly level throughout the day, and my toe felt better for it, being only sore, not exquisitely painful. Early in the day the trail presented yet another new face to me: waist high grass. A long section of the trail consisted of very thick, very high grass, with the trail being a mere six inch wide swath and hard to see. It was difficult to walk through, like wading through water. The heat and humidity once again became a problem for me as I pushed myself through the grass, using the trekking poles to move the grass aside, hoping there were no snakes down on the ground that I couldn't see. It was not possible to stop and sit down anywhere in the high grass, so there was no choice but to keep plowing through.

Coming out of the tall grass I found myself on the bank of the Elk River, which I walked alongside for awhile. I saw two buck deer standing in the river and excitedly grabbed for my camera and took their picture. They were magnificent. After following the river for a while I came to a side trail with a sign reading "Jones Falls, 0.1 mi." Unable to resist, I turned off the AT and followed the side trail to the waterfall, which was absolutely gorgeous, one of the biggest I had seen on the entire trail. I had the whole place to myself, and took off my shoes and socks while I ate my lunch. I didn't feel the oppressive heat or the pain in my toe with my feet soaking in the cold water. I just felt at peace and wished the whole world could experience what I was feeling right that minute. It was like twirling in Blue Tortoise Meadow or watching the sun rise at Little Laurel Shelter, a moment of transcendent joy and peace and the feeling that God creates these places and these moments just because He love us.

Eventually, though, I had to take my feet out of the water and let them dry thoroughly before I could pad up my injured toe, put my shoes and socks back on, pick up my pack, and walk on. By keeping a close eye on my guidebook, I knew where I was on the trail, so that when I reached Mountaineer Shelter, I knew that I had reached another milestone in my hike: 400 miles. I was all alone this time. There was no one at the shelter, and I didn't expect anyone to come along, as I hadn't seen any other hikers all day, so I contrived to take my own picture. The concept of the "selfie" wasn't as omnipresent then as it has become in the years since, but it was not unheard of, although I had never tried to take one. Still, I wrote the number "400" on a scrap of paper, then held my phone up over my head and managed to get a photo with both myself and the number in it. I was glad to have reached this milestone and couldn't help but compare it to my little celebrations at each of the other hundred mile markers. This was the only one I had celebrated alone.

I could feel that this would be my last hundred mile marker. I was enjoying the hike very much, but now with the type of enjoyment a person has when they take a little walk in the woods or along a stream, that is, it was enjoyment of the moment and the scenery, but in a very temporary or transient way, instead of as a part of a greater whole. I knew that I wasn't going to make it to Katahdin, at least not that year, and I was no longer part of a loosely-organized group of people who all thought they were going to Katahdin as well. Now I was just walking along, noticing how pretty the scenery was, yes, but seeing it with eyes of a person who would soon be back home, not the eyes of a person in the middle of a giant quest. Without a goal to focus on and work toward, I was just ambling along and enjoying the moment. Not that there's anything wrong with ambling and enjoying the current moment, but it's an entirely different feeling than pushing toward an ultimate goal. I had no goal now except to enjoy each day, and I knew that there weren't going to be many more of them. I didn't know when I was going to leave the trail, but I knew it would be soon.

I ended up walking 13 miles that day, my longest day since returning to the trail. The lack of big elevation changes made it easier to walk more miles, and I knew that if I stayed on the trail, and if my toe improved from its mysterious ailment, I would now be able to walk the big mile days that I hadn't been able to walk up to that point. The elevation profile in my guidebook looked like a gently curving line for the next few hundred miles instead of the jagged, steep, up and down peaks that had constituted it so far. I was glad for the gentle terrain in light of the heat and humidity that I struggled with.

I spent the night in yet another little hostel that I came across near a waterfall at Laurel Fork. The hostel was two tenths of a mile off the trail, but when I got there Jane was already there, and no one else came along. The cool shower felt refreshing. This hostel was located on a quiet country road, and there was no trip to town associated with it, so Jane and I ate supper from out of our food bags and enjoyed each other's company and being clean.

Upper Laurel Fork to Dennis Cove Road
June 22, 2013

Jane got ahead of me right out of the gate as we left the hostel in the morning. I saw her back (and Lola's) in a blur as she headed down the trail, and I didn't expect to see her until the evening. We had made a plan to hike almost twelve miles to Dennis Cove Road where there were two different hostels. Jane planned on staying at Kincora Hostel, because it is one of those iconic trail locations that every hiker has heard about. I wasn't sure if I would be staying the night, because I was feeling guilty about taking so many hostel stops, but I knew that my time on the trail was becoming shorter, and it's hard to turn down a cool shower and a colder drink at the end of a long, hot day.

Eventually I decided that hostel stays were justified since I was no longer planning to hike all the way to Maine, and we made loose plans to look for each other that night if we both decided to stay at Kincora.

I hiked on in fairly level terrain, but there were some rocky sections, and I quickly realized that the pain in my right pinky toe was back, and with a vengeance. As the day wore on it got worse and worse, until by the end of the day every step was agonizing, and I was limping badly, dragging my painful right foot.

Early in the day, before it got that bad, I was walking along and enjoying the beautiful scenery and pleasantly flat trail, when I met a group of Girl Scouts hiking with their leaders. They were from Louisville, Kentucky, and they brought a large group of girls out to hike every year. The girls were about middle school age and their leaders were very nice women and dedicated hikers. They stopped to talk and asked me a lot of questions about my hike. I was so glad that there were women like that to teach and train young girls, to show them a life outside of electronic entertainment. I thanked them for their service.

As the day went on, becoming continually hotter, my toe pain becoming unbearable, I knew that this was my last day on the trail. If it had just been the toe I knew I could take a day to rest it, maybe even see a doctor to find out what was wrong with it, and get back on the trail. But I just couldn't deal with the heat. I was sweating, and once again headachy and generally sick. I had to admit to myself that I couldn't hike in the heat and humidity. I loved the trail, but I wasn't having fun anymore, not when I felt so bad every day. I was sad and cried as I walked along, while at the same time feeling a great peace with my decision, knowing it was the right one.

Toward the middle of the day I came across two women sitting by the side of the trail, and I stopped to say hello. It was Deb and Lynn, the two teachers I had met at Greasy Creek. Deb was having a hard time with some GI symptoms that she thought might be norovirus, and also some severe back pain, which is obviously not a good thing when you have to carry a heavy pack on your back. They were looking for an opportunity to get off the trail to reassess their situation, and I told them about Dennis Cove Road coming up, with two different hostels to choose from, and that Jane was stopping there for the night at Kincora Hostel. Deb and Lynn looked at my guidebook and decided to go to the other one, Black Bear Hostel, because it had more amenities, including a camp store and cabins, which would be useful if they decided to call their husbands to come get them.

We all hiked on, and they were able to outpace me easily even with Deb's back pain, because my toe pain had me really hobbled by that time, and I limped painfully down the trail. I slowly inched forward, by now practically dragging my right foot and sweating profusely. My head hurt and I felt like I was going to be sick. Eventually I came out on Dennis Cove Road. Kincora Hostel lay three tenths of a mile to my left, and Black Bear Hostel was four tenths of a mile the other way. I turned toward Kincora, because I wanted to see that trail landmark. Black Bear was new and didn't have the trail history and tradition that Kincora had. I walked on the blacktop road which was much hotter than walking in the woods, something I hadn't thought was possible until that moment. Nevertheless, I limped to the hostel, up a long driveway, and onto the porch of the quaint, rustic hostel. There was Lola, lying patiently on the porch! No sign of Jane though, so I went inside. It was dark and quiet, and my overwhelming impression was of clutter and dust. "Hello!" I called out. Just when I decided that there was no one there, a sickly-looking young woman came hobbling out of a back bedroom, wrapped in a blanket, her hair sticking up in all directions. "Oh, hi," I said. "Where is everybody?"

"They've all gone to town," she said. "I didn't go because I'm sick with the norovirus. Don't get too close."

She didn't need to tell me twice. I felt bad enough without the dreaded virus. I was devastated that I had missed the trip to town—no ice cold Mello Yello for me. I was also very uncomfortable with the idea of staying in this dark, cluttered hostel, close to this sick young woman, so, reluctantly, I headed back out to the road to walk the now seven tenths of a mile to the other hostel. I saw Jane's Kindle on the picnic table on the porch, so I left her a note telling her I would be staying at Black Bear, and that Deb and Lynn would be there also. I added that I was pretty sure I was leaving the trail, the first time I had admitted it to anyone besides myself, and I didn't like the feeling of finality that it gave the end of my hike. With a heavy heart I limped down to the hot blacktop, back to the AT trailhead, and beyond, to the Black Bear Resort. I don't know if I have ever in my life been so glad to reach a destination as I was when I saw the sign for the hostel. It was a small cluster of buildings, all cute and clean and charmingly landscaped, consisting of a group of rental cabins, a camp store, a bath house, and a bunk room for hikers. There was a wide, welcoming porch populated with rocking chairs in front of the camp store and bunk room, which were connected. Deb and Lynn sat in two of the chairs, cold drinks in hand, looking much better than they had when I had last seen them. Deb said her GI symptoms weren't a virus after all, but just her body's reaction to her back pain, and both were much improved now. I wandered into the camp store and came back out with a Mello Yello and a bag of Doritos, and joined them on the porch, feeling better about my own decision.

EPILOGUE

I spent that night in the bunkhouse at Black Bear, and
St. Mike came to pick me up the next day and took me
home. I was happy to be home, and the extreme depression
that I had endured during my previous stay at home was
mercifully absent. I did not go back to nursing, but instead
found another part time job that I enjoyed more. I got
involved with my parish once more and with my fraternity
of the Secular Franciscan Order. I host a weekly book club
at my home and still lead the local dulcimer group. Life
has gone back to something close to what it was before my
hike, although I am forever changed by it.

Mike and I went back to eastern Tennessee the next
summer, so I could show him some of my favorite places
on the trail. We went to Max Patch, camped at Lemon
Gap, and hiked into Hot Springs from there, making up the
section I had skipped while hiking. I discovered what was
wrong with my little toe on that hike: my boots were too
small. Long distance hikers' feet grow by a half size to a
full size on a long hike, as the bones spread out, and they
never go back to their pre-hike size. I had known that
when I bought the shoes and so had deliberately gotten
them a bit too big, but not big enough. Mike and I limped

into Hot Springs at the end of that day hike with my little toe feeling just like it had at the end of my hike, and I removed the boots and left them in the hiker box at Laughing Heart Hostel. I never wanted to put them back on again. They were great boots, though, and still had a lot of wear left in them, even after 416 miles, so I went to the outfitter and bought another pair just like them, a full size bigger.

Mike hiked Hump Mountain and Little Hump, while I played shuttle driver and picked him up at Carvers Gap. We spent the night at Greasy Creek and found Connie to be just as sweet, just as warm, and just as funny as I had remembered.

I have not heard from Songbird, other than a short note that she was sorry about my mother passing, which she learned from reading my online trail journal. I never found out why she left so abruptly from Damascus.

It has been over three years since my hike now, and there is rarely a day that goes by that I don't think of it. To paraphrase Dickens, it truly was both the best of times and the worst of times. I have finally started to make sense of the things I learned along the trail, the lessons that God tried to teach me, and how they all fit together. I think that what I told the gentleman near Carvers Gap, that my biggest lesson had been to accept and love others without judging, was true to a point, but was only part of what He wanted me to know. I thank God for sending Chris and Mary to me in Bryson City in such a pointed way, to point out that He is sovereign over all, that we are *all* his children, a lesson I shouldn't have had to be taught. That lesson was a very important part, to be sure, but still just a part of the whole.

I understand now that the incident during the parade at Trail Days, followed by the harrowing night at Beauty Spot Gap, then by my mother's death, the three strikes that put me out, were all connected. At first I simply thought that the trauma of the hiker parade left me feeling particularly shaky and wobbly, enough so that the terrifying night at Beauty Spot shook me up enough to drive me off the trail. Because of that I spent that extra day at Greasy Creek, so that I was able to get the news about Mom's passing and make it to her funeral in time. Had I not been so shaken up, I might have been far enough into the woods that I would not have had either phone service or internet, as I frequently did not have for days at a time, and I could conceivably have missed the news *and* the funeral. I was grateful that events had conspired in such a way that I was able to go to the funeral and be with my family, but I felt that there was more to the story, that somehow I was still missing the big picture.

I couldn't help but think there was another lesson, a bigger lesson that God had for me. I looked for other meanings, other lessons, other explanations, other ways to make sense of the trauma, and for many months I came up short. My faith remained intact, though, and I had no problem with chalking it all up to "mystery," something beyond my comprehension.

In looking at my reactions to the events of my hike, I don't seem to have acquitted myself very well. I started the hike believing that I was a devoted Catholic, committed to living a life of whatever righteousness of which I was capable, and secure in my faith. Then, early on, I was confronted with the fact that I don't love as I ought, thus breaking one of the two great commandments, to love my brother as myself. While I was still coming to grips with that painful lesson learned at the NOC, I learned at Beauty Spot Gap that I was also breaking the other great commandment, to love the Lord my God with all my heart, soul, and strength. At least, I didn't trust Him, and don't love and trust go together? After praying for rescue from my fears during the storm, I turned for help from God to my phone in less than an hour. Where was my faith, why couldn't I hold on to my faith in His providence for more than an hour under testing? Could I really not watch with Him for one hour?

And yet, in spite of these two great failures on my part, God continued to show me great love and compassion and tenderness. He put events in motion so that when I received the devastating news of my mother's death I was in the most loving and gentle of places. I wasn't alone in an isolated campsite but surrounded by caring people who literally wrapped their arms around me and grieved with me. In addition, throughout my hike I was a daily witness to the grandeur of His physical creation, and stricken with awe too many times to remember or to recount. I am humbled with the revelation of my own sinful nature, so blatantly revealed to me on the trail. But I am even more humbled by the revelation of His great love and concern for me, even while I remained mired in the sins of the breaking of the two great commandments, with a generous scattering of pride, complacency, and selfishness to boot. But God proved His love for me in that while I was yet a sinner, He continued to answer my prayers, to show me His glory, to meet my needs on a daily basis, to send me all that I needed and was presumptuous enough to ask for. His eyes never left this little sparrow, even while my eyes were not on

Him. Love is always the answer, I have found myself saying so often in my life, when confronted with decisions to be made, or dilemmas to resolve. Yes, it's true, love is always the answer. And the greatest love of all is the love that God has for His creatures, of which I am just one. I failed to love Him, *or* my brothers, as I ought, yet He continued to love and watch and care for me. I have done nothing to deserve His love, yet He showers me with it daily. I am blessed beyond measure.

This wonderful mystery, the great boundless love of God, this is the great lesson to be learned from my walk on the strip of dirt.

GLOSSARY OF HIKING TERMS

AT   The Appalachian Trail

ATC   The Appalachian Trail Conservancy, the governing body of the AT, headquartered in Harper's Ferry, West Virginia

Blue blaze   Trail markers for a trail that is not part of the Appalachian Trail. It may be a side trail, a short trail to a shelter, or a shortcut around a difficult section. Hikers who routinely skip sections or take shortcuts are called, derisively, **blue blazers.**

Gorp   A favorite hiker food, like granola. It is an acronym, standing for "good old raisins and peanuts."

Hiker Box   A box, usually located in a hostel or other trail-related business, where hikers can leave any food, gear, or clothing they don't want, and other hikers are welcome to help themselves to anything in the box. I put my hiking boots, once they became too small, into a hiker box.

HYOH   stands for "hike your own hike." In other words, do it your own way. Don't judge others who hike differently than you do, and don't preach about it. *Hey, I know my pack is heavier than yours. HYOH, man.*

Nobo A person who hikes the trail from south to north, from Springer Mountain in Georgia to Mt. Katahdin in Maine if they are a thru-hiker. Most thru-hikers are nobos. It is short for "northbounder."

Ridge Runner An employee of the ATC who roams around a section of the trail to educate or aid hikers or collect data for the ATC

Section Hiker A hiker who hikes part of the trail, with no intention to hike the entire trail at that time. A section can be short, such as a weekend hike, or extremely long. Anything short of the entire 2,180 mile length of the trail is a section.

Shuttle A ride in a car from one point to another, that you pay for. A shuttle driver can be a person who lives locally and supplements his income during hiker season by giving rides, or it can be operated by a business, such as a hostel or outfitter who offers this service.

Slackpack To hike without your entire backpack. This usually involves leaving your backpack at a hostel while you hike between two pre-determined points with a ride at either end, carrying only what you might need during the day. *I plan on slackpacking that section, just have to call for a shuttle*

Sobo Short for southbounder, a person who hikes the trail from north to south, from Mt. Katahdin in Maine to Springer Mountain in Georgia. The overwhelming majority of thruhikers go from south to north to take advantage of the weather, getting an earlier start in the south, but there are also many sobos hiking the trail.

Thru-hiker A person who hikes the entire length of the trail in one hiking season, or one calendar year.

Trail Angel In general, anyone who helps a hiker can be called a trail angel, however there are some people, usually former hikers, who are dedicated trail angels, routinely taking food to road crossings, offering rides or stays in their own homes, etc.

Trail Magic The good fortune that frequently seems to come hikers' way. There is a saying, "the trail will provide," and things do seem to happen at the right time for hikers. Whether this is coincidence or God looking out for poor foolish hikers, I will leave for you to decide. In a specific sense, sometimes trail angels will set up a tent at a road crossing, or even just leave a cooler or plastic bin on the trial near a road, with food and/or beverages inside.

White Blaze The white rectangles that mark the AT. They are usually painted on trees, but in the absence of trees they can be painted on rocks, bridges, or other route markers.

Yellow Blaze This refers to the yellow dotted lines on a road. A hiker who skips sections of the trail, traveling from one point to another by car, is called a **yellow blazer.** This is cheating, and is looked down upon. *Oh yeah? Well, I'd rather be a blue blazer than a yellow blazer!*

Yogi To somehow convince a non-thru-hiker to give you some food, a ride, etc, without coming right out and asking for it. To make them think it was their idea to give it to you. *I yogied a bunch of bananas from the family reunion* *at the park.*

Zero A day when zero miles are hiked. This involves a two night stay in town, with the zero in between. Can be used as a noun or as a verb: *I think I'll take a zero in Hot Springs.* Or: *She zeroed in Damascus.*

MY GEAR LIST—WHAT'S IN MY PACK

Backpack My pack, the Green Monster, is a ULA Circuit, and I can't say enough good things about this pack. It is lightweight, rugged, comfortable, and functional. I still have it and use it, and after all the abuse it took it still looks like new. While on the trail I sometimes wished I had gotten a slightly bigger pack, the next size up, the ULA Catalyst, to have more room. But I actually did have enough room in the Circuit, and if I'd had more room I might have just brought more stuff, which I evidently didn't need. I apply the same concept to purses. I carry the smallest purse I can get away with, because the more room I have the more unnecessary items I tend to collect. I put a trash compactor bag inside my pack to keep things dry, and I believe it works better than a pack cover.

Shelter I carried a Hennessy Ultralite Backpackers hammock, and I loved it. I modified it before my hike by replacing the suspension system with tree straps and hardware from Dutchware, and the ends of the hammock itself with whoopee slings. The tree straps and whoopee slings make hanging the hammock easy and fast. If you're interested, I would suggest looking at the forums on www.hammockforums.net, or at the Youtube videos by Shug Emory. I just can't explain whoopee slings!

I replaced the tarp that comes with the Hennessy because it's just too small. I bought a Tadpole tarp from Wilderness Logics. Bigger is better when it comes to tarps, but like everything else a hiker carries, weight matters. I found the Tadpole to be a good compromise, big enough for adequate coverage, small enough to carry. It kept me dry in Beauty Spot Gap!

Sleep System The only drawback to a hammock over a tent, to me at least, is that they can be colder, since you do not have contact with the ground. So the sleep system becomes very important. An underquilt, which hangs on the *outside* of the hammock, is better than a sleeping bag on the inside of the hammock, because your body weight compresses the sleeping bag under you, taking away the insulation value. My underquilt was a ¾ length synthetic called Jarbridge from Arrowhead Equipment. It is fine for what it is, but I am a cold sleeper and found myself wishing I had a full length quilt, made of down instead of synthetic. These were two compromises I made, the synthetic for price savings and the length for weight savings. I did better after I added a pad to the inside of my hammock, for more insulation on the bottom.

My top quilt was a Mamba by Warbonnet, and it was phenomenal. Lightweight, compact, and warm, it's proof that down is really worth what you pay for it.

In addition, I had a synthetic fleece sleeping bag liner my daughter made for me. It was bulky and took up a lot of room in my pack, but on those cold nights I was very glad to have it. It added enough extra warmth to make it worth the space.

Pad I didn't start out with a pad, as technically you're not supposed to need them in a hammock. BUT I now think pads are indispensable, especially if you are a cold sleeper like I am, unless you're hiking in really hot weather. Having a pad also gives you the flexibility to sleep in a shelter. I spent too many nights on hard shelter floors without a pad! I started with a cheap blue Walmart style pad, which served the purpose. In the Smokies I bought a Therm-a-Rest Z Lite pad, which was smaller, more compact, and easier to carry, but not any more comfortable. After my hike I bought a Therm-a-Rest NeoAir XLite pad, which is inflatable, and I wish I had had it with me from the beginning. It is so comfortable and even smaller. It is good for both cushioning on a shelter floor and insulation in a hammock. I will never hike without it again.

Stove I started out with a homemade alcohol stove, but in the Smokies I switched over to the Jetboil and never looked back. There are a lot of different kinds of stoves, and each has their advantages and disadvantages. The Jetboil has some distinct disadvantages, such as cost, size, and weight, but the ease of use outweighs all other considerations for me for this piece of gear. I love my Jetboil. The only criticism I could possibly make is that I find it difficult to regulate the heat on low. Along with the stove I carried a plastic spork and a two inch square piece of scrubber to clean it with.

Water filter There are even more different kinds of water filters than there are stoves. I used a Sawyer Squeeze, and I loved it. It's small and light, and it works well. I put it inside my jacket pocket to sleep with at night in the cold weather to keep it from freezing, along with my phone and lighter. My water bottles were two Smart Water bottles, because they are lighter than Nalgene or other bottles you can buy at an outfitter.

My clothes I had minimal clothes, but I know people who hiked with less clothes than I did. If I were to do it again, I might pare my list down a little, but not much. Here's my complete list:

Underclothes Let's just get this one out of the way first. I carried two set of underclothes, two panties, two sports bras. The only important factor is that they contain no cotton. They don't have to be expensive items from an outdoor specialty company-- I bought mine at WalMart. I just had to do a little digging to find panties without cotton in the lining of the crotch.

I had two sets, thinking that I would wear one set and wash the other set out on a daily basis, in camp at night, and change into the clean, dry, set every day. In reality, that doesn't happen. For one thing, it's too much trouble to wash undies and socks every night and for another, nothing ever really dries on the AT in the spring anyway. But mostly, hygienic standards just change when you live in the woods. Only sissies wash clothes between weekly town stops. I'm sorry to put this image in your mind.

Socks I had three pairs of thick wool socks. Two pairs alternated as hiking socks, and one pair I kept separate to wear in camp at night, so that I always had a clean, dry pair to sleep in.

Pants   I only had one pair of convertible hiking pants, which I wore every single day.

Long underwear   I had one pair of black wool long johns, which I slept in at night. Like my sleeping socks, they stayed relatively clean. I did not hike in them except in the Smokies when I was very cold and my pants were split down the back.

Tops   I had three tops. Two were short sleeved and a lightweight wool that felt like cotton jersey. I alternated them to hike in. The third top was a synthetic top with long sleeves, and I kept it separate to sleep in. I kept all my sleeping clothes rolled up together.

Shorts   I had a cheap pair of nylon shorts that I wore over my long johns while in camp for modesty reasons. No one wants to see the outline of my back side prancing around camp.

Jacket   My fleece jacket was worn every single day until

the weather got hot, and even then I wore it at night.

Down jacket I had a puffy down jacket that I wore in camp at night, and I slept in it. I did not hike in it because it was too warm for that, except for that horrible day in the Smokies going to Clingman's Dome in the sleet and rain. I wore it under my rain jacket that day.

Hat and gloves Also for nighttime in camp, I had a wool hat and gloves. I also wore the gloves to hike in cold weather, and when it was cold *and* raining I covered them with waterproof mittens

Rain gear and waterproof mittens I had an inexpensive rain suit, jacket and pants, from Frogg Toggs, and expensive waterproof mittens. Both worked fine up to a point, but my personal belief is that when the rain is blowing in sideways, you are going to get wet, no matter what you're wearing. A hiking guru named Sir Packsalot told Songbird, when she asked him for his best piece of hiking advice, "If you don't have to walk in the rain, don't." This is excellent advice.

Crocs My camp shoes. Worn after I'd quit hiking for the

day, to give my feet a rest from the hiking shoes, and to allow both feet and shoes to air out and dry out.

Knee braces I guess I can put my knee braces in this category. I bought them at a CVS drug store, and I believe that they saved my knees and enabled me to hike. I wore them every day, taking them off only when I reached camp for the night. When it got hot out they started to irritate my skin a little, but I wore them anyway. I wouldn't hike any distance without them.

Buff This little sleeve of lightweight wool was one of my favorite items of clothing, and my most versatile. It was a headband when it was hot, keeping my hair out of my face, and a hood when it was cold. It kept my wool hat on my head while I was sleeping in the worst of the cold weather. It kept my dirty unkempt hair out of sight at all times. There are a hundred ways to wear a buff. I wore it every single day.

Bandanas I had two bandanas, which had a million different uses: wash cloth, towel, pot holder, etc.

Shoes My hiking boots were not actually boots, they were

hiking shoes. Footwear on the trail is evolving, like everything else, getting smaller and lighter, and few people wear the old-school, heavy leather hiking boots anymore. More and more people are wearing very lightweight shoes called trail runners. My shoes were somewhere in the middle of these two extremes—I like the idea of lightweight, but I believed I needed more support than trail runners provide and more durability. I wore Oboz Sawtooth B-Dry, and I loved them so much that after I threw them in a hiker box I went out and bought another pair just like them. (I only threw them in a hiker box because they had become too small. They did not wear out.) Shoes are very personal, and hikers can become passionate on the subject, but I love my Oboz.

Technology I carried only my phone, an LG Optimus G, and an external battery for charging. With the extra battery, which was smaller than a deck of cards, I could charge my phone about two and a half times between town stops, and I never had a battery go dead. I kept the phone on airplane mode most of the time to save battery, and I was without a signal much of the time. This phone served me well as phone, camera, computer to check my email and update my online trail journal, and Kindle. My carrier was

Sprint. Verizon is the carrier with the best coverage in the area of the southern AT.

Trekking Poles   Like my knee braces, I think trekking poles helped to save my knees. I would never hike without them. My poles were fairly inexpensive ones that I got from REI, and by the end of the hike they both needed replaced. They are so indispensable that my next set will be better, more expensive.

First Aid   My first aid kit was tiny. I just carried a film canister with ibuprofen, that magic vitamin I that I also credit with sparing my knees and enabling me to hike, and another canister with diphenhydramine in case of an allergic response or poison ivy, with a secondary use as an aid to sleep. I also had a few bandaids, a bit of moleskin, and a small tin of my homemade Healing Salve (remember that I am an herbalist who makes soaps and lotions and potions) for wounds. I had some iodine tablets as a backup to my water filter, because crushed and mixed with water they become an anti-infective.

Toiletries   I carried remarkably few toiletries, most of which I had made. I had a small comb, a toothbrush, another film canister with baking soda, and a small bottle of my homemade liquid soap. I have dry skin and was worried about hiking without cream or lotion, which I use every day at home, but was reluctant to take because of the weight. I finally compromised and took a very small jar of my thickest cream, but found that I didn't need it. Once I was out in the natural humidity of the outside air and away from the over-dried inside air, my skin was never dry. I used the cream on my feet, just to baby them. I had a tiny bottle of my waterless hand cleaner (also homemade, not alcohol. It also worked to some extent to deter the North Carolina Bugs.) I brought a small bar of jewelweed soap in case I got into any poison ivy, once the weather warmed up. I also had a tube of lip balm and a small nail clipper.

Toilet paper and baby wipes For toilet paper I carried paper towels, each sheet cut into quarters. Before my hike I had purchased large boxes of baby wipes, which I took out of the box and hung all around my house to dry out. I kept a stash of these dried wipes in with my toiletries for quick wash-ups. When moistened with a splash of water they "come back to life", and smell clean and feel soft, and make for a spa experience when washing up on the trail.

Miscellaneous   The other odds and ends I carried:

Headlamp   A headlamp is indispensable to a hiker. I had an inexpensive, lightweight one from REI and extra batteries.

Sewing kit, eyeglass repair kit   I really debated about carrying these two items, while trying to get my pack weight down, and I'm glad I wasn't crazy enough to decide against them. They were tiny, the size of a pack of matches, and I used the sewing kit twice. I did not use the eyeglass repair kit, but if I had needed it I would have been thrilled to have it.

Food Bag   My food bag was made of cuben fiber, from Z Packs. Along with the food, I had in it a length of paracord and a carabiner, to use as a bear bag when I had to throw my own over a tree branch. Most shelters had a cable system to hoist your food bag up so you didn't have to throw a bear bag. I was glad mine was made of cuben fiber, which is listed as "rodent resistant." While hanging side by side with Songbird's food bag, on two separate occasions hers was chewed through, and mine was untouched. I also had a gallon size Zip loc bag in the food bag, to be used for trash, and emptied when in town.

Fire Starters I had one Zip loc bag just for my fire starting material. In it I had two small lighters and a handful of homemade fire starters. I made them by filling the egg cups of a cardboard egg carton with lint from the dryer and pouring melted paraffin in them. After cutting them apart, they make lovely fire starters, easy to light, and each one will burn probably twenty minutes, which is more than enough time for the kindling to catch.

Knife I had bought a small, cute Swiss Army knife, with a lot of blades I knew nothing about, but replaced it before my hike even started with a little knife bought at a cash register in a convenience store for about a dollar. It was tiny and had a single, razor sharp blade. The only thing I ever used it for was to slice cheese for lunch, and it worked perfectly for that.

Sudoku I had one quart size Zip loc bag that I carried a few pieces of paper in, as well as two ink pens and several pages torn from a book of Sudoku puzzles. These kept me entertained when stuck in shelters alone.

Duct tape   I had a length of duct tape wrapped around each water bottle. It's useful for many things, but the only time I remember using it was to repair my rain jacket when it ripped.

Chamois   I had a small (four inch square) piece of "shammy" that I used to dry off my tarp the morning after a rain before packing it up. The shammy saw a lot of use.

Money belt   I carried my cash, ID, rosary, and credit cards in a money belt around my waist. There was zero chance of me losing any of it that way.

My Guidebook   This was another absolutely indispensible piece of gear I could not have hiked without. There are several types of guides out there, but most hikers used the same one I did: The AT Guide by David Awol Miller.

87151618R00261

Made in the USA
Lexington, KY
20 April 2018